FEAST OF LOVE

FEAST OF LOVE:

Pope John Paul II on Human Intimacy

Mary G. Durkin

A Campion Book
Loyola University Press
Chicago
1983

IN MEMORIAM

To Edith Roberts

*Her loving friendship and support
across the miles from Martinez, California,
for these past seven years taught me much
about the femininity of God.*

Contents

Acknowledgments

Many people have contributed ideas and support during the development of this book. I want to thank them for this contribution while, at the same time, absolving them from any responsibility for the way in which I have used their ideas. In particular, I would like to thank the following:

Pope John Paul II for developing a theology of the body and sexuality that, because it is rooted in an analysis of key scriptural passages, so readily lends itself to a vision and a spirituality. I have tried to give an accurate summary of the Pope's work in the first section of each chapter and, in many instances, I have used his exact words. Any summary, however, by its very nature, runs the first risk of emphasizing some important points while excluding others. Readers who are interested in pursuing the Pope's work in more detail will find the specific references for each of his audience addresses in Appendix A.

Andrew M. Greeley for bringing these audience addresses to my attention and encouraging me to summarize and apply the ideas in the Pope's addresses.

John Cusick, Laura Durkin, and participants in the Chicago Young Adult Ministry Conference, Weekend Conference on Sexuality, for enthusiastically responding to my early articulation of a vision based on the Pope's addresses. These young adults made it obvious that they were looking for a vision, and they found that the vision which is rooted in the audience addresses spoke to their needs.

The people of St. Raphael's Parish, Bay Village, Ohio, who, through their participation in a Lenten series in 1981, confirmed the possibility of a local church addressing this crucial area of human life.

Dismas Beique, S.S.P., and Edward Donaher, S.S.P., of Alba House Communications for encouraging me to do a series of abbreviated reflections on many of the ideas from the Pope's analysis of Genesis and Matthew 5:27-28. Their help in recording and editing the cassette series, *Reflections on Intimacy and Sexuality:*

Biblical and Spiritual Insights (Canfield, OH: Alba House Commun
ications, 1981) was especially valuable as I was trying to develop ar
interpretation of the papal material.

Georgiana Duffy whose typing—and retyping—was an invalu
able assistance throughout the entire project.

Foreword

At the 1980 Synod of Bishops which dealt with marriage and the family, I made several inverventions which called for the development of (1) a richer, more positive theology of sexuality and (2) a spirituality of marital intimacy. I was prompted to do this because of two events which had occurred earlier. One was Pope John Paul II's Wednesday audience talks which began a year before the Synod and continued until the following spring. The second was a series of informal and unofficial meetings of theologians and social scientists, several of which I had attended, which had addressed the question of the spirituality of sexuality.

Dr. Durkin has responded to this invitation. In each chapter of *Feast of Love,* she first analyzes the Holy Father's remarkable audience talks which developed a theology of sexuality and the body. Then, in her spiritual reflections, she explores the implications of this theology for the people of our day. Her work is marked both by professionalism as a trained theologian and a realism which stems from her own twenty-seven years of experience as a wife and mother.

Her book should make an important contribution to the Church's effort to support people as they face the issue of sexuality in their lives. It should also challenge Catholic thinkers and scholars to continue exploring, within the context of our Catholic tradition, this vitally important topic.

Joseph Cardinal Bernardin
Archbishop of Chicago

Introduction

Enough is not as good as a Feast—Eugene O'Neill,

A Long Day's Journey into Night

This is a book about feasts—about preparing for, participating in, and inviting others to the feast that God planned for us when he created humankind male and female.

Everywhere we turn these days we are reminded of the fact that we humans find it extremely difficult to deal with the confusion we experience because of our masculinity and our femininity, because we human beings come in male and female varieties. The man who lives down the street, for example, ends his marriage of 25 years; he wants to have a meaningful relationship with his 23-year-old law partner. Or the neighborhood ideal homemaker walks out on her husband and four children; she wants to "find" herself and has discovered that this is impossible in her present home situation.

Even though we know more about human sexuality than any previous generation of parents ever knew, we are still uncomfortable with assuming the role of sex educator for our children. In addition, we hear that Phyllis Schlafly, an ardent opponent of the Equal Rights Amendment (ERA), has testified that women who are sexually harassed on the job are obviously "nonvirtuous." We also hear that a group of male celebrities have banded together in support of ERA. The confusion increases when we discover that our own resolve to control our own strong sexual desires is shattered when we meet a particularly attractive person of the other sex. Our own experience, plus all the media reports about the troubles people have with their sexuality, make us somewhat skeptical about the possibilities of human sexuality being a feast.

Pope John Paul II, in his series of weekly audience addresses, has invited us to put aside our skepticism. Beginning on September 5, 1979, and continuing through April 8, 1981, the Pope gave a total of 56 addresses on sexuality and the body during his weekly general audience.[1] In these addresses, he discussed 18 different topics that form a theology of sexuality and the body. (See the Appendix for a complete list of the titles and dates of all 56 addresses as well as the dates of the issues of *L'Osservatore Romano* in which the translations first appeared.) The Pope's theology gives direction to our search for the feast, which was originally planned for us by God, even when we are not aware of the possibility of participating in such a feast. In this book, the Pope's theology will serve as a basis of a spirituality that will assist us as we try to put some order into the chaos we discover in our experiences of our own sexuality.

Books and articles that give us ideas on how to be sexually mature are plentiful today; there seems to be no end of advice on how to be sexy, for example, or how to be good in bed or how to avoid sexual harassment or how to have a successful two-career marriage or how to be a sex educator for our children. Every aspect of our life that is affected by the fact that humans come in two varieties[2] has been analyzed and discussed by professionals and nonprofessionals alike. Facts and opinions are presented in both scientific journals and the popular media; TV and radio talk shows that present guests who eagerly discuss some aspect of sexuality regularly attract large audiences; men's magazines and women's magazines, as well as the tabloid newspapers, design covers that promise some new tidbits of sexual information. There certainly seems to be "enough" secular, scientific information about sexuality.

Undoubtedly, this secular, scientific understanding of human sexuality has opened for contemporary men and women the possibility of appreciating their sexuality much more than had their ancestors, whose understanding of what it meant that they had been created male and female was largely influenced by stereotypes and myths. Of course, all this knowledge about human sexuality, knowledge that is the fruit of scientific investigation, can indeed contribute to a more positive use of the sexual dimension of our personality. But, in many instances, this knowledge merely seems to be "enough." It is, in short, not "as good as a feast."

Certainly, as we compare contemporary attitudes toward human sexuality with those of previous eras of human history, we can say that we have come a long way toward understanding how sexuality can be a positive force in our lives and in our relationships with other people. We now know, for example, that women are not naturally inferior to men. We also know that women do not have to reproduce the optimum number of children in order to contribute to the continuation of the human race. And, furthermore, we know that one of the stages of human growth and development—growth into mature adulthood—is the stage in which a man and a woman share their identities in a relationship of intimacy. These three bits of knowledge have profound implications for marital relationships in modern society. Men and women are now free to combine the roles of friend, lover, and parent in one relationship. And, as life expectancy has increased and, with it, the prospect of a marriage lasting fifty years, the possibility of being friend, lover, and parent along with your spouse seems to offer a security that our ancestors lacked.

This example of combining friend, lover, and parent in one relationship over a fifty-year span, however, raises an extremely important question: How is it possible to be intimate with one person for such a long time? Here, too, scientific, psychological knowledge about personality growth and development, life-cycle stages, male-female role identity, and the biological basis of sexual attraction, gives many positive insights into how to achieve happiness in a marriage. So, too, almost every other aspect of our sexuality has been carefully analyzed, and now there are suggestions in plenty telling us how to order the sexual dimension of our lives.

Still, all this knowledge, all this advice, which seems to be enough to get us through the ordinary challenges of masculinity and femininity, is not sufficient for those times when we experience our sexuality as an *extraordinary* dimension of our lives. And it is during those extraordinary times—those times when we are overjoyed in the experience of lovemaking, dismayed at the loss of a loved one, enraptured at the birth of a baby, surprised by the passion of a new love, discouraged by sexual discrimination, or affirmed by the fidelity of a spouse—that we discover the mysterious dimension of our sexuality. During experiences such as these, or during the reflection upon these experiences, we begin to encounter the mysterious dimension of our sexuality. We feel awed, for example, at the wonderful possibilities that are revealed in these moments, or we experience terror at the possible loss of identity that is bound up with rejections, or we find ourselves wondering why such things happen. At these moments, we discover that all our secular, scientific understanding of sexuality does not adequately quiet the restlessness we feel. We are encountering Mystery in this extraordinary dimension of sexuality.

When we acknowledge this extraordinary dimension of our sexuality, when we encounter Mystery in our experience of our own masculinity and femininity, when we acknowledge that our plentiful secular understanding does not have an adequate answer to our question ("why?")—we are then at the point where a religious vision of the meaning of human sexuality might be of assistance. Religious vision helps us develop an appreciation of the Mystery we encounter in an extraordinary experience. Religious vision encourages us, inspires us, so that we might respond to this Mystery in a positive manner.

Pope John Paul II's theology of the body and of sexuality provides a vision that challenges us to recognize that our encounters with Mystery, which we experience in the extraordinary dimensions of our human sexuality, are actually invitations to participate in the feast that God had originally planned for man and woman. This vision gives the basis for a spirituality of sexuality, a spirituality that will allow us to recognize the extraordinary dimension of our sexuality. A spirituality of sexuality also helps us respond to the invitation to the feast of our sexual identity by helping us establish guidelines for behavior, which will be a positive response to the creative potential of our masculinity and femininity.

This book about feasts, therefore, is also a book about a spirituality of sexuality. We will examine the experience of human sexuality in light of the vision that is uncovered by reading the Pope's addresses. We will consider how it is that reflecting on the experiences of human sexuality from the perspective of the Pope's addresses can provide a new basis for insights into the depth of the meaning of human femaleness and maleness. At the same time, we will develop values and attitudes out of the new understanding that is emerging from the conversation between our experience and our vision. Spirituality actually bridges the gap between our human experiences and the faith we affirm in our Christian beliefs. Spirituality assists us in our struggles with the sexual dimension of our personality by allowing us to place our experiences of masculinity and femininity into the broader story of life and its meaning that we affirm when we call ourselves Christians.

Thus, a spirituality allows us to integrate the experiences of our life around a central meaning of life. In the process of bridging the gap between our experiences and our beliefs, it is also possible to uncover a significance to these beliefs that is deeper than what we had previously understood. This approach to a spirituality has a snowballing effect. As we engage in a conversation about our experiences and our beliefs, we become more conscious of the extraordinary in our lives and more aware of how important our religious vision is for our appreciation of the depth of the Mystery we encounter. At the same time, as we bring the question "why"—a question discovered in our encounter with Mystery in the experience of our human sexuality—to our religious belief system, we often find a depth in this belief that we had not previously appreciated. As we discover more about our God, we come to an appreciation of how our experience reveals new aspects of God to us.

This book about both feasts and spirituality seeks to carry on a conversation between the experience of sexuality in a modern technological society and the beliefs of our Catholic Christian tradition, especially as these beliefs have been formulated into a theology of the body and of sexuality by Pope John Paul II. Actually, our conversation joins the Pope's conversation with certain scriptural passages that he feels contain a positive perspective of the divine plan for our masculinity and femininity. These particular passages are stories that illustrate, uncover new depths to, and, at the same time, limit some of the basic symbols of the Christian tradition. Thus, when we look at the story of creation in the Book of Genesis, we find the symbol of the Creator-God coming alive, but, at the same time, being limited. Our God, the God we discover in the creation myth of Genesis, created good but not evil. The placing of a limit on this symbol of our faith is not so much a limiting of the possibilities of the Creator-God as it is a limiting of the possibilities of our human interpretation of the meaning of the Creator-God. Thus, the story of the creation and the fall in the Book of Genesis makes it impossible for us to attribute the creation of evil to the God we find there.

The conversation we will be carrying on with the Pope's addresses has its own background. This background illustrates the method that will be used in this book and should be helpful for the reader who wishes to fully participate in the conversation. I was a participant in, and the final co-author of, the report of the Human

Intimacy Colloquium—a four-part gathering of social scientists and theologians that tried, over a two-year period, to correlate the experience of human intimacy, especially marital intimacy, and the Catholic Christian tradition. The method of the colloquium was to let the human experience of intimacy speak through the lives of the individual participants as well as the perspectives of the social scientists before the theologians offered a response. The theologians in the group listened to the experiences of intimacy, then reflected on and connected to our Catholic tradition the insights that had arisen from the group, and finally wove religious meanings from the analysis of the experiences. Participants in the colloquium were seeking an integrated wisdom, a blending of the insights of theology and the social sciences that would help Christians who wished to understand the importance of the experience of intimacy from a faith perspective. For me, this interdisciplinary approach—that is, reflecting on human experience, seeking understanding from scientific perspectives, and integrating these two with a religious understanding of the meaning of life—provides the basis for both a pastoral theology and a spirituality.

The vision of marital intimacy from a Catholic perspective that was developed in this colloquium is, in fact, a pastoral theology based on this interdisciplinary method. The vision articulated in the colloquium report, *Marital Intimacy: A Catholic Perspective*,[3] also challenges me to be more attentive to the religious dimension of my own attempt at marital intimacy, following the process used in the colloquium. Thus, I find that a spirituality of marital intimacy requires, first, reflection on the experience of intimacy in my own life; second, some consideration of what the secular, scientific understanding of intimacy says about my particular experience; and, third, an examination of what my Catholic Christian beliefs, particularly as they are expounded in the stories of my faith, say to me about the mysterious dimension of my search for intimacy.

Some of the participants from the first colloquium continued this interdisciplinary approach to a pastoral theology—that is, to a religious vision about the practical aspects of a religious community—in a study of pastoral leadership in the local church under the auspices of the Lilly Foundation. The participants in this study felt that here, too, the correlation of life and faith resulted in an understanding of pastoral leadership that was much broader than one that would have been achieved by either discipline on its own. Again, we began, first, with our experience of parish and pastoral leadership in a local church; then, we examined the insights into local community and leadership in local religious communities that are found in the social sciences; and, finally, we asked theologians to reflect, to connect the insights from the social sciences with our religious tradition, and to weave religious meaning from our analysis of the religious experience. The report of this study, *Parish, Priest & People,*[4] represents what, for those of us who participated in the study, was an enriching experience in the use of this interdisciplinary method. And, as a consequence, the participants have become more adept in using this method when they consider the religious dimension of various experiences.

So, I brought to my reading of the Pope's addresses on a theology of the body and of sexuality an interdisciplinary understanding of human sexuality, which I had developed in the intimacy colloquium, as well as a methodological approach to a religious problem, which uses a correlation of life and faith. These two factors strongly influence not only how I enter into the papal conversation, but also the way in which I both interpret the Pope's analyses of these scriptural references and apply them to the experience of our contemporary technological society.

In the chapters of this book, I hope to take the reader with me as I read the Pope's addresses and apply them to my understanding of the experience of sexuality in our contemporary society.

Each chapter begins with a summary of the contents of the Pope's addresses on a particular topic. In these talks, the Pope seems to be entering into a conversation with Scripture from the perspective of phenomenology and personalism and also, undoubtedly, from the experience of a twentieth-century Polish Catholic bishop. He is not undertaking a strictly exegetical exercise; rather, the Pope seems to be engaging in the kind of criticism that has been called "in front of the text" criticism. That is to say, although the Pope is undoubtedly familiar with the current exegesis of the particular scriptural passages he has analyzed, he is not attempting to perform a strict interpretation of the specific passages. Instead, the Pope examines the scriptural passages from the broader perspective of the faith of the whole tradition. Thus, the Pope brings to his experience of faith his understanding of the experience of human sexuality—an understanding that is conditioned by both his experience as a contemporary Polish Catholic bishop and his phenomenological and personalistic analysis of that experience. He attempts to correlate life and faith by examining some of the doctrines of faith from the perspective of the stories in Scripture that give flesh and meaning to these doctrines. The end result is double enrichment—an enrichment of the experience of human sexuality and an enrichment of our understanding of the doctrines of faith.

Following the summary of the Pope's ideas on a particular topic, we will not only examine how the Pope's ideas might trigger our own reflections on our understanding of human sexuality, but also consider insights that flow from the interaction between our experiences and the Pope's vision. My understanding of the experience of human sexuality is rooted in both my own experience and the insights concerning human sexuality that I have acquired from the social and biological sciences. Different understandings of human sexuality might easily emerge from different experiences.

There is room for many more voices in the conversation between the human experience of sexuality and the faith of the Catholic Christian tradition. The interpretation in this book is one voice in this conversation—a conversation that also needs to hear scientists and theologians, pastoral ministers and laity, voice their concerns and experiences.

Social and biological scientists, by continuing their investigation of human sexuality, can help us more readily understand the powerful influence that sexuality is in our lives. Theologians who listen to those who speak of all the dimensions of the experience of human sexuality should be prepared to spot the extraordinary manifested in the experience and then begin to place it within the context of our beliefs. This will not always be an easy task for there are, as theologian John Hotchkins has observed, two topics that theologians have a very hard time dealing with—one is death and the other is sexuality. Both of these experiences are so intimately a part of each of our lives that it is difficult for us to move beyond the emotional impact that is entailed in reflecting on the experiences.

Pastoral ministers and laity in a religious community bring to the conversation a most intimate understanding of both the creative possibilities and the destructive potential of our masculinity and femininity. And, after they have participated in the conversation, they bring back to the experience of human sexuality some suggestions for transforming this experience. In this way, a spirituality of sexuality begins to develop.

Before we proceed, it must be acknowledged that, at this level, we encounter two particularly noteworthy obstacles to the conversation.

1. There is an obvious fear of tackling so complex and highly charged a notion. Pastoral ministers and laity alike will argue that sexuality is not an appropriate topic for inclusion in religious conversation. Seldom do we hear reference to sexuality in homilies or in comments during liturgical celebrations, and efforts to encourage its inclusion often meet with strenuous resistance. In effect, the revelatory potential of our sexuality is short-circuited. Previous hang-ups regarding sexuality, coupled with present disappointment over official church positions on certain issues of sexual behavior, combine to form a conspiracy of silence on issues that are related to sexuality. An important dimension of human experience is therefore being ignored.

2. There is a second, equally destructive attitude that denies the need for a spirituality of sexuality. The need is often denied because either the laity have not expressed an interest in the topic, or the minister may feel that the need for a spirituality of sexuality is a very low priority for his people. In the latter case, particularly in communities that are financially depressed, pastoral ministers—both bishops and local leaders—often dismiss a plea for consideration of the issue of sexuality with the following remarks: "My people are hungry and oppressed. It is this issue that I, as their pastor, must work with. We have no time to waste on other issues." Such an attitude demonstrates a remarkable naïveté about human sexuality. First, even in oppressed conditions—save, perhaps, those that result in near starvation—issues of sexual identity and the use of one's sexual capabilities are crucial issues. Individual men and women in oppressed conditions still face the question of sexual identity, and their reactions to both oppression and sexual identity formation are often intimately related. Second, there is no guarantee that, once the oppressed condition has been removed, men and women will automatically be able to come to grips with sexual identity. Contemporary American society, after all, has achieved a

high level of technological development and affluence but is not noted for its sexual stability.

All of us—theologians, scientists, pastoral ministers, and lay persons—will have to undergo what theologian John Shea has called a "conversion" if we are to join in the conversation. We must open ourselves to the possibility that God is revealed in the experience of human sexuality. Admittedly, this is not an easy task for those who are used to rigid interpretations of rules for sexual behavior or for those who view sexuality as a way of exploitation. We must be willing to believe that reflection on the experience of sexuality is an important aspect of Christian spirituality, and, more important, we must be willing to begin this process of reflection. Again, this is not an easy task for those of us who have avoided reflection, especially reflection on sexuality.

In conclusion, both the theology of the body and of sexuality that is found in the addresses of Pope John Paul II, and the beginning spirituality that flows from our participation in the conversation with Scripture, seek not only to uncover the possibilities in human sexuality of a feast but also to find the revelation of God available in the extraordinary dimension of our femininity and masculinity.

ONE
In the Beginning

And Pharisees came up to him and tested him by asking, "Is it lawful to divorce one's wife for any cause"? He answered, "Have you not read that he who made them from the beginning made them male and female and said, 'For this reason a man shall leave his father and mother and be joined to his wife and the two shall become one flesh'? So they are no longer two but one flesh. What therefore God has joined together let not man put asunder." They said to him, "Why did Moses command one to give a certificate of divorce and put her away?" He said to them, "For your hard-ness of heart Moses allowed you to divorce your wives but from the beginning it was not so. *(Emphasis added by the Pope.)*
—Matthew 19:3-8 (Cf. Mark 10:2ff)

Summary of the Pope's Addresses

The Synod of Bishops, which met in Rome in the fall of 1980, considered the role of the Christian family. The Pope decided to accompany from afar the preparations that preceded this synod not by addressing the specific topic of the synod, but by turning our attention to the beginning of the family, to the deep roots from which the Christian family springs. When the Pharisees ask Jesus the question about the indissolubility of marriage, he does not accept the discussion at the level at which his questioners try to introduce it. Rather than get caught up in a juridical, casuistical controversy, he twice refers his listeners to "the beginning," thus directing them to the relevant words in the Book of Genesis which they, too, knew by heart.

Referring to Genesis 1:27 ("God created man in his own image, in the image of God he created him, male and female he created them") and Genesis 2:24 ("Therefore a man leaves his father and his mother and cleaves to his wife and they become one flesh," and adding the following, "So they are no longer two but one flesh. What therefore God has joined together, let not man put asunder," Jesus interprets Genesis 2:24, which sets forth the principle of the indissolubility of the marriage union, as the very content of the word of God expressed in the most ancient revelation.

Jesus does more, however, than set forth a normative principle. The repetition of the expression "from the beginning" (vv. 4 and 8) directs Jesus' listeners, and us, to the way in which mankind was formed in the mystery of creation as "male and female." If we reflect, therefore, on "the beginning," we will be able to correctly understand the normative sense of the words of Genesis.

Thus, we find the words spoken by Jesus to the Pharisees set in the context of (1) the so-called first account of the creation of man, which is inserted in the seven-day cycle of the creation of the world (Gn 1-2:4); (2) the so-called second account of the creation of man (Gn 2:5-25); (3) indirectly, the entire third chapter of Genesis; and (4) at least the first phrase of the fourth chapter of Genesis, which treats of the conception and birth of man from earthly parents. This context will form the basis of our present analysis.

The Pope mentions that we know that the first account of man's creation, which is derived "from the priestly and 'elohist' tradition, from 'Elohim,' the term used in that account of God," is chronologically later than the second account, that is, the Yahwist account with its rather anthropomorphic image of God. When we compare the two accounts, we find the priestly and elohist account much more mature regarding both the image of God and the presentation of essential truths about man.

The account of man's creation inserted into the seven-day cycle of creation in the first chapter of Genesis contains only objective facts and defines objective reality. Man, though strictly bound to the visible world, is not like the rest of creatures, but is created "in the image of God" (Gn 1:27). The objectivism continues with the words of the first blessing: "Be fruitful and multiply and fill the earth, subdue it and have dominion over it" (Gn 1:28). This account, however, which is theological in nature, conceals within it a powerful metaphysical content. Man is defined, first of all, in the dimensions of being and existence.

Corresponding to the mystery of man's creation "in the image of God" is the perspective of procreation, that is, being fruitful, multiplying, and filling the earth. Both of these are related to the value judgment that appears in this story after all the days of creation reach their culmination in the creation of man when "God saw everything that he had made, and, behold, it was very good" (Gn 1:31). The metaphysical fact that *being* and *the good* are convertible has a special significance for the theology of the body. This expression, "theology of the body," will receive a more exact explanation as we continue our analysis.

First, however, we must consider the second account of creation, which, with its subjective and psychological profundity, has a quite different character. The second chapter of Genesis may be said to contain the most ancient description on record of man's self-knowledge, and, when it is linked with the third chapter of Genesis, it is the first testimony of human conscience. This narrative, with its primitive mythical character, presents the creation of man in its subjective aspects and provides us with nearly all the elements of the analysis of man to which modern and contemporary philosophical anthropology is sensitive. The subjectivity of this second account corresponds to the objective reality of man created "in the image of God." In subsequent analyses, the Pope will explain how this correspondence is also important for the theology of the body.

Although Jesus initially refers the Pharisees to the first account of creation (Gn 1:27), his later quote from Genesis (2:24) indicates that the words that directly describe the unity and indissolubility of marriage are found in the immediate context of the second account of creation. Its characteristic feature is the separate creation of woman (see Gn 2:18-23), whereas the account of the creation of first man is found in Genesis 2:5-7. By referring to Genesis 2:24, Jesus links "the beginning" with the mystery of creation and also leads us to consider man's original innocence and original sin, since the second description of man's creation is placed in this context. The narrative of the separate creation of man and woman is immediately followed by the account in chapter three of the first fall of the man and the woman, which is linked with the mysterious tree that is already called "the tree of the knowledge of good and evil."

Thus, the tree of the knowledge of good and evil becomes the line of demarcation between the two original situations described in the Book of Genesis. In the first situation of original innocence, man (male and female) exists outside the sphere of the knowledge of good and evil until he transgresses the creator's prohibition and eats the fruit of the tree. In the second situation, man, having disobeyed the creator's command, finds himself within the sphere of the knowledge of good and evil. By contrasting these two situations, the Yahwist text clearly differentiates these two original situations. The description of the events, which are recorded in the second and third chapters of Genesis, reveals two different states of human nature—the state of *integral* nature and the state of *fallen* nature—and, thus, has a fundamental significance for both the theology of man and the theology of the body.

When Jesus directs his questioners to Genesis 2:24, he orders them to go beyond the boundary that, in the Yahwist text of Genesis, runs between the first and second situation of man. Despite the questioners' "hardness of heart," the original divine regulation has not lost its force. Because Jesus' reply is decisive and unequivocal, it has a normative significance not only for ethics, but especially for the theology of the body, which is constituted on the basis of the revealed word of God.

Jesus' words that refer to "the beginning" also enable us to find in man an essential continuity and a link between the two different situations or two different states or two different dimensions of the human being. The state of sin, which is part of historical man and includes those who questioned Jesus in Matthew 19 and man today, has its roots for every person, without question, in our human theological prehistory, that is, in the state of original innocence. It would be impossible for us to understand the state of historical "sinfulness" unless we also refer to the state of original and fundamental innocence. Our state of sinfulness bears a relationship to the original innocence of man created "in the image of God." We, as historical persons, are rooted in our revealed theological prehistory. That is to say, original sin signifies, in every historical person, a state of lost grace; however, original sin also contains a reference to that grace, the grace of original innocence.

When Jesus refers to "the beginning," he is not merely indicating the state of a lost horizon of human existence; he also has in mind the whole eloquence of the mystery of redemption. We live not only in the history of human sinfulness but also in the history of salvation as its subject and co-creator. Because of our sinfulness, we are closed to original innocence; at the same time, however, we are open to the mystery of redemption that was accomplished in Christ and through Christ.

We are reminded of Paul's description in his letter to the Romans, that speaks of "groaning inwardly as we wait for the redemption of our bodies;" (Rm 8:23). If Jesus had only directed us to "the beginning" and had not, at the same time, opened us to the perspective of a "redemption of the body," we would not be able to adequately understand his response to the Pharisees. The perspective of the "redemption of the body" guarantees a continuity and unity between the hereditary state of man's sin and his original innocence, although this innocence has been lost irremediably.

Jesus' answer to the doctors of the law and the convenant is from the perspective of the redemption on which the covenant itself rests. It directs us to a method for further analyzing the revelation of "the beginning." In our interpretation of the revelation of man, especially about the body, we must refer to experience. Corporeal man is perceived by us mainly by experience. Even though we have seen that our historical experience must, in a certain way, stop at the threshold of man's original innocence, we also arrive at the conviction that our human experience is, to some extent, a legitimate means for theological interpretation. It is, in a certain sense, an indispensable point of reference that we must keep in mind in any interpretation of "the beginning."

Subsequent analysis of the first chapters of Genesis will reflect the truth of our "groaning inwardly" as we wait for the redemption of the body. In this position of groaning—a position that is so deeply familiar to our own experiences—we look to "the beginning" for the great richness of light which not only comes from revelation, but to which, above all, theology wishes to be accountable. Our further analysis will demonstrate why we need a theology of the body.

In concluding this summary of the first four papal addresses, we emphasize four main points that will be important for both a theology and a spirituality of sexuality.

1. The normative sense of Jesus' response to the Pharisees has its basis in the account of human creation and fall that appears in the first chapters of Genesis, especially in the Yahwist account.

2. The "beginning" narrative tells of two different situations: (A) original innocence, and (B) original sin. We know about original sin from our own experience; we learn about original innocence from reflection on God's revelation.

3. By directing us to the "beginning," Jesus not only links our historical experience of our body to its roots in that "beginning," but also indicates the importance of reflection on our experience of our body for an understanding of the revelation of the "beginning."

4. In the Genesis narrative we seek to uncover the depths of the revelation of the body, because Jesus' words promise us that his gift of the "redemption of the body" guarantees a continuity and unity between ourselves and that time of original innocence.

Spiritual Reflections

As we reflect on the ideas in these first four papal addresses and call to mind our own experiences of our femininity and masculinity, we feel the sense of "groaning inwardly." We find ourselves part of the crowd that is following Jesus. Like them, we hope that Jesus will say something useful for our search for meaning in life, for our need to make some kind of sense out of so many of the situations we encounter in our day-to-day experiences.

The Pharisees' question strikes a responsive chord in us. How often we have looked for rules for specific sexual behavior and yet ignored the full significance of our masculinity and femininity, not wanting to admit that it has implications for much broader aspects of our lives. Like the Pharisees, we are virtually convinced that, if we only had the magic answer to a particular question, we would have a complete understanding of how to be a sexual being. We fail, however, to perceive the necessity for an integrated understanding of our masculinity and our femininity.

We are not unlike the woman who, for example, calls a radio talk show that is focusing on the religious aspects of sexuality. She is convinced that if the official church were to change its stand on birth control, then all the difficulties that Catholics have had with their sexuality will disappear. We, too, often tend to focus on a single issue. Although we might never consider the possibility of a divorce, we nevertheless are content with a marital relationship in which each spouse adheres to stereotypical expectations for male-female and wife-husband roles because then we do not have to bother relating to the *person* of our spouse. Or, we might consider ourselves much more sexually mature than "others" who contribute to the spread of pornography, but we see no problem with using sexual attraction as a basis for getting or giving promotions. Or we might be ardent supporters of women's liberation—perhaps we even pride ourselves on our support for ordination of women—but when it comes to giving a woman a promotion in our department, or allowing her to function as a pastoral minister in our community, or accepting her vision and expertise in our own area of endeavor, we find ourselves feeling threatened and setting up obstacles to her progress. Or we might keep our marital relationship open to the possibility of children, but, when those children arrive, we find ourselves unable to help them develop positive attitudes toward their own sexuality.

The woman who calls the radio talk show to complain about the church's position on birth control fails to see sexuality as more than the ability to control reproduction. Similarly, sexuality is more than avoiding divorce, more than not contributing to pornography, more than supporting women's liberation, and more than being open to having children. Sexual maturity requires that we respect the personhood of the other, that we do not assign people roles that are based on stereotypes, or manipulate those who are sexually vulnerable for our own advancement, or discriminate against another's ideas simply on the basis of the other's sex. Likewise, it would be difficult to claim that we are completely at ease with our sexuality when we are unable to offer our children positive models of sexual identity. Yet, we still tend to focus on a narrow view of sexuality that equates sexual maturity with following "rules." Generally, however, these "rules" do not supply the key for discovering a positive, integrated plan for our sexuality.

Reflection on the contradictions in our own behavior and on the fact that half the human race comes in one variety and the other half comes in another variety often makes us aware that all is not right in our world. Although there are times when we have positive feelings about our masculinity and femininity, we often "groan inwardly" over our inability to experience our sexuality as a positive force in our lives. We do not understand why it is that we so often find it difficult to control our strong sexual drive or live up to our ideals about male-female relationships; in short, we do not understand why we find it so difficult to be at ease with our own sexuality. So, like the Pharisees, we wait for Jesus' answer; we want him to confirm the "rightness" of our present actions, but we also hope he might say something that will help us make sense of the confusion we so frequently experience about our sexual identity.

When Christ directs us to "the beginning," to the roots of human sexuality in the original divine plan, we feel the call to expand our perspective, to try to see sexuality as more than the particular problem of our own situation at this particular time. We feel challenged to consider *why* there were males and females in the first place. The need to discover the origins of human sexuality and to consider sexuality as a multidimensional phenomenon has received attention from scientists. Scientific insights on these matters give us a foundation for a better appreciation of the importance of Jesus' answer to the Pharisees.

The *Report of the Project on Human Sexual Development,* for example, captures what most of us feel about sexuality when it observes: "For many people sexuality means 'sex' or sexual intercourse and brings to mind a brief and limited encounter, that begins and ends at a certain time, that occurs with a certain person, in a certain place, that involves specific parts of the body."[1] And if you think this description is inaccurate, try telling someone that you are reading a book on sexuality and then notice the look that you get. Or suggest that issues about sexuality should be discussed from the pulpit and then observe the nervous reactions you encounter. This narrow view of sexuality is extremely limiting. The report continues: "Understanding sexuality is essential to genuine self-knowledge and integral to the formation of satisfying human relationships. Sexuality is expressed through erotic behaviors, life styles, social roles, demonstration of affection, raising of children, and everyday life processes" (ibid.). The fact that we come in male and female varieties affects so many areas of our lives, and, if we hope to be sexually mature, we need to integrate our behavior in all of these areas.

This insight into human sexuality is also supported by the American Medical Association's statement:

> Human sexuality is involved in what we do, but it is also what we are. It is an identification, an activity, a drive, a biological and emotional process, an outlook, and an expression of the self . . .. It is an important factor in every personal relationship, in every human endeavor, from business to politics.[2]

Perhaps some of our problems with sexual identity occur because we lack an appreciation of its pervasiveness. Our masculinity or femininity is deeply connected with who we are and with the way in which we understand who we are. We cannot compartmentalize our behavior, ignoring the need for a cohesive approach to our sexuality, without negatively affecting all our human relationships.

Still, even this understanding of the multidimensional character of human sexuality does not relieve the anxiety we feel over our inability to be "in control" of our sexuality. In fact, when we ponder the pervasiveness of our sexual identity, we can't help but wonder why human sexuality is so different from animal sexuality. Why, for example, do we humans have to bother being concerned about more than erotic behavior and reproduction? Why do we experience a strong sexual attraction to members of the other sex, yet so often fail in attempts to establish long-term relationships with them? Why do we so often play "sexual games"?

Here, too, new scientific insights about the roots of human sexuality help us appreciate the important role the human brand of sexuality has played in the evolution of our species. Physical anthropologists, primatologists, sociobiologists, archaeologists, and others find the survival of the human species attributable to the unique form of human sexuality. Richard Leakey, in *People of the Lake,* pinpoints how important sexuality has been:

> Heightened human sexuality evolved as emotional cement to an economic contract in which the product is children. In other words, sex became sexy for humans—particularly for females—as an essential ingredient in the uniquely interdependent child-rearing bond of *Homo Sapiens.* If our ancestors had not invented the food-sharing economy of gathering and hunting around three million years ago, we would be neither as intelligent as we are today, nor as interested in each other's sexuality.[3]

Donald Johanson in his book, *Lucy,* finds the beginnings of hominid sexuality going back nearly three million years.[4] The particular kind of "quasi-pair bonding" that is unique to humans and the emotional contract that evolved out of it have assumed different characteristics in different cultures. Although we are pair bonded—that is, our male ancestors would not have mated with more than the number of women they could protect for the period of childrearing—we are free to break that bond; it is not instinctual.

Again, to quote Leakey, "we were conceived in the animal world but we came to maturity under the influence of a self-generating culture."[5] For most of human history, our powerful sexual attraction has been used to ensure, first, the survival of the species and, then, the survival of the community. Consequently, heavy emphasis has been placed on the reproductive aspects of human sexuality. Societal rules concerning erotic behavior have served the need of community survival. Likewise, religious attitudes about human sexuality have aimed at reinforcing the correct use of our reproductive capabilities in order to serve the common good of community survival.

Today we find ourselves experiencing a unique kind of sexuality that, in order to ensure community survival, aims at an emotional bonding that was begun perhaps as long ago as three million years. We are, however, in a societal situation that no longer requires the strict control of our reproductive capacity. Thus, we are free to begin considering some of the implications of those aspects of our sexuality that are concerned with emotional bonding. This investigation of the "beginnings" of human sexuality gives us some hints about why we might encounter difficulties in integrating our masculinity and femininity into our search for identity.

Given this understanding of the roots of human sexuality, we are somewhat better prepared to understand the rationale behind Jesus' concern with "the beginning." We now feel a sense of awe at the magnitude of our sexuality, at the extraordinary possibilities within an experience that we have tried to render quite ordinary by limiting it to something that a few rules can control. Like the Pharisees, we know that "the beginning" Jesus refers to is a religious interpretation of the common and unique human experience of masculinity and femininity. We see that our "hardness of heart" has made it impossible for us to appreciate the potential of our own sexuality.

The Pope's initial interpretation of Jesus' words to the Pharisees challenges us to be reflective about our experiences of sexuality. We therefore feel the need to undergo a conversion, a transformation of our ordinary way of responding to our sexuality. We feel called to consider both our bodies and our sexual potentialities as good, as integral parts of creation, as components of God's plan. We sense the need for a more thorough investigation of both our experiences of sexuality and the divine plan. Though we might remain somewhat skeptical about the possibilities of a feast of human sexuality, we are ready to investigate "the beginning" so that we might have a better appreciation of the foundations of Jesus' directive.

Thus, we conclude our initial conversation with the first four papal addresses aware that the task ahead requires us to reflect on our experiences of sexuality and on the religious dimension of these experiences. We must begin to tell ourselves the story of our sexuality, and we must also begin to listen to the divine story about human sexuality. As we become more familiar with both these stories, we hope to gain more insight into Jesus' promise of a "redemption of the body" and a deeper appreciation of the Mystery we encounter in the extraordinary dimension of our femininity and masculinity. Responding to Jesus' words and looking to "the beginning," we now feel the inadequacy of our attempts to both compartmentalize our sexuality and follow the "rules" without completely understanding the rationale behind these rules. As we "wait with eager longing," we find ourselves anxious to continue our conversation with the Scriptures. We fervently hope this conversation will end in a feast.

TWO
Original Solitude

*There was no one to till the land or to make
channels of water spring out of the earth to
irrigate the whole land . . . The Lord God
formed man of dust from the ground, and
breathed into his nostrils the breath of life;
and man became a living being.*
—Genesis 2:5b-7

*"You may freely eat of every tree of the
garden; but of the tree of the knowledge of
good and evil you shall not eat, for in the day
that you eat of it you shall die." God-
Yahweh said, "It is not good that the man
should be alone; I will make him a helper fit
for him." So the Lord God formed out of the
ground every beast of the field and every bird
of the air, and brought them to the man to see
what he would call them. Whatever the man
called every living creature, that was its name.
The man gave names to all cattle, and to the
birds of the air, and to every beast of the
field; but for the man (male) there was not a
helper fit for him.* —Genesis 2:16-20

Summary of the Pope's Addresses

The Pope begins his next three reflections on a theology of the
body and of sexuality with an invitation to reread, in a wider con-

text, the narrations of the first and second chapters of the Book of Genesis. In this way, he hopes to establish a series of meanings in the ancient text, meanings to which he feels Jesus referred in his response to the Pharisees. The first characteristic of original innocence that we will examine is man's original solitude.

The starting point for this papal reflection comes from the second, or Yahwist, account of the creation of man: "It is not good that man (male) should be alone; I will make him a helper fit for him" (Gn 2:18). In the Yahwist text, we find the creation of man (male) in a separate passage (Gn 2:7), which preceeds the account of the creation of the first woman (Gn 2:21-22). The first man (*'ādām*) is defined as a "male" (*'iš*) only after the creation of the first woman. When Yahweh speaks of solitude, therefore, it is the solitude of the first *human*, not just the solitude of the first male.

When we consider the solitude of Genesis 2:18 in the wider context of the whole creation story, however, we find that it is a solitude of "man" (male and female), not just the solitude of the male caused by the lack of the woman. Actually, the solitude has two meanings: one is derived from man's very nature, and the other is derived from the male-female relationship. A detailed analysis of the description of this first solitude will demonstrate how this is true.

The first account of creation does not consider the problem of solitude; man is created in one act as "male and female" (Gn 1:27). But the second account concentrates our attention on the fact that "man is alone," and this aloneness is a fundamental human problem that precedes the problem caused by the fact that man is male and female. When we consider the wider context of the statement in Genesis 2:18, we find that the creation of man is connected, first and foremost, with the "need to till the ground" (Gn 2:5), which corresponds to the first account of creation in which man's vocation is to subdue and have dominion over the earth (see Gn 1:28). In the second account of creation, man is then put into the garden; he is in a state of original happiness as the object of the creative action of God-Yahweh, who has established the conditions of the first covenant with man.

Next, the Lord God gives man a specific test, which helps to define the first meaning of man's original solitude. In Genesis 2:19, we find that "whatever the man called every living creature, that was its name." But even after man has named all the birds of the air and the beasts of the fields, there was still not a helper fit for him.

Although all of this is undoubtedly a preparation for the account of the creation of woman, it also has another, deep meaning. Man, from the first moment of his created existence, finds himself in a search for what we and our contemporaries would call his own "identity." Man is "alone" in the midst of the visible world, particularly among living beings. There is a negative significance to man's search, since it expresses what he "is not"; however, the search has a positive aspect in that it constitutes one of the elements of humanity, which, in addition to "aloneness," is "self-knowledge." Solitude signifies man's subjectivity, which is constituted through self-knowledge. Man is alone because he is "different" from the visible world, from those beings to which he has given names. As we analyze the text of the Book of Genesis, we see not only how man "distinguishes himself" before God with his first act of self-consciousness, but also how he reveals himself to himself and asserts himself as a "person" in the visible world.

In addition to self-consciousness, the concept of original solitude reveals man as both conscious of his body and capable of self-determination. Unless we understand the significance of man's original solitude, we cannot possibly grasp what it means for first man to have been created "in the image of God," that is to say, we cannot understand God's first covenant. This man is manifested in the second narrative as the subject of the covenant, as a partner with the Absolute. He must consciously discern and choose between good and evil, life and death. Man is "alone." He is in a unique, exclusive, and unrepeatable relationship with God himself.

Man realizes this relationship because he is conscious of his body. Man, created "in the image of God," is a body among bodies. It is through his body that man participates in the visible world. At the same time, however, his body makes him conscious of being "alone." Actually, the first man might have concluded, on the basis of his experience of his own body, that he was substantially similar to other living beings; instead, however, he concluded that he was "alone." Although the Yahwist text never directly speaks of the body, when the narrative is considered as a whole it is clear that man is created in the visible world as a body among bodies. On the basis of his experience of original solitude, therefore, man has a consciousness and an awareness of the meaning of his own body.

We discover the importance of the body when we read in Genesis 2:5-6 that there was no one to "till the land" or to "make channels of waters to spring out of the earth." The narrative alludes to the work that man carries out in tilling the earth. The means to dominate the earth lie within man himself; he alone is capable of "tilling it" and transforming it according to his own needs. Thus it is that, through solitude, man, from the beginning, is in the visible world as a body among bodies who discovers the meaning of his own "corporality."

We find that man is a subject not only because of his self-awareness and self-determination, but because of his own body. The structure of his body permits him to be the author of a truly human activity, an activity through which the body expresses the person. Consequently, when we analyze man's original solitude, we discover a fundamental perception of the meaning of the body.

Man, the subject of the ancient covenant with the Creator, has this perception of his body when he is placed before the mystery of the tree of knowledge. Although man had never experienced the meaning of the word "die," he hears the words of Genesis 2:16-17 as a radical antithesis of everything with which he has been endowed. He must associate the meaning of "death" with that dimension of life which he has enjoyed up until this particular time. The words of Genesis 2:16-17 confirm a dependence in man's existence that makes him a limited being who, by his very nature, is now liable to nonexistence.

Man, when he hears the words "you shall die," has to find the truth of these words in the structure of his own solitude. It depends on him—on his own decision, his own free choice—whether he will partake of the tree of knowledge of good and evil and thereby make his own experience of death and dying. The man, hearing the words of God-Yahweh, should realize that the tree of knowledge has roots, not only in the "Garden of Eden," but also in his own humanity.

Thus, man, who has discovered the fundamental meaning of his body—its distinction from all other creatures—knows that the "invisible" determines him more than the "visible;" man is then presented with the alternative that is attached to the tree of the knowledge of good and evil, the alternative of death or immortality.

This alternative goes beyond the essential meaning of the body because it grasps the eschatological meaning of humanity itself as distinguished from all living beings, from "bodies." But this alternative still concerns the body that has been created from "dust from the ground." This alternative, therefore, enters the definition of man and belongs, from "the beginning," to the meaning of man's solitude before God. This original meaning of solitude, permeated by the alternative between death and immortality, has a fundamental meaning for the whole theology of the body.

The Pope concludes his reflections of the meaning of man's original solitude by calling for further reflection on both the text and man, who, in the Pope's words, is "too little conscious of the truth that concerns him and which is already contained in the first chapters of the Bible."

There are six key points for a theology and a spirituality of the body and of sexuality found in the three papal addresses on original solitude.

1. The Yahwist account of original solitude is a key revelation concerning the meaning of human existence; it is the story of the human search for identity *before* it is a tale of human search for a mate.

2. In the story of Adam alone in the garden, we find human nature containing the dimensions of self-knowledge, self-determination, and consciousness of the body.

3. The first human, who alone of all creatures can "till the earth," recognizes that he cannot identify with the creatures he has named; this self-knowledge allows him to discover his identity as being "in the image of God"—in a complete relationship with God-Yahweh.

4. The first human alone in the garden, in a state of original happiness, becomes aware of his capacity for self-determination; he is free to enter into the covenant relationship with God (immortality), or he may enter into the world of "the tree of the knowledge of good and evil" (death).

5. The first human is conscious of his solitude, his self-knowledge, and his self-determination because of his body, which permits him to be the author of truly human activity—activity that allows him to be a partner with the Absolute.

6. This interpretation of the Yahwist account of human solitude challenges us to reflect on the deeper meanings in the biblical text and on the deeper meanings in the human experience, especially in the experience of the body.

Spiritual Reflections

When we think of solitude, many of us immediately recall the innumerable instances when we have felt a great affinity for Greta Garbo and her famous request—"I want to be alone."

Perhaps, to cite a few examples, we think of solitude at the end of the summer. Although we love our school-age children and have enjoyed many experiences of family life during the summer, a certain edginess sets in around this time of year; we find ourselves counting the days until the children return to school. We expect a certain sense of order to return to our family life. Secretly, we look forward to an increase of "alone time"—time in our lives during which we can relax in peace and quiet and listen to the sounds of our own thoughts uninterrupted by the noise and confusion that the children generate.

Or maybe we live in a big city; we are surrounded, in both our work time and play time, by large crowds of people, bombarded by all kinds of noises, seldom able to snatch a few minutes of "alone time" for ourselves. Periodically, the hustle and bustle of the crowds as well as the pitch of the noise jangles our nerves, and we silently scream: "I've got to get away! I need time to smell the flowers, listen to the crickets and the birds, feel the warmth of the sun and the coolness of the breeze."

Or maybe we are experiencing a bad time in our marital relationship; our spouse seems to be demanding more of us than we want to give. The pressure has been mounting over the last few months, and as we continue to resist our spouse's new attempts at intimacy, he or she becomes hurt and angry. Hostilities build up on both sides; as a matter of fact, little in the way of meaningful communication has occurred between us for some time. We are tense, yet listless and depressed. Eventually, we begin to feel sorry for ourselves; we long to be able to walk out the door and go someplace where we could be all alone. We say to ourselves: "What's the sense of staying around here when she (or he) doesn't even talk to me? If I could just be by myself, I wouldn't have to put up with all this hassle."

And so it is. We all have many tales of times when we have wanted to be alone in order to free our minds and our bodies from the demands, the hassles, the tensions, the pressures of everyday life. Solitary walks, retreats, vacations, back-to-nature movements, monastic enclosures, and isolated hermitages are all manifestations of the powerful human need to be alone from time to time. When we begin to feel a drain on our ability to function in a human way, we sense, though not always consciously, a pull toward solitude, toward a place or a time that will afford us an opportunity to "get our life in order."

Much as all of us might dream of our own garden of Eden on some tropical island whose sandy beaches are peopled only by palm trees swaying in the gentle breezes, however, the solitude we long for is a solitude on our own terms. We want to be "in charge" of our own experiences of solitude. We do not want to have these experiences dictated to us by any outside source.

We are, of course, aware of the other side of the coin of solitude, and we do not long for an experience of enforced loneliness. It is difficult, painful, sometimes almost impossible, to recall experiences of loneliness in our life, and we do not consciously seek repetitions of these experiences. In short, we do not fantasize about being lonely.

Maybe we have experienced the loneliness that follows the death of a spouse or a parent or a child or a sibling. Although we may have survived the loss, and the intensity of the loneliness may have lessened, we would not look forward to encountering such a loss again. Or maybe we have experienced the heartbreak that comes with the rupture of an important relationship—perhaps between a husband and wife, or between a parent and child, or between friends, or between lovers. The physical ache we experience with the realization that we cannot mend the relationship takes such a heavy toll that we often find it difficult to fully trust another person again. Or maybe, as a teen-ager, we had experienced that terrible loneliness of desperately wanting to be part of a crowd, yet feeling that we were not pretty enough, strong enough, talented enough, or friendly enough to really be accepted. And then, when we were not invited to the big event of the season, we grieved over this rather dramatic confirmation that we were an "outsider." No one would want to go through that experience again.

Or perhaps we have observed the isolation of the infirmed and the aged in our society, and we promise ourselves that we are going to prepare ourselves so that we can be active in our golden years. We do not want to have to depend on our children or on society or on anyone, but we do want to be sure that our final years will not be spent alone, confined in either a nursing home or our own home endlessly waiting for others to visit us.

Understandably, then, our initial reaction to the Pope's mention of solitude is to say, Yes, we often want to be alone. In fact, we would like to program more "alone time" into our life. But we do not want to be lonely. We hesitate to embrace the concept of solitude because we fear the experience of loneliness. Consequently, for the most part, we do not give ourselves much time for being alone. We do not act on the signals our bodies and our minds give us that we need to be alone. We take vacations, but every moment is filled with activity; we go on retreats, but group discussions dominate. We end up avoiding solitude out of fear of loneliness.

Our mixed response to the suggestion that solitude is an important part of the understanding of man that is revealed in the Yahwist creation story makes sense when we consider the development of human consciousness as both a phenomenon of the species and the experience of individuals within the species. Studies of the development of human culture indicate that in the most primitive of human societies there was no sense of individuality. One's identity was determined by one's participation in the clan, the tribe, or whatever unit one belonged to. There was no sense of self. The demands of human existence were such that group solidarity did not allow for the development of an individual identity. In some situations, conditions eventually allowed for the gradual emergence of a sense of self, and then great leaps forward in the development of human consciousness occurred. Accompanying this emergence of a sense of self, however, was the loss of an assigned identity, and, for the first time, the possibility of loneliness became a reality.[1]

So, too, we all know the mixed sense of joy and sorrow we have felt when we have "cut the apron strings." Perhaps we recall some of the fear we felt going off to our first day of school. Yet, in going off to school, we also experienced the emergence of the sense of self, we were able to keep "secret" from our parents some of the things we had done in that far off world of school. Or we might recall the sense of freedom that accompanied our move into the world of high school. No longer were we part of the baby world that was watched every moment by teachers and parent. We would be less than honest, however, if we did not admit that we also often felt a desire to return to the security of those younger years. And so it is with each move forward in the process of growth and development; we are excited over new challenges, but, at least initially we sense a loss of the security that had been connected with our previous experiences.

The self that is alone is a self that must make choices; the person who has a group-assigned identity need not be troubled with decisions about appropriate behavior. A clear example of this reality in our contemporary society emerges from the difficulties that most of us are experiencing in understanding recent changes about male-female roles. The old stereotype of "man's world" and "woman's place" relieved men and women of the responsibility of working through appropriate behavior in individual relationships. Now that many persons are questioning the stereotype that had emphasized man as the intellectual creature who was to succeed in the world of work, and woman as the emotional creature who was responsible for the caring functions in the home, there are innumerable possibilities for how an individual man and woman might relate. But, at the same time, it becomes necessary for this individual man and woman to assume responsibility for their relationship—a task that is not always easy.

Reflection on our own experiences of solitude, then, causes us to realize that the experience of being alone is, for the human being, a two-edged sword. We long for solitude and can grow as a result of it; at the same time, we fear loneliness and often long for the security of a group-imposed identity. If we place our own experiences of solitude within the story of original solitude, as related in the Genesis account of creation, we begin to appreciate the times when we are alone as opportunities to develop a deeper sense of our own identity, a sense of who we are as a human being and as an individual. And, as we come to a greater appreciation of that sense of identity, we can become better equipped to make choices about appropriate behavior. Times of solitude—whether they are freely chosen or enforced—are, in fact, times for us to discover what it means to be made "in the image of God," namely, that we are partners in a covenant relationship with God-Yahweh. Although we might not be as tempted in the same way our first parent was tempted to identify with the creatures he named, we nevertheless do not often give ourselves the opportunity to discover how we might identify with God. Times of solitude, times for reflection are crucial if we are to develop the capacity for self-knowledge that is revealed in the Yahwist account of creation.

The Pope's reflections on original solitude also make us conscious of the importance of our bodies in our search for identity and self-determination. Certainly our bodies are affected by the stress that builds up and causes us to long for opportunities for solitude. Indeed, the weariness of our bodies often makes us aware of our need to be alone. And the physical pain that accompanies the trauma of loneliness has led researchers to observe that the "broken heart" is not merely a figure of speech.[2] If we are to use our bodily capacities to "till the earth," that is, to be creative caretakers of the earth, then we must listen to what our bodies tell us about our identity and our capacity for self-determination.

We end our reflections on the Pope's analysis of solitude conscious that our religious story encourages us not only to find times for solitude in our own lives, but also to use these times to reflect on our identity, our covenant relationship with Yahweh, and what it means to be created "in the image of God." We also realize that periods of enforced loneliness are times to discover the real meaning of our covenant relationship with Yahweh. Instead of running away from these periods of loneliness, instead of trying to use other people as a way of avoiding feelings of loneliness, we should see these times in the same way that Adam saw his loneliness, that is, as times for examining what it means to be created "in the image of God." Oftentimes, when we have been cut off from some support system that gave us a sense of identity, we avoid the loneliness of our new situation by immediately attaching ourself to another group that will give us an identity. The teen-ager, for example, who feels freed from his or her family identity, rather quickly grabs onto the identity of the peer group. So, too, the rejected divorcee might turn to promiscuity in an attempt to fill the void she experiences as a result of being rejected by her mate. We all know the experience of avoiding the issues that confront us during periods of loneliness.

This examination of original solitude challenges us to be reflective, to uncover God's plan for us through meditation on both revelation in the Biblical text and revelation in our own experiences. We are now ready to return to the Scriptures.

THREE
Original Unity

*"It is not good that the man should be alone;
I will make him a helper fit for him." . . . But
for the man (male) there was not found a
helper fit for him. So the Lord God caused a
deep sleep to fall upon the man, and while he
slept took one of his ribs and closed up its
place with flesh; and the rib, which the Lord
God had taken from the man, he made into a
woman. Then the man said, "This at last is
bone of my bones and flesh of my flesh; she
shall be called woman because she was taken
out of man." Therefore, a man leaves his
father and mother and cleaves to his wife, and
they become one flesh.* —Genesis 2:18-24

Summary of the Pope's Addresses

The words of Genesis 2:18 are a prelude to the narrative of the creation of woman, and, when they are combined with that narrative, the sense of original solitude becomes part of the meaning of original unity. The key point of original unity is found in the words to which Jesus refers in his talk with the Pharisees, "A man shall leave his father and mother and be joined to his wife, and the two shall become one flesh" (Mt 19:25). For this reason, it is important to clarify the meaning of original unity.

The Yahwist text of Genesis 2, unlike the narrative of Genesis 1, authorizes us to think first only of the man, who, by means of his body, belongs to the visible world, but goes beyond that visible world; then the text makes us think of that same man through the dualism of sex. We see, then, that corporality and sexuality are therefore not completely identified. Although the human is, by its nature, male and female, the "body" belongs to the structure of the person more deeply than the fact that the human is, in its somatic constitution, also male and female. Original unity is based on masculinity and femininity, on two different "incarnations," on two ways of "being a body" or being "in the image of God." When we read this Yahwist narrative, we must continually have before our eyes the overriding fact that we were created "in the image of God."

As we read the tale of the separate creation of woman (Gn 2:21-22), the fact that God-Yahweh immerses man in a sleep in preparation for the new creative act gives us food for thought. The man (*'ādām*) falls into that "sleep" in order to wake up "male" and "female." Perhaps the analogy of sleep indicates a return to nonbeing (sleep contains an element of annihilation of man's conscious existence), a return to the moment preceding the creation so that, through God's creative initiative, solitary "man" might emerge in his double unity as male and female. Whatever the reason, we know that man falls into "sleep" with the desire of finding a being like himself. Perhaps he dreams a "second self," which is also personal and participates in his original solitude. In this way the circle of solitude is broken because the first "man" awakens from his sleep as the first "male and female."

The fact that woman is made with "the rib" from the man indicates that there is a homogeneity of the whole being of each one concerning, above all, the body, the somatic structure. This homogeneity is also confirmed by the man's first words to the woman, "This at last is bone of my bones and flesh of my flesh"; these words must be read in the context of the affirmations made before the creation of woman, which described her as "a helper fit for him" (see Gn 2:18 and 20).

Woman is created on the basis of the same humanity as man, and this somatic homogeneity is so evident that the man's words in Genesis 2:23 are dominated by joy and exultation in the other human being, in the "second self" who, despite the sexual difference in constitution, has the same humanity as the man. The narrative of the Book of Genesis shows that the "definitive" creation of man consists in the creation of the unity of two beings, a unity that indicates the identity of human nature. But these two beings also have a duality that manifests what constitutes masculinity and femininity.

From Genesis 2:23, which is set within the context of the creation narrative, we learn that man was created as a particular value for God and as a value for man himself—first, because he is "man" and, second, because the "woman" is for the man and the "man" is for the woman. The first chapter of Genesis expresses this value in a purely theological form (Gn 1:31), but the second chapter reveals this value through man's experience. Certainly the text of Genesis 2:23 can be considered the biblical prototype of the Canticle of Canticles. If it were possible to read impressions and emotions into the remote words of Genesis 2:23, we would have to say that the original "emotion" of the male "man" in the presence of the humanity and the femininity of the other human being seems unique and unrepeatable.

Thus, the meaning of man's original unity through masculinity and femininity is expressed as an overcoming of solitude and, at the same time, as an affirmation for both human beings of everything that constitutes "man" in solitude. Solitude is the way that leads to that unity which Vatican II calls *communio personarum* (communion of persons). Man, who discovered in original solitude his "distinction" from all living beings, opens himself to a "helper fit for him." In a negative sense, man in his solitude, expects a "communion of persons." Communion of persons could be formed only on the basis of a "double solitude" of the man and the woman. Both, through subjectivity and consciousness of the meaning of their bodies, have self-knowledge and self-determination and can exist as one person "beside" another person.

Although the second creation narrative does not speak of "the image of God," it nevertheless reveals that the complete and definitive creation of "man" is expressed in giving life to that "communion of persons" which man and woman form, thus agreeing with the content of the first narrative. We can deduce, then, that man became the "image and likeness" of God not only through his own humanity, but also through the "communion of persons" that man and woman form right from the beginning.

An image reflects the one who is the model; it reproduces its own prototype. Man becomes the image of God, not so much in the moment of solitude as in the moment of communion. We could say that, from "the beginning," man is not only an image that reflects the solitude of the Person who rules the world, but also—and essentially—an image that reflects an inscrutable divine communion of Persons. Thus, the second narrative contributes to an understanding of the Trinitarian concept of the "image of God," which is also significant for the theology of the body.

At this point, we find ourselves at the very heart of the meaning of "body." The male "man" utters the words of Genesis 2:23 as if, only at the sight of the woman, would he be able to identify and call by name that which makes them visibly similar to each other and, at the same time, manifests their humanity. Of no other being could man say "flesh of my flesh." It is the body, therefore, that reveals man.

The body, then, has not only an anthropological significance, but also a theological meaning. The theology of the body, which is bound up with the creation of man in the image of God, also becomes the theology of sex, or rather, the theology of masculinity and femininity. The original meaning of unity through the body possesses a multifaceted dimension—an ethical dimension, which is confirmed by Jesus' answer to the Pharisees in Matthew 19, a sacramental and a theological dimension, which are found in St. Paul's words to the Ephesians and also in the tradition of Hosea, Isaiah, and Ezekiel.

The human is presented, right from the beginning, with a deep consciousness of corporality and sexuality, which is an inalienable norm for the understanding of man on the theological plane. The meaning of the original unity of man who is created "male and female" is found by knowing man in the entire endowment of his being as one who, at the beginning, is "alone" and must always pass through duality, that is, "communion." Masculinity and femininity are two ways of being "a body" and, at the same time, "a man," two complementary dimensions of self-consciousness and self-determination, and two ways of being conscious of the meaning of the body. So it is that femininity finds itself in the presence of masculinity, and masculinity is confirmed through femininity. Sex, which is a constituent part of the person, proves how deeply man, in addition to his spiritual solitude, is constituted by the body as "he" or "she." The presence of the female element and the male element signifies an enrichment for man in his whole history, including the history of salvation.

The unity of Genesis 2:24 is undoubtedly that of the conjugal act. Sex—that is, femininity and masculinity—is the characteristic of man—that is, male and female—that permits them, when they become "one flesh," to submit their whole humanity to the blessing of fertility. Thus, we cannot stop at the surface of human sexuality or consider the body and sex outside of the "communion of persons." The expression, "a man cleaves to his wife" so intimately that they become "one flesh," refers us back to the words of Genesis 2:23. When they are "one flesh," they return to that union in humanity which allows them to both recognize each other and call each other by name. Becoming "one flesh" is a powerful bond that has been established by the Creator to allow the man and the woman to discover their own humanity, both in its original unity and in the duality of mutual attraction. At the level of the mutual relationship of persons, sex expresses an ever new surpassing of the limit of man's solitude, which contains within it a certain assumption of the solitude of the body of the second "self" as one's own.

Genesis 2:24 indicates that the unity through which the man and the woman become "one flesh" has had, from "the beginning," the element of choice. Although Genesis 2:24 refers to the first man and the first woman, it does so in the perspective of the whole earthly future of man. Jesus appeals to this text as relevant for his age. The first man and woman, who had been formed in the image of God as a true communion of persons, constitute the beginning and the model of that communion in which all men and women are so intimately united as to be "one flesh." The body, which helps the man and the woman find themselves in the "communion of persons," becomes the constituent element of their union when they become husband and wife. This union takes place through mutual choice, the choice that establishes the conjugal pact.

Choice, as the expression of self-determination, rests on the foundation of man's self-consciousness that was uncovered in original solitude and now is actually a "two-fold solitude." Man is a "body" and, through the body, male and female. When man and woman unite as "one flesh," their conjugal union presupposes a mature consciousness of the body. In every conjugal union, there fore, the same original consciousness of the significance of the body in its masculinity and its femininity is rediscovered. In each of these unions, the mystery of creation is renewed in all of its original depth and vital power. In Genesis 2:24, we find woman, first, "taken out of man" as "flesh of his flesh," next becoming his "wife," and then eventually becoming the mother of the living through a motherhood that has its origin in him. Procreation is rooted in creation, and reproduces its mystery.

Chapter 7, on knowledge and procreation, will cover this subject in greater depth. The Pope concludes his analysis of original unity with the realization that the unity of man and woman, part of the mystery of creation, was meant to apply, from "the beginning," to all future unions of this nature.

This summary of the Pope's three addresses on original unity contains the following six important points for a theology and a spirituality of sexuality.

1. The "definitive" creation of man consists in the creation of the unity of two beings in which solitary "man" emerges in a double unity as "male" and "female"; man and woman share the same humanity because woman is a "helper fit for him."

2. Genesis 2:23, the prototype of the Song of Songs, shows how human solitude is overcome in a communion of persons that reflects a divine communion of persons; the body reveals humans as persons who, even in their corporality, are "similar" to God.

3. The theology of the body, which, from the beginning, is rooted in the creation of man "in the image of God," now becomes the theology of sex or the theology of masculinity and femininity.

4. Masculinity and femininity are two "incarnations" of the same solitude; two ways of being "a body" and, at the same time, "a human," two complementary dimensions of self-consciousness and self-determination; and two complementary ways of being conscious of the meaning of the body.

5. Becoming "one flesh" is a powerful bond established by God through which the first humans, and all others who join as one flesh, are able to discover their own humanity by

surpassing the limit of their solitude and assuming the solitude of the body of the second "self" as their own.

6. The unity of one flesh is the unity of choice; the body, through its own masculinity or femininity, becomes the constituent element between the union of a husband and wife through mutual choice.

Spiritual Reflections

We ended our thoughts on original solitude much like the person who has just successfully resolved an identity crisis. We recognized the challenge of our solitude as a reminder that we are persons created "in the image of God." There is a sense of excitement in discovering the possibility that we can choose to be *persons*—that is to say, beings with both bodies and interior perceptions—who reflect the divine image; but, like the person who has discovered his or her own identity, we are somewhat bewildered. What do we do with our new-found identity? In psychological language, how do we share this identity with another in a relationship of intimacy?

We discovered that we wanted "alone time" but we did not want to be lonely. We are, even in the midst of our solitary times, people who want to share ourselves with others. We want to communicate so much to others, especially to those others who are most important to us, but oftentimes it seems difficult, if not impossible, to *really* share ourselves with another.

Think of what happens when we plan a vacation. Perhaps it is a long-awaited trip to Europe, or a camping expedition in the wilderness, or a visit to Grandma's, or a cross-country trek with the family, or a return to the place of our childhood. Whatever vacation we are planning, the preparation time is generally filled with an air of excitement; friends, family, and co-workers express an interest in how things are going and wish a hearty *bon voyage* as we embark on our adventure. The actual trip, whether it lasts for one week, two weeks, or perhaps even three weeks, is a time filled with different experiences and different people and passes quickly.

Generally, we take pictures to help jog our memory when this exciting time begins to grow dim. When we return home and go back to work, we are eager to tell everyone about what we did and the things and people that we saw. Quite often, however, we discover that our friends, relatives, and co-workers have only minimal interest in hearing about our vacation. The level of interest that others give to our vacation could be characterized as follows: "Did you have a good time? What was the weather like? How was the food? And what were the important sights you saw? But please don't take more than five minutes of my time answering these questions."

We quickly realize that it is impossible to "share" these experiences with those who were not traveling with us. They have been busy about their own lives during our absence, and, just as we will be unable to appreciate what happened to them while we were away, it will be impossible for them to enter into the spirit of our vacation. This realization makes us aware of our human "limits," at least when it comes to sharing experiences with others.

Our solitary "self," therefore, wants unity but finds the search for this unity a difficult task. Indeed, discussions of unity usually focus on experiences of disunity because we seem to experience disunity so much more than we experience unity. In fact, we would have to be hermits to escape the ever present phenomenon of disunity in our contemporary world. The media, our family, and our friends all supply us with examples of disunity: armed conflicts in all corners of the world, violence in our cities, disagreements on political issues, a lack of consensus on religious matters, quarrels in both our communities and our families, divorces, child abuse, disagreements among work associates, and breakups of long-time friendships—these are but a few of the myriad experiences of disunity that come to mind.

And few, if any, of us are happy with disunity; virtually everyone longs for an end to strife and conflict, be it in our family, our community, or the wider world. Disunity is a reminder of the loneliness we experience in our solitude. We feel our sense of identity, which we uncovered in our original meditations on solitude, threatened by our experiences of disunity. If, at a psychological level, we come through an identity crisis with a strong sense of who we are, we also carry with us the memory of the disintegration we have experienced during our times of personal conflict. The disunity around us can, at times, threaten us with the same type of chaos that we had experienced during our crisis. So, too, if our theological identity or our spiritual identity is linked to the fact that we are created "in the image of God," we cannot help recognizing that the conflict that is present in so many instances of disunity does not seem to fit what we understand to be the divine plan for human existence.

The Yahwist creation narrative reminds us that our bodies supply us with powerful hints on how to overcome our sense of isolation. In short, we need "a helper." We need to learn how we can share our identity with another, how we can, with another, truly reflect the image of God.

Our bodies seem to long for "a helper fit for us." Comparative primatologists, sociobiologists, and physical anthropologists maintain that a sustained, sexually motivated relationship between male and female was necessary for the emergence of primitive hominids into *homo sapiens*. This sustained relationship provided a longer socialization period for the offspring that allowed them to adapt more readily to environmental changes. The quasi-pair bonding of humans therefore, ensured the survival of the next generation, despite external obstacles. At the scientific level, it would seem safe to suppose that we are genetically programmed for unity. The human female has a sexual attractiveness that is unique to our species.

The human readiness to respond to the sexual attractiveness of the person of the other sex serves as the basis of the "sex sells" approach to advertising. Such an approach would never work in the animal world because fantasies about future sexual encounters do not seem to be part of the experience of other species. Animal sexuality is instinctual. Animals do not have the need or desire to find some greater meaning in their sexual instinct.

For most of us, however, even though we don't often try to articulate it, our sexuality means more than simply a romp in bed. We remember past sexual encounters, and our anticipation of future sexual experiences is colored, positively or negatively, by our reflection of these past experiences and how they have satisfied our human longing for unity. Even if we have not yet had a sexual encounter, we can nevertheless spend a great deal of time fantasizing about future encounters; just remembering our teen-age years can cause a blush among adults.

In addition to forcing us to make decisions about our identity, solitude also makes us conscious of the power of the physical sexual attraction we feel toward members of the other sex. In light of the Pope's analysis of original unity, we could say that both our bodies and our strong, genetically programmed desire for unity point toward the possibility of a "communion of persons." As we all know from our own experience, however, every response to the stirring of our sexual drive is not a search for "communion of persons."

The biblical story of the first man and the first woman encourages us to be more reflective about the meaning of this important dimension of our human personality. We need to ask ourselves how we might use our bodily responses as an aid in forming a "communion of persons." If our bodies are propelling us toward unity, what more must we do to achieve that unity which will allow us to reflect the divine communion of persons.

Even those experiences of human unity that are rooted in the powerful sexual attraction of man for woman and woman for man are colored by limitations on our desire for unity. Consider what we experience when we fall in love. Our bodies begin to react in strange ways: the physical presence of our beloved causes our heart to race and our bodies to be filled with sensual joy; what is more, just thinking about this person we love causes our palms to sweat and our nervous system to work overtime. Being in love makes us acutely conscious of our bodily desire for unity, and, at the same time, makes us aware of the limits of our human attempts at unity because we cannot be with our beloved every minute.

Consider, too, our fantasy life when we are in love, and then compare these fantasies with our actual encounters with our beloved. In our fantasy world, our attempts at unity are much more successful because we control the response of our beloved to our overtures; in the real experience of our meetings with our beloved, however, she or he often reacts in ways we had never imagined in our fantasies.

Even at those times when our bodies are supporting our quest for unity, we nevertheless have difficulty achieving the intimacy we long for. And today, when people are living for an average of seventy years or more, the idea that a communion of persons will survive a marital relationship of fifty years presents us with many difficulties. "Cleaving to another" is not so easy as we had thought it would be. And if the relationship of a husband and wife—these two persons who become one flesh—is to be the model for all human unity, we seriously wonder about the possibilities for unity. So many marriages are filled with disunity; we cannot imagine how marriage could possibly point the way to God's plan for human unity.

When we consider the Pope's observation that masculinity and femininity are two "incarnations" of the same solitude, two ways of being a body, two complementary dimensions of self-consciousness and self-determination, and two complementary ways of being conscious of the meaning of the body, we begin to realize why it might be extremely difficult for those of us who live in "historical" time to enter into a marital union that will reflect the image of God. Self-consciousness, self-determination, and an awareness of the meaning of our body are issues that many of us choose to ignore both before and after we are married, even though these issues contribute to the forming of our unique identity. As psychologists are quick to point out, it is impossible to be intimate (that is, share our identity with another) if we do not have an identity to share.

Because an intimacy relationship of any duration is clearly bound to have "highs and lows," we cannot afford to ignore the importance that self-consciousness, self-determination, and an awareness of the meaning of the body have in our own lives and in the life of our mate. Because each one of us has a distinct identity, any marriage is bound to have dimensions of disunity. The vision that is presented in the creation story seems to challenge us to emphasize the complementary dimensions of our marriage relationship rather than the inevitable experiences of disunity.

We must therefore look beneath the surface of the Yahwist creation story if we are to understand the man-woman relationship as a model for human unity. We need to "unpack" the mythical, archaic way of trying to express a deeper content. We want to know what it is that Adam and Eve discovered when they found themselves no longer "alone." We need to reflect on the meaning of "bone of my bones and flesh of my flesh." Adam discovers the meaning of femininity in the body of Eve while, at the same time, Eve discovers the meaning of masculinity in the body of Adam. This discovery of the "other" way of being a body helps each one to uncover more definitively what it means to be a human, to be in the "image of God."

So, too, in our "historical" time, it is possible to see the joining of a man and a woman in a successful conjugal union as a way in which we can learn more about the meaning of human existence through reflection on how we share our bodies. The joy of sexual union, which is similar to the unique and unrepeatable joy of Adam when he discovers Eve, is a joy that is based on joining two different ways of being human into a unity that (1) is enriched by these differences and (2) allows each of us to overcome the loneliness of our own solitude.

When, as the Pope says, we assume the "solitude of the body of the second self as our own" in an act of sexual union, we have the opportunity to experience a hint of the complementariness of masculinity and femininity in God's original plan. As human beings, we have the opportunity to reflect on the meaning of such an activity. If, in the act of sexual intercourse, we assume some of the solitude of the other, what effect does this have on how we relate to that other person apart from the instance of physical sexual union? Does the joy of union carry through into other aspects of our relationship? Or have other aspects of our relationship begun to interfere with our ability to appreciate sexual intimacy as a discovery of someone who is "bone of my bones and flesh of my flesh"?

The Genesis story reminds us that, in a marital relationship, the union of our bodies is meant to help us enter a "communion of persons." We are "helpers" fit for each other, fit to help each other discover the real meaning of human existence. We need to more fully explore how it is possible to be "helpers." We need to learn how to be a "helper."

According to the Pope's analysis, the story of original unity, in which Adam and Eve are "bone of my bones and flesh of my flesh" and cleave to each other in such a way that they enter into a "communion of persons" that allows them to be "in the image of God," has all the necessary ingredients for overcoming disunity in human relationships. The story challenges us to reflect on how our bodies—alone and in union with another—reveal the divine plan for human unity.

We know that the union of our bodies does not require so complete a sharing that one or both partners might lose their individual identities. This model of unity helps us to understand why it is so difficult to *really* share ourselves with another if that sharing ignores the other's experience of solitude, that is, the other's self-consciousness or identity. If the sexual union of man and woman is the model that will point the way toward overcoming some of the disunity that seems to threaten us with chaos, our experiences of our masculinity and femininity, as well as our experiences of the very unity we strive for, are important experiences for religious and spiritual reflection. They are important experiences not just because they will help us to understand sexuality, the body, and marital intimacy, but also because such reflections might be useful for developing models for other forms of human unity.

Just as in Genesis 2:24, the element of choice, the element of self-determination is present right from "the beginning." A husband and wife today, through their bodies, establish a conjugal pact in which they strive to be a "communion of persons." This element of choice, which differentiates humans from the other "visible" world, colors our ability to enter into all relationships that involve unity. We are free to choose whether to attempt unity and how deep a unity we want; so, too, the other person or group is free to choose the unity they desire. Because the body, through its masculinity or femininity, is presented in the Genesis story as the constituent element that allows the husband and the wife to mutually choose each other, an awareness of our bodies and of our sexuality takes on an added importance at this juncture of our development of a spirituality.

We conclude our reflections on original unity with an acute awareness of both our longing for unity and the difficulties we experience in our attempts at unity. We also hear the Yahwist narrative telling us that God's plan for human unity calls for a joining of different ways of being human into a "communion of persons." We need, therefore, to continue to reflect on both the human experience of sexual unity and the biblical narrative of God's original plan for that unity. We in "historical" time gain a perspective from these original stories even though we cannot hope to enter into such a perfect unity ourselves. We can be inspired to strive for a "communion of persons" in which God will be present.

FOUR
Original Nakedness

*And the man and his wife were both naked
and not ashamed*—Genesis 2:25

Summary of the Pope's Addresses

As background for his analysis of the experience of original nakedness, the Pope reminds us that when we are speaking of original human experiences, we are referring to the basic significance of these experiences rather than to the fact that they belong to man's prehistory. These experiences are always at the root of every human experience, even if they do not receive much attention. The beginning "revelation of the body" helps us to discover the extraordinary side of what is ordinary. In the biblical text, man's experience of his body is on the threshold of the whole "historical" experience that will follow it. Man does not perceive the depth of this experience in his everyday life; however, he presupposes it as part of the formulation of his own image.

This understanding of the meaning of original nakedness enables us to analyze Genesis 2:25, which, at first glance, seems a misplaced statement. A deeper analysis, however, shows us that Genesis 2:25 presents one of the key elements of the original revelation that is as decisive as original solitude and original unity. This third element, clearly stressed in this story, is not something accidental; it is, in fact, the key for a full and complete understanding of biblical anthropology.

The account of original nakedness in Genesis 2:25 requires that reflections on the theology of the body should be connected with man's personal subjectivity. The text, according to which the first human beings—man and woman—"were naked" and yet "were not ashamed," unquestionably describes their state of consciousness as

39

a state within which the meaning of the body develops. Saying that they "were not ashamed," the author tries to describe the mutual experience of the body, that is, the man's experience of the femininity that is revealed in the nakedness of the woman's body, and, likewise, the woman's experience of that masculinity that is revealed in the nakedness of the man's body. The phrase, "naked and not ashamed," reflects a basic experience of man in the "common" and prescientific sense; this description also meets the requirements of contemporary anthropology, which likes to examine such fundamental experiences as the experience of shame.

In referring to "the beginning" (Mt 19:4 and 8), Jesus indirectly establishes the idea of continuity between the state of "historical" man and that of original innocence, allowing us to move back from the threshold of man's "historical" sinfulness to his original innocence. Genesis 2:25, placed as it is within the context of the entire Yahwist narrative, emphasizes the need to cross that threshold. In Genesis 3:7, we read: "Then the eyes of both were opened, and they knew that they were naked; and they sewed fig leaves together and made themselves aprons." "Then" indicates a new moment, a new situation, and implies a new content, a new quality of the experience of the body.

There is a significant difference in the formulations of Genesis 2:25 and Genesis 3:7. This difference takes place at a level that is deeper than the pure and simple use of the sense of sight. It is not simply a question of whether, in the first instance, the man and woman did not "know that they were naked," and, in the second instance, they "knew"; rather, there is a radical change in the meaning of original nakedness that emerges from the conscience of the man and the woman as the result of having eaten the fruit of the tree of the knowledge of good and evil. This change directly concerns the experience of the meaning of one's body, of the man-woman, femininity-masculinity relationship. We will analyze this change in a later chapter. Now we must ask if it is possible to reconstruct the original meaning of nakedness, which, in the Book of Genesis, constitutes the immediate context of the doctrine about the unity of the human being as male and female. This reconstruction seems possible if we understand the experience of shame in the biblical text as a "liminal" experience.

Contemporary analysis of shame indicates the complexity of this experience in which the human being experiences fear about his "second self" (as, for example, the woman before the man), a fear that is substantially fear for his own "self." Shame in a human being reveals the need for affirmation and acceptance of this "self" according to its rightful value. Another complexity in the experience of shame arises from the fact that, although it "almost" keeps one human being away from the other (woman from man), it also seeks to draw them closer personally and influences the formation of *ethos* in human society, particularly in the man-woman relationship. Thus, we find that shame is deeply rooted in mutual relations; shame expresses the essential rules for the "communion of persons" and touches the dimensions of man's original "solitude." We still need to ask, however, why it is absent from Genesis 2:25.

First, Genesis 2:25 speaks of a real non-presence of shame rather than a lack or underdevelopment of shame. On the contrary, Genesis 2:25 indicates a particular fullness of consciousness, experience, and understanding of the meaning of the body that is bound up with the fact that "they were naked." We must try to uncover what this fullness of consciousness, experience, and understanding of the meaning of the body indicates.

To do this, we must keep in mind our analysis of the Yahwist passage up to this point. We saw man's original solitude as "non-identification" of his own humanity with the world of living beings around him. This non-identification made way for the discovery of one's own humanity "with the help" of the other human being, the woman. Their discovery act flows from a perception of the world that is carried out directly through the body ("flesh of my flesh"). We can see, then, that nakedness corresponds to that fullness of consciousness of the meaning of the body which is derived from the typical perception of the senses. This fullness of consciousness reveals a truth of reality according to which man and woman were originally given to each other. We cannot ignore this participation in the perception of the world in its "exterior" aspect, which is a direct and almost spontaneous fact that virtually precedes any "critical" complication of knowledge.

We must go beyond consideration of man's participation in the exterior perception of the world, however, in order to find the meaning of original nakedness. Genesis 2:25 introduces us to the level of the depth of man and wants us to explore, at that depth, the original innocence of knowing. It is at the level of human interiority that we can understand the particular fullness of interpersonal communication that allows man and woman to be "naked and not ashamed." The concept of "communication" is connected with subjects who "communicate" precisely on the basis of the "common union" that exists between them—a union that enables each of them to express the reality that is peculiar and pertinent only to each one's own sphere. Thus, the human body acquires a completely new meaning that is different from the "external" perception of the world. The personal, human "self" derives its "exterior" perception from within.

The whole biblical narrative of creation, but especially the Yahwist text, shows the body, through its own visibility, revealing man and enabling man and woman, right from the beginning, "to communicate" with each other according to the *communion of persons* that had been willed by the Creator for them. This perspective allows us to understand the correct meaning of original nakedness, which Genesis 2:25 shows as something extraordinary, that is, outside the limits of the shame that is known through human experience, and, at the same time, contributing to the fullness of interpersonal communication that is at the very heart of *communion of persons*. The words, "they were not ashamed," convey an original depth in affirming what is inherent in the person, what is visibly female and male through which the "personal intimacy" of mutual communication is formed. The fullness of "exterior" perception, which is expressed by means of physical nakedness, corresponds with the "interior" fullness of man, who is created in the "image of God." The act of the man and the woman seeing each other also has an "interior" dimension—a participation in the vision of the Creator himself who "saw everything that he had made, and, behold, it was very good." (Gn 1:31).

"Nakedness" signifies the original good of God's vision through which the "pure" value of humanity as male and female, the "pure" value of the body and of sex, is revealed. The situation of the man and the woman that is described in Genesis 2:25 does not know an interior rupture, that is, an opposition between what is spiritual and what is sensible, between what constitutes the person humanly and what is male and female. Man and woman see each other more fully and distinctly through the very mystery of creation than they do through the sense of sight itself. They have the peace of the "interior gaze," which creates the fullness of the intimacy of persons. If "shame" brings limitation to seeing through the eyes of the body, this is because personal intimacy is disturbed by this sight. The man and the woman in Genesis 2:25 "communicate" in the fullness of humanity precisely because they are "male" and "female." When they "communicate" on the basis of that communion of persons in which, through femininity and masculinity, they become *gift* for each other, they reach a mutual and special understanding of the meaning of their own bodies. Thus, we find that the original meaning of nakedness leads to an understanding of the meaning of the body that is at the very heart of the man-woman community-communion. We will refer to this meaning of the body as "nuptial" in the next chapter.

Our analysis of the creation of man and woman in the Elohist and Yahwist narratives has allowed us to establish the original meaning of solitude, unity, and nakedness. The biblical text contains the essential elements of an anthropology that tries to understand and interpret man in the theological context of the "image of God," which is revealed through that "beginning" to which Jesus refers the Pharisees (Mt 19:4 and 8). Man, whom God created "male and female," bears the divine image printed on his body "from the beginning;" man and woman constitute two different ways for the human to be "a body" in the unity of that image.

When Jesus used the words "created" and "Creator," he indicated a new dimension of understanding, which we will call "hermeneutics of the gift," that determines the essential truth and depth of meaning of the original solitude, unity, and nakedness. It is this dimension of gift that enables us to construct the theology of the body "from the beginning" while, at the same time, it demands that we should construct it in this way.

The Creator is he who "calls to existence from nothingness" because he "is love." Although we do not find the word *love* in the creation narrative, we do know that God saw what he had made and that "it was very good" (Gn 1:31). Because only love gives a beginning to good and delights in good, we understand that love is the divine motive for creation. Creation signifies not only an initial *calling* to existence from nothingness, but also a fundamental and radical *giving* in which the gift comes into being from nothingness.

Every creature bears within him the sign of the original and fundamental gift. This concept of "giving," however, does not refer to a nothingness; rather, it indicates the one who gives the gift and the one who receives the gift and the relationship that is established between them. We discover this relationship in the creation account when man is created—"God created man in his own image, in the image of God, he created him" (Gn 1:27). In the narrative that describes the creation of the visible world, the concept of giving has meaning only with regard to man; the visible world was created "for him." Creation is a gift because there appears in it man who is both "the image of God" and capable of understanding the very meaning of *gift* as the call from nothingness to existence. And man is capable of answering the Creator. Man appears as "created," as the one who, in the midst of the world, received the other as a gift. In the next chapter the Pope will analyze more deeply this dimension of the gift.

The following are the main points for a theology and a spirituality of the body and of sexuality that emerge from the Pope's three addresses on original nakedness.

1. Original experiences are at the root of every human experience, even when we do not pay attention to them; our study of the "revelation of the body" helps us discover the extraordinary side of what is ordinary.

2. The "nonpresence" of shame in original nakedness indicates a radically different perception of the meaning of the body and a different relationship between man and woman in "original" time as compared to our "historical" experience of shame.

3. In the Yahwist narrative, the body enables man and woman to communicate according to the communion of persons that has been willed for them by the Creator because their physical nakedness corresponds to the interior vision of man created in the "image of God"; there is, in short, no rupture between what is spiritual and what is physical.

4. The personal intimacy of man and woman that is implied in Genesis 2:25 is possible because, through masculinity and femininity, man and woman become a gift for each other; they bear the divine image upon their bodies and

constitute two different ways of "being a body" in the unity of that image.

5. We fully understand the depth of original solitude, unity, and nakedness when we realize that God created the world as a gift because he "is love"; creation is a gift because man, created in the "image of God," understands the meaning of gift and responds to that when he receives the other as a gift.

Spiritual Reflections

How do we as "historical" people react to nakedness? A study of various cultures indicates that there are a variety of responses to the situation of physical nakedness. As Richard Leakey has observed: "We were conceived in an animal world but came to maturity in self-generating cultures."[1] Our reactions to physical nakedness, therefore, seem conditioned by the standards that are accepted by our society at large. Certainly many of our ancestors would be shocked at the degree of dress (or undress, as some might judge) in today's society. And, of course, what is acceptable exposure of the human body in one culture could easily be ruled nonacceptable in another.

Kenneth Clark, in his work *The Nude,*[2] seems to capture the response of many people in western society when he observes that many of us who appreciate nudity in art would be uncomfortable in the presence of the same degree of nudity in real life situations. Clark maintains that nudity in art is considered beautiful because the artist's rendition of the naked body eliminates all of the imperfections that are visible in a real encounter with a naked body, be it our own or that of another person.

The degree of physical arousal that is engendered by nakedness also seems to be conditioned by previous learning and by present expectations. Members of nudists colonies claim to have overcome the tendency to associate nudity with sexual availability. Health care workers, who regularly deal with people in various degrees of nakedness, indicate little, if any, problem with the sexual aspects of physical nakedness. Actors and actresses who perform "nude" scenes, at least for conventional movies, claim that the technical aspects of preparing for and executing such a nude scene divest it of any potential sexual explosiveness.

It seems, then, that our individual reactions to the naked body vary greatly, and the basis of these reactions, which is conditioned by culture and family, might be so deeply buried that we would have a difficult time articulating why we react as we do. We realize, however, that our response to nakedness, like the response of our first parents, is influenced by an interior perception of the sexuality of another, a perception that seems to require further examination when we reflect on the Pope's analysis of original nakedness.

When we reflected on original solitude in Chapter 2, we realized that the Christian response to a search for identity needs to be considered within the context of persons who have been created "in the image of God." Reflection on original unity (Chapter 3) reminded us that God's plan for our identity includes an ability to join with another, to have a unity with our fellow human beings— either the exclusive unity of a male-female relationship, or the more general unity of intimate relationships with others. Now, as we consider the reaction of original man and woman to their nakedness, we find hints about what we must do if we are to achieve unity; if, in other words, after we establish our own identity, we are to be able to share that identity with another in an intimate relationship.

The Pope's emphasis on how the man discovered another way of being human when he looked on the femininity of the woman, and how the woman discovered another way of being human when she observed the masculinity of the man, indicates that the unity of man and woman "in the image of God" is the unity of two different ways of being human. The self that wants to be alone and yet fears loneliness is reminded that we can be "in the image of God" when we are open to appreciating the "nakedness" of the other, that is, the "difference" of the other.

Those who are somewhat uncomfortable in the presence of physical nakedness find it difficult to imagine that reflecting on human nakedness would help us discover the meaning of existence. Our background is such that we make aprons out of fig

leaves and cover not only our bodies but also any consideration of the goodness of our bodies and our sexuality in the divine
plan for human existence. When we do this, however, we rob our
bodies of some of their revelatory significance. The unity of two in
one flesh is a unity of two different persons, a unity that forms the
"image of God," a unity that seems to require an interior unity as
well as an exterior, physical joining. Only then can that unity help
us grow in our capacity for intimacy, in our capacity to be "in the
image of God." If we begin to consider this unity of two in one
flesh and the meaning of nakedness for this unity, we can begin to
understand something about the unity of humankind that will
reflect God's plan.

Even when we delight in the joy of sexual intercourse, a joy that
is greatly enhanced by our perception of our spouse's nakedness,
we still find it difficult to accept that there is something in our
erotic engagement that speaks to us of how we are to understand
all human relationships. We easily appreciate our partner's difference in sexual play, but it becomes rather difficult to accept that
same partner's differences when they are differences in point of
view or personality or lifestyle, or ideas about male-female roles.
Yet we know that when we appreciate both the masculinity of our
spouse and the joy it can bring us, as well as the pleasure our
femininity can bring him, we can be a better lover. The exploration
of the other, of the other's differences, is a part of sexual play that
not only is pleasurable at the moment, but also contributes to
enjoyable fantasies, which sustain the bonding aspects of our relationship. Reflection on our own experiences of lovemaking can, in
fact, enhance the quality of our relationship as well as contribute
to increased pleasurability in our sexual intimacy. If we can learn
to appreciate the interior "differences" that seem to separate us
from our spouse by seeing them as possible ways of enriching us
and our relationship, we will be allowing our physical intimacy to
act as a catalyst for our whole life of intimacy.

The intimacy we seek in a marital relationship that is modeled
on our first parents' communion of persons is not always an easy
task. The fullness of interpersonal communications, which allowed
the first man and woman to be "naked and not ashamed," requires
a blending of differences that is rooted, first of all, in the conviction that difference is not bad. Yet humans have difficulty with

47

communication, especially the kind of interpersonal communications that are required for intimacy, precisely because we have problems with "differences."

Consider the great frustration we all experience when we try to communicate with someone, and that person is unable to grasp what we are trying to tell them. The parents of teen-agers, for example, want their children to know that they are loved. Part of this loving includes setting restrictions on driving while drinking. The teen-agers in this example, however, love their parents, but nevertheless "know" they can handle the situation and do not want their parents' overprotective concern. Both parents and teen-agers have the best of intentions, but they bring such different perspectives to the discussion that it becomes impossible, or at least terribly difficult, to overcome barriers to understanding each other's point of view.

To cite another example, consider the persons who live in a changing neighborhood. They worry that newcomers to the community, who come from an ethnic background that is different from theirs, will destroy the sense of neighborliness that has been such an important part of the community's life. Or consider the newcomers to a community who are concerned about maintaining their strong sense of family in the midst of what they perceive to be the vastly different values of the people already settled in their community. Fears stirred up by "differences" in the other prevent them from discovering the common interest in living in peace and safety that is the goal of most families.

All too often, we find ourselves distrusting the "differences" of another political party, of a business competitor, of the "big city" when we live in a small suburb, of other parts of our country or other nations. Moreover, we allow this distrust over a different point of view to be an obstacle to unity rather than a contribution to a more rewarding unity.

We do not easily embrace the concept of pluralism as a positive value in human societies. Our American experience celebrates the concept of the melting pot according to which every ethnic group supposedly gave up its identity in order to become American. Our religious experience in the post-Reformation church put heavy emphasis on unity meaning *oneness*. Both of these influences, however, have caused us to ignore the reality of our own experience in which a unity that has been freely chosen, for example, and has contributed to either personal or community growth and development has been a harmonious blending of differences. Reflection on the unity "of two in one flesh" and the unity of marital intimacy leads us to see the importance of a "nakedness" that is an openness to a different way of being—whether a physically different way of being a human or a different point of view or some other interior difference.

Thus, we find that the Genesis story offers us a pattern for all human relationships when it focuses on the primordial relationship of man and woman. We humans, when we reflect on the story of our bodies and God's plan for our bodies, find a deep significance in the fact that God made us "male" and "female." We who are "alone" will appreciate our own identity and the meaning of human existence when we are able to be "in the image of God." Through a unity with our fellow human beings and through a communion of persons that celebrates the different ways of being human, our bodies—that is, our masculinity and our femininity— are meant to assist in the continual revelation of this divine plan. We who were created by a God who is love can appreciate the meaning of the gift of creation; we are therefore challenged by both the biblical story and our own bodies to respond to this gift by giving ourselves to the other.

Although our reflections help us to more fully appreciate the meaning of God's original plan, we who are "historical" people nevertheless find it very difficult to imagine how humankind could ever begin to approximate the original appreciation of differences. We even find it difficult to imagine how our first parents were able to have the interior unity that allowed them to be "not ashamed" about their obvious physical differences.

With these thoughts, we conclude our reflections on this third element, original nakedness, in the theology of the body and sexuality which has been uncovered by the Pope in his analysis of the creation stories in Genesis. Inspired by this vision of the possibilities for human relationships, perhaps more open to the revelatory possibilities of our bodies, and somewhat hopeful about the potential for a feast of human sexuality, we see more of the interaction that can take place between the story of our masculinity and femininity and the divine story that has been related by the narrators of the Book of Genesis. We see the direction that our spirituality should take, but we also feel the gnawing question: "How will it ever be possible for us?"

FIVE

Nuptial Meaning of the Body

The Lord God formed man of dust from the ground, and breathed into his nostrils the breath of life; and man became a living being—Genesis 2:7

"It is not good that the man should be alone. I will make him a helper fit for him"
—Genesis 2:18

But for the man (male) there was not found a helper fit for him. So the Lord God caused a deep sleep to fall upon the man, and while he slept took one of his ribs and closed up its place with flesh; and the rib which the Lord God had taken from the man he made into a woman. Then the man said, "This at last is bone of my bones and flesh of my flesh; she shall be called woman, because she was taken out of man." Therefore, a man leaves his father and his mother and cleaves to his wife and they become one flesh. And the man and his wife were both naked, and were not ashamed. —Genesis 2:20b-25

Summary of the Pope's Addresses

As background for the analysis of the nuptial meaning of the body, the Pope suggests that when we reread and analyze the Yahwist narrative of creation we ask ourselves if the first "man," in his original solitude, really experienced the world as a gift. When we analyzed original solitude, we found a certain lack of good; both God and the man agreed that it was *not good* for man to be alone (Gn 2:18). Man needed a "helper fit for him." Two words—the adjective "alone" and the noun "helper"—are the key to understanding the essence of the gift that is contained in the truth of the "image of God." There is a particular characteristic of personal existence that man "alone" does not realize. He realizes this truth only by existing "with someone and for someone." The communion of persons thus means existing in a mutual "for," in a relationship of gift. Man's original solitude is fulfilled in such a relationship.

This fulfillment is beatifying because it constitutes original happiness. The phrase, "bone of my bones and flesh of my flesh," expresses the beatifying beginning of man's existence in the world and springs from the depths of his human solitude, which he lives as a person in the presence of all other living beings.

So it is that we discover an adequate anthropology in our study of "the beginning." When we attempt to verify this anthropology for its adequacy, we must consider the idea of "person" and of the "body-sex." If we separate sex from the person, the adequacy of the biblical anthropology would be destroyed, and the essential light of the revelation of the body would be veiled for our theological study.

We find a deep connection between the mystery of creation, a gift springing from Love, and the beatifying "beginning" of the existence of man as male and female in the whole truth of their body and their sex. In the phrase, "bone of my bones and flesh of my flesh," man emerges from the depth of original solitude into the dimension of mutual gift, the expression of which is the human body in all the original truth of its masculinity and femininity.

This masculinity-femininity—namely, sex—is the original sign of both God's creative gift and man's (male-female) awareness of a gift lived in an original way. So it is that sex enters the theology of the body.

The beatifying "beginning" of man as male and female is connected with the revelation and discovery of the meaning of the body which we call "nuptial." The joy of man's coming to existence as male and female (Gn 2:23) is followed by an account of their conjugal unity (Gn 2:24), and then by an account of their nakedness, which is devoid of mutual shame (Gn 2:25). This significant confrontation tells of the revelation and, at the same time, of the "discovery" of the nuptial meaning of the body. This meaning confirms that the creative giving, which springs from Love, has reached the original consciousness of man and has become an experience of mutual giving in which nakedness brings no shame.

Genesis 2:24 also speaks of the finality of man's masculinity and femininity in the life of the spouse-parents who unite in such a way that they will subject their humanity to the blessings of fertility, which are mentioned in the first creation narrative (Gn 1:28). Genesis 2:25 shows that man, who is conscious of this finality of his sexuality, is aware of the procreative capacity of his body. This sexuality is free from the "constraint" of his own body and sex. Both texts of the Book of Genesis connect the perspective of procreation with the human *person;* in both narratives, the analogy of the human body and sex in relation to the world of animals (analogy "of nature") is raised to the level of "image of God," to the level of persons and communion between persons.

As we try to understand what the nuptial meaning of the body expresses, we see that the revelation and the original discovery of the nuptial meaning of the body, as outlined in the Yahwist narrative, presents man (male and female) in the whole reality and truth of his body and sex ("they were naked"). At the same time, man is free from any constraint of the body and of sex ("they were not ashamed"). Created by Love, both are "naked" because they are free with the very freedom of the gift, a freedom that is at the basis of the nuptial meaning of the body.

The human body, with its sex and its masculinity and femininity, is a source of fruitfulness and procreation; from "the beginning" it has included the "nuptial" attribute—a capacity for expressing a love in which the man-person becomes a gift and, in this way, fulfills the very meaning of his being and existence. Here we are reminded of the text of the Second Vatican Council: "It follows, then, that if man is the only creature on earth that God has willed for its own sake, man can fully discover his true self only in a sincere giving of himself" (*Gaudium et Spes*, 24).

In the freedom of the gift, therefore, we find the root of original nakedness free from shame. Only in this way can they remain in a relationship that is based on the "sincere gift of themselves." By freedom we mean that *mastery of one's self* (self-control) which is indispensable if man is to give himself so that he may become a gift and, then, "fully discover his true self" in a "sincere giving of himself." So it is that the phrase, "they were naked and not ashamed," can and must be understood as the revelation and discovery of freedom that makes possible and qualifies the "nuptial" sense of the body.

But Genesis 2:25 says more than this. The man and the woman—interiorly free from the constraint of his or her own body and sex, free with the freedom of the gift—enjoy the whole truth about man, just as God-Yahweh had revealed these things to them in the mystery of creation. These truths are: (1) man is the only creature in the world that the Creator willed for "its own sake," and (2) this same man, "from the beginning," can find himself only in the disinterested giving of himself.[1]

At the root of the man's and the woman's nakedness, there is the interior freedom of the gift—the disinterested gift of one's self—which enables them both, man and woman, to find one another because each was willed "for his or her own sake." In the first meeting, man finds woman, and woman finds man. He accepts her "for her own sake," as she is constituted in the mystery of the image of God through her femininity; she, for her part, accepts him as he is willed "for his own sake" and constituted by means of his own masculinity. They, thus, discover the "nuptial" meaning of the body—the disinterested giving of one's self.

The human body, therefore, also reveals a value and a beauty that goes beyond the purely physical dimensions of "sexuality," completing a nuptial awareness of the body that is connected with man's masculinity-femininity. This meaning indicates a particular capacity of expressing love whereby man becomes a gift. It also points to a capacity for the "affirmation of the person," for living the fact that the other is, by means of the body, someone willed by the Creator "for his or her own sake." This "affirmation of the person" is an acceptance of the gift that, through reciprocity, creates the communion of persons, which is constructed from within but also includes the "exteriority" of man—the nakedness of the body in its masculinity and femininity.

The few verses in the Book of Genesis that speak of this beatifying "beginning" are full of a surprising theological and anthropological content. The revelation and discovery of the nuptial meaning of the body explains man's original happiness and also opens the perspective of his earthly history in which this indispensable "theme" of his own existence will be felt. That is to say, in the whole perspective of his own "history," man will confer a nuptial meaning on his own body. Even though this meaning has undergone distortions throughout history, it always remains a sign of the "image of God."

In original time, this "nuptial" meaning reveals the whole reality of the gift that is spoken of in the first pages of the Book of Genesis. The meaning of the body that we find in original solitude, original unity, original nakedness, and particularly in its "nuptial" meaning, is the fundamental element of human existence in the world. The "nuptial" meaning of the body can be understood only in the context of the person who is a creature willed by God for its own sake, who can fully discover its true self only in the sincere giving of itself.

The Pope ends this reflection on the nuptial meaning of the body with the observation that Christ's revelation of a vocation over and above the vocation of marriage—the vocation of renouncing marriage for the sake of the kingdom of heaven—highlights the same truth about the human person. If a man and a woman are capable of making a gift of themselves to the kingdom of heaven, this proves that there is the freedom of the gift in the human body; the body possesses a full "nuptial" meaning.

The following main points emerge from the two papal reflections on the nuptial meaning of the body and apply to a theology and a spirituality of sexuality.

1. We can only completely realize our essence by existing "with someone and for someone"; in this way, we form a communion of persons that reflects the "image of God."

2. The body—our masculinity-femininity, our sex— reveals this reciprocity and communion of persons. The body is the original sign of both the creative gift and human awareness of that gift.

3. The Yahwist text concerning "the beginning" reveals the giving of the gift as well as man's discovery of the body. In the text, procreation raises the analogy "of nature" to the level of the "image of God" when there is communion between persons.

4. The nuptial meaning of the body is the capacity of expressing love, through which we become a gift that fulfills the very meaning of our being and existence; we are able, in other words, to "fully discover our true self in a sincere giving of self."

5. The "nuptial" meaning of the body goes beyond the purely physical dimensions of "sexuality" because it shows that the body, free from constraints of shame, has a capacity for expressing love in which man becomes a gift, thus affirming the person of the other as someone who is unique and unrepeatable, someone who has been chosen by Eternal Love. This mutual "affirmation of the persons" creates the "communion of persons."

6. The "nuptial" meaning of the body affirms the gift of creation that is described in the first pages of the Book of Genesis. Together with the meaning of original solitude, original unity, and original nakedness, the "nuptial" meaning of the body gives us an understanding of the essence of human existence in the world.

Spiritual Reflections

As we begin to reflect on the meaning of our bodies, we are struck by the fact that perhaps we feel quite inadequate about our own particular body. We are either too tall or too short, too fat or too thin; we bulge where we are supposed to curve and curve where we are supposed to bulge, and as we begin to grow older, we buy clothes that we fervently hope will conceal the bulges. Even those of us who have near perfect bodies have a secret anxiety about some aspect of our physical make-up. Few of us would rate a "10" on a scale of 1 to 10, so we tend to feel inadequate when people start talking about bodies.

Our bodily self-image often relates to the way we compare our own body to that of the ideal male or female body. As a result, our identity as man or woman—our sexuality—and our bodily images are closely linked. Although we might not consciously consider it, our bodies are important in our search for identity; few of us, however, would ever think of our bodies as a source of revelation about the meaning of human existence.

We can usually trace our feelings of inadequacy about our own body back to the time of puberty, when our body began to act in strange and often uncontrollable ways. Just thinking about the discomfort we felt about our bodies during those early teen-age years can stir up feelings of inadequacy. Perhaps, from sixth grade through tenth grade, we were the only girl in our class who had attained her full height, and this phenomenon caused us to tower over all our classmates, both male and female. Or perhaps we were the boy in the class who began to think that we had missed out on our share of growth hormones as we struggled to reach the five foot mark at the end of our freshman year of high school. In addition, of course, we were all concerned about our sexual development. Some of us matured so rapidly that none of our peers were able to relate to the difficulties we were encountering; others of us were so far behind in our sexual development that we avoided any activity that might have required nude showering.

Now, in our adult life, we still find it difficult to be at ease with our bodies. Many of us are somewhat surprised when another person expresses an interest in our bodies. When we fall in love, and our lover tells us he finds our body attractive, we no longer feel bad that we will never be a perfect "10." Or when she tells us that we are physically attractive, it ceases to be important that we never made the football team. In our "solitude," we continually found things wrong with our bodies; when we are in love, we might not automatically consider ourselves perfect "10s," but our previous anxieties about our body seem to fade in importance.

Falling in love is a good example of how we experience the giftedness of creation. When we are affirmed by another, we are drawn out of ourselves and our solitude. We no longer fear that giving ourselves to another will rob us of our own identity; we feel safe about sharing ourselves with another. We want to do things for the person we love, not because it does something for us, but because we love her or him and want her or his happiness. We find that we are existing *with* someone and *for* someone, and this experience gives us several hints about the way we are to exist "in the image of God."

No one can really attempt to explain why we fall in love with a particular person. Although we might tend to feel that our match was "made in heaven," others take a less romantic view of the situation. One commentator on marriage has observed that "we fall in love with and marry the person we meet when we are ready to get married—assuming, of course, that the other person is also ready." This less-than-romantic assessment of the situation, however, does not completely rule out the possibility that our attraction to our beloved has its roots in some divine plan.

In general, we are "ready" to fall in love and marry when we are able to trust our ability to respond in a positive manner to the powerful force of our sexual drive. When we feel that we are able to integrate our bodily attraction for another person with our "interior" perception of this person, the other becomes a possible partner in an intimacy relationship. Few of us can deny the power that sexual attraction has played in those instances when we have fallen in love. When we consider sexual attraction from the viewpoint of "the beginning" that is described in the Book of Genesis, we can see it as part of the gift of creation.

All of us have had experiences of sexual attraction, however, that have been unrelated to any interior sense of love. Consequently, we find it difficult to listen to the message of our bodies when we reflect on the meaning of human existence. Listening to our body's message has often caused us more trouble than joy, so we prefer to ignore the body's potential for revealing a divine plan.

Delores, the heroine in Marilyn French's novel *The Bleeding Heart,* bemoans the fact that her body constantly betrays her. Her mind is definitely made up; she will terminate an unsatisfactory relationship. But she is unsure about whether she can trust her body or whether it will countermand the decision of her mind. We can feel a certain sympathy for this position when we consider our own infatuations, crushes, and initial responses to overtures from particularly attractive members of the other sex. Although we can see our powerful sexual attraction as a positive force toward building and sustaining a love relationship, we also know this powerful attraction can sometimes cloud the issues in a relationship and cause disappointment and heartache.

The Yahwist creation narrative in the Book of Genesis suggests that our bodies have a "nuptial" meaning; our powerful sexual drive is meant to help us join with another person and form a "communion of persons" in which we live *with* someone and *for* someone, in which we are willing to be a *gift* for someone. It seems that we can trust our bodies if the communion they seek with another is a "communion of persons" that includes the body, as opposed to a communion of bodies that excludes the persons.

The following questions confront us, therefore, when we consider the "nuptial meaning of the body": How do we exist *with* and *for* someone; how are we to be a disinterested gift, that is, an unselfish gift, in a "communion of persons"? In psychological language, we ask: How do we *share* ourselves with another in an intimacy relationship? As we observed earlier, when we fall in love, we are more readily able to let down our defenses in the presence of our beloved and to exist with him or her. At the same time, affirming him or her as a person of worth comes easily during this phase of a relationship because we tend to be blinded to the negative implications of any of our beloved's shortcomings. We are willing to live *for* him or her in the sense of being the person who tells our beloved of his or her worth.

The act of existing with someone and for someone, which goes on in the beginnings of a love relationship, uncovers hints that help us more fully appreciate the nuptial sense of our bodies. Unfortunately, as the relationship develops, we begin to have second thoughts about how far we want to go in this sharing of ourselves with another. We set up new barriers when we feel that the other is getting too close to us. Although familiarity might not breed contempt in most love relationships, familiarity often leads to new obstacles in the search for unity. At that point in our relationship, it is helpful to have a vision of the nuptial meaning of the body that will encourage us to recapture the romantic sense of our initial falling in love. The vision of existing *with* someone and *for* someone as a *disinterested gift* challenges us to overcome the obstacles to intimacy that will be part of any long-term relationship.

We need to consider the implications that sexual intimacy has for other areas of our life together. We have been given our masculinity and femininity as both a sign of God's love and a way for us to be lovers the way God is a lover. Our sexuality, which is a gift of creation, points the way to and, in a sense, explains how we are to be a communion of persons. When we reflect on physical sexual intimacy, we appreciate how we can improve as lovers when we are able to be a gift to the other, when we are able to exist *for* and *with* the other. This nuptial meaning of our bodies invites us to reflect on what we must do to be lovers in the same way that God is a lover.

Yet even in this age of so much secular scientific knowledge about how to achieve sexual intimacy, a high degree of misunderstanding surrounds this area in many marriages. Inadequate sex education undoubtedly accounts for some of our difficulties. Quite often, however, sex therapists discover that problems in sexual intimacy are linked to an inability of the partners to communicate about their bodily needs. Some of this lack of communication is rooted in ignorance about one's own body and can be quickly dispelled through an understanding of the facts. Sex therapy clinics have had considerable success in relieving problems of sexual dysfunction.

In many marriages, however, the problem is not sexual dysfunction; for many of us, problems of sexual intimacy seem to be rooted in previously developed ideas about our bodies. Good sexual communication in a marriage requires that each partner have a sense of self-worth, especially regarding the body. Although it might be possible to have periodic experiences of sexual intimacy that are unrelated to the interior person of either partner, long-term relationships of sexual intimacy require a concerted effort to overcome the "solitude" of our body. For many of us, this solitude is actually a negative sense of the body, which is often rooted in a fear that the body will betray us or that we will be unable to contain the power of our sexual attraction. For many of us, holding back on sexual intimacy is closely linked with our desire to retain "control" over our own identity, our own solitude. We are not willing to run the risk of sharing ourselves with another; we hold back on the gift of our bodies; that is, we do not give so as to "affirm the other." We will not be committed to a unity that will cause a "communion of persons."

Although most of us do not articulate, even to ourselves, the significance of our attempts at sexual intimacy, the idea of the nuptial meaning of the body causes us to realize how often we fail to realize that sexual intimacy is a way of affirming the person of the other. We begin to recognize the need to examine our "interior" views on our sexual activity. In short, we need to reflect, alone and with our spouse, on the significance of sexual intimacy in our relationship. Perhaps, in this way, we will discover the nuptial meaning of the body as Eve and Adam discovered the gift the Creator gave them.

The Yahwist creation story also invites us to put aside any negative attitudes we might have toward our body and toward masculinity and femininity. We are to be free from the constraints of our bodies so our sexuality will be raised to the "image of God." We also must learn how to rid ourselves of bad bodily images that either interfere with our ability to be a good lover with our spouse or make it difficult for us to relate to anyone of the other sex. Only when we have overcome bad bodily images will we begin to appreciate the giftedness of our bodies and gain some hint about the Love who was the cause of creation.

Negative attitudes toward the body and toward masculinity and femininity often influence the way in which we care for our body. Some researchers claim that once a man or a woman no longer wants to be "sexually attractive," he or she begins to lose interest in caring for his or her body. If a woman fears the sexual attraction of her body, for example, she might, upon entering into a marital relationship, use weight gain as a means of signaling other males of her lack of availability. Or a man might fail to keep his body "in shape" after he marries because he no longer feels it is necessary to be sexually attractive. Or a person might fear the sexual demands of his or her spouse and fail to care for his or her body as a way of resisting these demands. Whatever the case, the idea that our bodies have a "nuptial" meaning causes us to examine how we feel about the sexual attractiveness of our bodies. It encourages us to reflect on the fact that the care we take of our body reflects our attitude toward our body and toward our sexuality.

We do not live in the original garden of Adam and Eve, but our bodies have a "nuptial" meaning even in this "historical" time. The joy of marital intimacy, an intimacy that is both exterior and interior, is not automatically achieved, however. We have been given the gift of our bodies and the gift of the other in a love relationship; we need to continually examine how we are to respond to both gifts and how we, in turn, are to be gift for our beloved. The Yahwist creation story reveals God's plan to us and encourages us to continually reflect on experiences of intimacy, especially marital intimacy, in order to discover God's continual gift to us in our present situation. Our bodies and our experiences of intimacy continue to be a source of revelation of the divine plan.

SIX

Original Innocence

*Then the man said, "This at last is bone of my
bones and flesh of my flesh; she shall be called
woman, because she was taken out of man."
Therefore, a man leaves his father and mother
and cleaves to his wife and they become one
flesh. And the man and his wife were both
naked, and were not ashamed.*
—Genesis 2:23-25

Summary of the Pope's Addresses

Another mystery uncovered in reflection on the Genesis story is
the mystery of man's original innocence, that is, the mystery of this
existence *prior to* the knowledge of good and evil and almost *outside*
it. As background for understanding original innocence, we must
remember that the first verses of the Bible speak about the consistent giving that is both reflected in the mutual "experience of the
body" and rooted in Love. These first verses speak not only of
creation, but also of grace, that is, the communication of holiness
that is rooted in the Spirit, and produces in the first man a special
state of "spiritualization." The original happiness of the first man
indicates that he both emerged from Love and initiated love in an
irrevocable way, despite the subsequent sin and death. And because
of love, man and woman did not know shame. We find that happiness, therefore, is rooted in Love.

We also find in the first chapters of Genesis that creation is a gift
to man. His fullest and deepest dimension is determined by grace,
which is a participation in God's holiness—the interior life of God
himself. This grace is also the foundation and source of man's original innocence.

In order to understand the theology of the body, the Pope is reflecting on the mystery of man's awareness of the body in his original state, because this awareness reveals the peculiarity of original innocence. The body is, in a way, the *eye*-witness of the original innocence that the first man and woman bear in a unique way. Only in Genesis 2:25 does the Bible ever refer to nakedness without the corollary of shame.

We search Genesis 2:25, therefore, for a trace of the mystery of original innocence that belongs to the dimension of grace, to that mysterious gift made to the human "heart." It is the "heart," the inner man with the gift of grace, that enables man and woman, from "the beginning," to exist as disinterested gift. They discover the nuptial meaning of the body through original innocence; as they discover this meaning, the mystery of original innocence is revealed.

But original innocence belongs to "the beginning" from which "historical" man was separated. "Historical" man understands the mystery of original innocence by means of contrast with his experience of sin. In order to understand original innocence as an essential characteristic of the theology of the body, historical man starts with the experience of shame, which original innocence excludes from the body and the "heart" of the man and the woman. Although original innocence speaks of the grace that makes it possible for man to experience the meaning of both the world and the body, it seems to refer, above all, to the interior state of human "heart," that is, the human will.

From our historical perspective, we are trying to reconstruct the characteristic of original innocence that conditions the nuptial meaning of the body. We see this innocence as a particular "purity of heart" that allows an interior faithfulness, that is, the gift of the nuptial meaning of the body. Original innocence, thus, is a tranquil testimony of conscience that precedes any experience of good and evil.

The human will is originally innocent, and this innocence facilitates the reciprocity and exchange of the gift of the body according to its masculinity and femininity. The innocence of Genesis 2:25 is the innocence of the mutual experience of the body. It inspires the interior exchange of the gift of the person, which, in fact, is the real source of the experience of innocence.

Interior innocence consists of reciprocal "acceptance" of the other so that a mutual donation creates the "communion of persons;" it is a question of "receiving" the other human being and "accepting" him or her. In the mutual relationship of which Genesis 2:23-25 speaks, the man and the woman become a gift for each other through the whole truth of the body in its masculinity and femininity. The innocence of the "heart," which leads to an innocence of experience, means a moral participation in the eternal and permanent act of God's will, an act that not only expresses and sustains, in mutual nakedness, the meaning of the gift, but also deepens the mutual dignity of it.

When the man and his wife are not ashamed, the exchange of the gift of their whole humanity (body and soul, femininity and masculinity) is actualized by preserving the interior innocence of both the donation of one's self and the acceptance of the other as a gift. The giving and accepting of the gift interpenetrate so that giving becomes accepting, and acceptance is transformed into giving.

The woman who is given to the man by the Creator is, in original innocence, "received" as a gift. At the same time, the man's acceptance of the gift becomes the first donation. In giving herself, the woman "rediscovers," at the same time, "herself" because she has been accepted and welcomed by the man "for her own sake." The man's acceptance of the whole dignity of the gift of the woman's humanity—her body, her sex, and her femininity—allows her to reach the inner depth of her person and, consequently, becomes a new source of giving of herself.

It seems that the second creation narrative has assigned man, from "the beginning," to be the one who, above all, receives the gift. The woman is entrusted to him, and he must ensure the process of the exchange of the gift; the mutual interpenetration of giving and receiving will create a real communion of persons. Even though the woman is the one who was "given," the man, who enriches her by accepting her as a gift in the full truth of her person and femininity, is also enriched through her gift and through the gift of himself. The exchange is mutual; in it, the reciprocal effects of both the "sincere gift" and the "finding one's self again" are revealed and grow.

This experience of the body, which is inferred from Genesis 2:23 and 25 with its different degree of "spiritualization" of man, involves another composition of the interior forces of man himself.

It is almost another body-soul relationship, another inner proportion between sensitivity, spirituality, and affectivity, another degree of the sensitiveness to the gifts of the Holy Spirit, when it is compared to the state of man in "historical" time. Although an insuperable barrier divides us from that first man and woman who, through the gift of grace, are united in the mystery of creation, we try to understand that state of original innocence and grasp the connection between the original meaning of the body and the nature of original innocence. We do this not only because it is important for man's "theological prehistory," but also because of the possibility that it reveals to us the permanent roots of both the human and the theological aspects of the *ethos* of the body.

Man enters the world with the awareness of the nuptial meaning of his own body, his own masculinity and femininity—a meaning that, according to original innocence, is conditioned "ethically" and constitutes the future of the human *ethos*. For this reason, it is important that we construct the theology of the body from "the beginning." We know that man and woman were "given" to each other by the Creator. This influences the whole perspective of the existence of mankind and the human family. The fundamental fact of this existence at every stage of man's history is that God "created them male and female": he always creates them in this way. It is therefore important to understand the fundamental meanings in "the beginning" stories; they are important and indispensable if we are to know who man is, who he should be, and how he should mold his own activity. This knowledge is essential for the human *ethos*.

Genesis 2:24 indicates that man and woman were created for marriage; it opens the great creative perspective of man's existence, which is continually renewed by means of "procreation" ("self-reproduction"). This perspective is deeply rooted in a consciousness of humanity (Gn 2:23) and in the particular consciousness of the nuptial meaning of the body (Gn 2:25), which allows the man and the woman to form a "communion of persons." The first man and the first woman, then, grow as persons or subjects; they grow mutually, one for the other, through their bodies and through their "nakedness," which is free of shame. If they cease to be disinterested gift for each other, they recognize that they are "naked", and a shame not felt in original innocence will spring up in their hearts (see Gn 3). So it is that original innocence manifests and, at the same time, constitutes the perfect *ethos* of the gift.

Through the *ethos* of the gift, the "subjectivity" of man—a subject who is made in the image and likeness of God—is partly outlined. The woman is not merely "an object" for the man, though they are objectively both naked. Only the nakedness that makes man an "object" for woman, or vice versa, is a source of shame. Interior innocence, or "purity of heart," makes it impossible for one to be a mere object. The words "not ashamed" means that the man and the woman are united by an awareness of the gift; they are mutually conscious of the nuptial meaning of their bodies.

After original sin, man and woman lose the grace of original innocence; the nuptial meaning of the body, then, ceases to be a simple reality of revelation and grace. The meaning, however, will remain as a commitment given by the *ethos* of the gift and inscribed in the depths of the human heart as a distant echo of original innocence. Human love, in its interior truth and subjective authenticity, will be formed from a basis of that nuptial meaning. Man will continually rediscover himself as the guardian of the mystery of the subject so as to defend the subject from any reduction to the position of mere object.

Before man and woman cross the barrier to the knowledge of good and evil, they are immersed in the mystery of creation. The depth of this mystery, which is hidden in their hearts, is innocence, grace, love, and justice (see Gn 1:31). Man appears in the visible world as the highest expression of the divine gift; he bears within himself the interior dimension of the gift; he brings into the world his particular likeness to God with which he transcends and dominates his "visibility" in the world—that is, his corporality, his masculinity or femininity, his nakedness. Reflected in this likeness is the primordial awareness of the nuptial meaning of the body, which is pervaded by the mystery of original innocence.

So it is that we find a primordial sacrament, a sign that effectively transmits in the visible world the invisible mystery that is hidden in God from time immemorial—the mystery of truth and love, the mystery of divine life in which man really participates. Original innocence begins this participation and is a source of original happiness. The sacrament is a visible sign through man as a "body," by means of his "visible" masculinity and femininity. Only the body is capable of making visible what is invisible—that is, the spiritual and the divine. The body was created to transfer into the visible world the mystery that has been hidden in God since time immemorial.

The sacramentality of creation, the sacramentality of the world is revealed in man who is created in the "image of God." Man, by means of his corporality—his masculinity and femininity—becomes a visible sign of the economy of Truth and Love, which has its source in God himself and was already revealed in the mystery of creation. Thus, we can understand "the beginning" of the sacrament of marriage found in Genesis 2:24.

We also understand that the words of Genesis 2:25, with their anthropological meaning, indicate that holiness entered the visible world together with man. Original innocence, which is connected with the nuptial meaning of the body, is the same holiness that enables man to express himself with his own body by means of the "sincere gift" of himself. An awareness of this gift conditions the "sacrament of the body"; in his body, as male or female, man feels that he is a subject of holiness.

We conclude this analysis of original innocence by observing that man's consciousness of the meaning of his body shows him entering the world as a subject of Truth and Love. Genesis 2:23-25 tells of the first feast of humanity in all the original fullness of the nuptial meaning of the body. This feast draws its origin from the divine source of Truth and Love in the very mystery of creation. Although sin and death eventually extend over the original feast, right from "the beginning" we draw a first hope—namely, the fruit of the divine economy of Truth and Love, which was revealed at "the beginning," is not death, but life, and not so much the destruction of the body of man, which was created "in the image of God," but rather the "call to glory" (cf Rm 8:30).

The following points for a theology and a spirituality of the body emerge from the Pope's four audience addresses on original innocence.

1. Our fullest and deepest dimension is determined by grace, by participation in the interior life of God, which is the interior source and foundation of original innocence; the first human existed in a special state of "spiritualization."

2. In "the beginning," the body is an *eye*-witness to the gift of grace that is made to the human "heart"; the discovery of the nuptial meaning of the body not only is

possible through original innocence, but also reveals that innocence.

3. In the process of making a "gift of one's self," the giving and the accepting of the gift interpenetrate so that the giving becomes accepting, and the accepting is transformed into giving; this mutual exchange leads to a finding of one's self in the giving of one's self that then becomes the source of a new giving of one's self.

4. The fundamental fact of human existence at every stage of human history is that God "created them male and female"; understanding the fundamental meanings (original solitude, original unity, original nakedness, and the nuptial meaning of the body) is important and indispensable for the future of human *ethos;* interior innocence, or "purity of heart," made it impossible for the man and the woman to reduce each other to the level of a mere object.

5. Only the body is capable of making the spiritual and the divine visible; by means of masculinity and femininity, we become a visible sign of Truth and Love, which have their source in God himself. Thus, the body is a primordial sacrament, that is, a sign that effectively transmits in the visible world the invisible mystery that is hidden in God from time immemorial.

6. Genesis 2:23-25 tells of the first feast of humanity in all the original fullness of the nuptial meaning of the body; the holiness that enters the world through the human body and contributes to the possibilities of the feast of humanity is also the source of our first hope that we are not bound for destruction, but rather called to glory.

Spiritual Reflections

At this point in our consideration of the Pope's reflections on the Genesis creation story, we might begin to wonder what all this might mean for us. As the Pope indicates, all of these experiences are experiences of "original" time, but we live in "historical" time.

How can we be expected to find a plan for our human sexuality in a situation that we can never hope to emulate?

We might be like the man who protested that the creation stories in Genesis have no meaning whatsoever because, after all, they are "only" myths. As a youngster, he was undoubtedly taught that they were actual accounts of the beginning of the world. Now that he is an adult, however, and has been exposed to scientific understandings about the possible beginnings of the world, he finds these mythical stories meaningless for his spiritual life.

But "the beginning," with its original solitude, original unity, original nakedness, nuptial meaning of the body, and original innocence, speaks to us at another level that is different from the scientific level. It addresses those questions of meaning that we encounter when scientific explanations are inadequate for our particular search for meaning. The "beginning" speaks to our religious imagination; it asks us to imagine how things would be if there were no disruption between man and God. If God's plan for existence had worked, what would the world now be like, what would the male-female relationship be like?

Mircea Eliade, in his study of myths of beginnings, maintains that all primitive religions have, in addition to their creation story, stories about how things were in the beginning, what relationship existed between God and man, between man and the world.[1] These paradise myths not only tell of how things were at a time when the relationship between man and God was good, they also serve to encourage people to want to recapture that kind of a relationship. Religious communities have a hope that "end times" will be similar to "beginning times." There will be an idyllic time in the future during which humans and God will be on friendly terms, humans and the animal world will no longer be adversaries, and the trials, pains, and sufferings of our present situations will be wiped away.

Myths, such as the Genesis story, are true in that they tell us what the author and the religious community believe about their God. They represent the way in which the communities have tried to explain their God and their relationship to that God, and their understanding of the meaning of life in light of that relationship. As the Pope indicates, the creation story in Genesis has many layers; its particular value is in the fact that it can challenge every generation to "imagine" what it is saying to their particular prob lems. Thus, even though we today might not accept as scientifically accurate the Genesis account of the creation of the world and the beginning of human existence in the world, the story still has meaning for us.

If we, like the Pope, bring contemporary questions of meaning to the biblical story, the revelation of God present in that story will speak to our search. Obviously, the person who first narrated this story did not think in the categories of original solitude, original unity, original nakedness, the nuptial meaning of the body, and original innocence; but the storyteller undoubtedly did have experiences of both solitude and unity that were not only connected with the male-female relationship but also related to the narrator's and the community's understanding of their God. The account of creation in the Book of Genesis reflects the fact that these experiences led the storyteller to a deeper understanding of both God and the meaning of life. When John Paul II reads the account of creation, he recognizes the universality of the experiences that have been captured in the short creation narrative. The words he attaches to these experiences, and the explication he offers of the meaning of these original experiences, are "trigger-words" that can assist us as we try to relate the story of our own sexuality to the biblical account of God's plan for the body and sexuality.

We will be able to respond to the Pope's analysis of the creation story only when we are willing to allow our religious imagination an opportunity to speak of meaning. Evolution, or some other theory, might give a scientific explanation about the beginning of our world and the beginnings of man and women, but this explanation does not give us a basis for understanding how we are to relate to one another. The idea of the unity of "one flesh" as the first feast of humanity can inspire us if we see it as a model for all human relationships.

The narrator of the Yahwistic account of creation obviously sees the sexual relationship of man and woman as a positive experience that revealed something of the plan of Yahweh. In trying to explain Yahweh's relationship to Israel, the storyteller calls upon the positive aspects of this relationship. The sexual feast of "one flesh" is the process of giving and accepting—finding one's self in the giving of one's self—that gives hints about God. The storyteller uses analogy in trying to recount the community's understanding of its God. This use of the analogical imagination challenges us to consider how we might describe our participation in the interior life of God. Though we do not exist in a special state of "spiritualization," we do have experiences when we are "enspirited," when our hearts are touched by God. It might be helpful for us to consider these enspirited or graced moments in our lives. We could then imagine how we would go about telling the story of our God, our relationship to our God, and our relationship to other human beings.

Let us imagine, therefore, that we have been given the task of writing the tale of the God-human, human-human relationship. Let us stop and consider the graced moments in our experience of ourselves as persons with bodies and with sexuality, that is, with masculinity or femininity. What are some particularly graced experiences of human sexuality, and how might that grace permeate our lives? If we could say that, during "the beginning" time, humans were fully graced, then their relationship with each other and with God was identical to our experience of grace, but carried to the ultimate.

Reflecting on what it means for us to be male or female will eventually lead us to remember times when our femininity or masculinity has made us aware that we are related to a larger reality. At the time, we might not have thought in those terms, but now that we are examining our experiences we do uncover times when being a woman or being a man has made us aware of something that transcends our understanding of the particular situation. We have encountered Mystery in our experience, and this encounter with Mystery offers us the possibility of grace.

The experience of sexual intimacy, of becoming "two in one flesh," is one experience of masculinity and femininity that, for those of us who join in such a unity, at some time, has probably been a graced moment, a time of wonder, a time of awe, a time when relationship with our partner has been positively influenced by our physical union. The sexual feast has been more than the grabbing of a quick bite to sustain us for a few hours; rather, it has been a feast, a party, a celebration, the memory of which lingers on. Not every particular experience of sexual union in a long-term relationship is an experience of the "gift of one's self." But, at those times when our sexual union leads to the finding of ourself and the giving of ourself, these experiences become the source of a new giving, that is, they enrich our relationship. And these experiences are occasions through which we can discover hints about the "nuptial meaning of our bodies."

Consider the aura that surrounds us after an experience we could label a "sexual feast." Perhaps we have a weekend away, or maybe a second honeymoon, or maybe just a period of uninterrupted lovemaking during which we have been able to affirm each other as persons, not as objects. More than likely, others who would observe us shortly after such an experience would notice something special in the looks we exchange, the unity we demonstrate by our close bodily contact, or the intensity of our verbal exchanges. Love shines through lovers who have experienced the gift of Eternal Love in the course of their lovemaking; God is revealed and holiness is made present as the result of their bodily union.

Oftentimes, the realization that such experiences of lovemaking are indeed graced moments is not obvious to us until we have reflected on the experience. We have to admit, however, that all of us have had experiences of lovemaking—good experiences of lovemaking—that have not always been graced experiences. We have failed to carry the wonder of the sexual feast into other areas of our relationship; we have let the presence of God, which was available in the moment, be buried by our fear of an interior union in which we give ourselves and accept the other. We have not acted on the grace of the moment.

But when we stop to consider how we might tell the story of male-female relationships that are totally graced, we cannot help feeling that a relationship between a woman and a man that continually reflected the positive experience of one of our "graced" moments would be an ideal. We can then begin to understand the female-male relationship and might even try to capture it in our own creation myth.

We also begin to understand that our Yahwist narrator must have known of, or actually had, such an experience. Like the original storyteller, we would rather live in a situation where the wonder of the good experience of lovemaking would permeate our lives—both in our relationship with our partner and in all human relationships. The model of "two in one flesh" that we know from our own experience—especially when that two-in-one-flesh experience is a graced moment—offers us hope that there is life rather than death.

The model of sexual union is just that, a model. Because most humans, at some time in their lives, have the possibility of experiencing graced moments in sexual unity, the Yahwist narrator's choice of the sexual union as the first feast of humanity is an apt choice. Those of us who join our bodies as two in one flesh, but fail to be aware of graced moments in our sexual union, do, nevertheless, reflect on this lack of continuity between our exterior experience and our interior understanding of male-female relationships and eventually arrive at an understanding of how we would like it to be.

There are other graced moments that arise from the fact that half of us are female and half of us are male. By reflecting on the experiences of the eagerly awaited birth of a child, we realize that the "moment" of motherhood and fatherhood—both the initial moment and the ongoing moments of parenthood—forcefully confronts us with Mystery. Parenthood, with its joys and sorrows, draws our attention to the fact that our sexual union has caused unbelievable results in our life. We are called beyond ourselves, both in the joyous moments and in the sorrowful moments. If we were to try to tell the story of the ideal parenthood relationship, however, we would often fall back on the wonder of the joyous moments—especially the moment of birth. In our relationships with our children, the memory of the moments of joy often sustains us through moments of sorrow, especially when a situation seems hopeless; we are reminded of the joy of the graced moment, and this recollection overpowers the helplessness of the dark moments. Our sexuality—our masculinity and our femininity—which reaches its generative potential in fatherhood and motherhood, is not always felt as an experience of grace; but when we try to describe the ideal, we portray it as the graced moments lived to the maximum. Again, we feel an affinity with the Yahwist narrator.

When we reflect on our femininity and masculinity, another experience that is noteworthy emerges. There is a powerful sexual drive that attracts us to another even before we join with that other in a sexual union; perhaps this drive even attracts us to another with whom we will never join in a sexual union. The "crushes" of our early puberty days, the infatuations with unattainable public figures, the numerous "falling-in-love" experiences of our teen-age years—all these experiences of our sexual drive often lead to great frustrations rather than revelations of God. But if we reflect on these experiences, we can appreciate the way our bodies and our sexual drive call us out of our solitude and open us to the possibility of both receiving a gift and being a gift. This reflection can help us appreciate the wondrous possibilities of our bodies and, at the same time, make us aware of the element of choice in human sexual relationships. Much of our response to our teen-age experiences of the sexual drive, however, was not based on a harmony between internal perception and external feelings. Although we do not wish to depreciate the infatuations of our youth, we realize that, for the most part, a narcissistic tendency caused us to fall in and out of love every other week. The model for an ideal male-female relationship, therefore, would have to go beyond adolescent infatuations and demonstrate accord between internal perceptions and external experiences. The level of "image of God," in which a "communion of persons" grows out of mutual giving, seems quite apt.

The Song of Songs celebrates the sexual union. Its marvelous conclusion—"For love is as strong as death; passion as fierce as Hell. . . . Mighty waters cannot quench love; no torrents can sweep it away" (S 8:6,7)—is an example of how a biblical writer reflected on the experience of romantic love that culminated in sexual union. Biblical scholars argue whether this is simply an erotic poem that was used by the religious community to point toward God and God's relationship with Israel, or whether it is truly an account of the God-Israel relationship. In either case, we find the biblical community—and, later, the Christian community—using the sexual feast as a way of talking about God. The union of a man and a woman that leads to the conclusion that love is as strong as death seems to be one in which the partners experience the "gift of one's self" and neither is an object.

As our earlier reflections on romantic love indicated, the call out of solitude that is issued to us in romantic love makes the giving of ourselves a joyous experience. The Pope sees Genesis 2:23-25 as the biblical prototype of the Song of Songs. Our experiences of romantic love, and the sexual union that evolves from that romantic love, give us hints about an ideal female-male relationship, about all human relationships, about the God-human relationship, and about the meaning of human existence. Not all experiences of sexual union that flow from romantic love, however, would lead us to compose our own Song of Songs; but those experiences that call us out of ourselves, and unite our "hearts" and bodies in an affirmation of persons, bring holiness into the world and are sacramental. And this romantic love relationship, which characterizes our "beginning" sexual unions of "two in one flesh," points toward a model that we might include in our own story of Paradise.

In these and in other graced moments that flow from the fact that "God created us male and female," we find hints of how we participate in the interior life of God. We can begin, then, to imagine what it might be like in a state of original innocence in which the "spiritualization" of man and woman is grounded in total participation in the interior life of God, and they are fully graced. We might not use the same terms that the Yahwist narrator used, but we would certainly want to capture the same ideas.

The Pope's analysis of original innocence—with its solitude, unity, nakedness, and nuptial meaning of the body—helps us to realize the depth of meaning that is present in the short Yahwist account. We who live in "historical" time can use the Pope's phenomenological and personalistic analysis of the tale to spark our own experiential reflection. Our religious imagination responds to the creation narrative when we examine our own graced moments of sexuality and appreciate them as hints of a divine plan.

Jesus directed us to "the beginning" (Mt 19:4 and 8) so that we might appreciate the basic fact of human existence—namely, that we are woman and man. We cannot read the biblical account of creation and ignore the fact that our masculinity and femininity are at the root of human experience. We are challenged to evaluate our own actions and the actions of our society according to how they contribute to our discovery of the nuptial meaning of our bodies. Do we learn to recognize the personhood of the other? Sexual union based on the model of the sexual feast directs us to an understanding of human existence that leads to an "affirmation of persons" in all human relationships. The fact that our human sexuality is conditioned by the possibility of choice and, when it is raised to the level of "the image of God," contributes to a "communion of persons" points toward a need for freedom of choice in all human relationships.

The Pope's analysis invites us to examine our own experiences of our masculinity and our femininity from the perspective of the grace of original innocence. We are called upon to put aside false ideas about masculinity and femininity, about sexuality. We are invited to celebrate our bodies because they bring holiness into the world.

SEVEN

Knowledge and Procreation

Adam knew Eve his wife; and she conceived and bore Cain, saying, "I have gotten a man with the help of the Lord." And again, she bore his brother Abel. —Genesis 4:1-2a

Summary of the Pope's Addresses

The last characteristic of original innocence analyzed by the Pope is that of "knowledge and procreation." Thematically, this discussion is bound up with the blessings of fertility (Gn 1:27-28), but, historically, it is inserted in the period of sin and death.

There's a certain poverty in archaic language; it lacks varied expressions to define different facts. Still, the situation in which husband and wife united so closely as to become "one flesh" has been defined as "knowledge" and seems to express a depth of meaning which derives from our previous analyses.

The term "knowledge," which is used in Genesis 4:1 and in many other places in the Bible, indicates that the conjugal relationship of man and woman—the fact that they become, through the duality of sex, "one flesh"—is raised and introduced into the specific dimension of persons. Although Genesis 4:1 speaks only of "knowledge" of the woman by the man, which seems to stress the activity of the man, it is also possible to speak of the reciprocity of this "knowledge."

In Genesis 4:1, the biblical use of "knew" is our first encounter with the direct expression of human intentionality (because intentionality is characteristic of knowledge) and also with the whole reality of conjugal life and union in which man and woman become "one flesh." In this way, the Bible indicates the deepest essence of the reality of married life, which appears as an element and, at the same time, a result of those meanings we have been trying to follow. We find man and woman experiencing in a particular way the meaning of the body. Together, they almost become the one subject of that act and that experience; yet, at the same time, they remain, in this unity, two distinctly different subjects. When they "know" each other, they reveal themselves to each other with a specific depth of their own human "self" that is also revealed by means of their sex and their masculinity and femininity. Thus, in a unique way, the woman is "given" to the man—and he is given to her—to be known.

To help maintain a continuity with our previous analyses, we need to point out that, according to the Book of Genesis, *datum (knowledge)* and *donum (gift)* are equivalent. In Genesis 4:1-2, *datum* is stressed. We find that, in conjugal "knowledge," the woman is "given" to the man, and he is given to her, because the body and sex directly enter the structure and the very content of this "knowledge." The reality of the conjugal union, therefore, shows a new and, in a way, definitive discovery of the meaning of the human body with its masculinity and femininity. But we are not speaking only of "sexual life together." Rather, we must take into consideration that each of them—the man and the woman—is not just a passive object that has been determined "by nature." Because they are a man and a woman, each one is "given" to the other as a unique and unrepeatable subject—a "self," a person. Consequently, sex not only is part of the somatic individuality of man; sex also defines his personal identity and concreteness. "Knowledge" reveals the deepest roots of this identity and concreteness, both of which man and woman owe to their sex.

Biblical "knowledge" establishes a kind of biblical archetype of corporality and human sexuality. The term "knew" synthesizes the whole meaning of the body that has been uncovered in our analysis thus far. The man who, for the first time, "knows" the woman, his wife, in conjugal union is the same man who "differentiated himself" by "knowing" and imposing names on the whole world of living beings and, thus, affirmed himself as a person and a subject. The "knowledge" of Genesis 4:1 does not take away from the level of the fundamental self-awareness of original solitude. It is not speaking of a passive acceptance of one's determination by both the body and sex. On the contrary, the "knowledge" is a further discovery of the meaning of one's own body, a common and reciprocal discovery. "Knowledge," which was at the basis of man's original solitude, is now at the basis of the unity of the man and the woman.

According to Genesis 4:1, the one who *knows* is the man, and the one who *is known* is the woman, as if to show that the specific determination of the woman through her own body and sex hid what constitutes the depth of her femininity. It should be noted that, in the "knowledge" of Genesis 4:1, the mystery of femininity is manifested and completely revealed by means of motherhood. The woman stands before the man as a mother, that is, she is the subject of the new human life that is conceived and developed in her. At the same time, the mystery of man's masculinity, the generative and "fatherly" meaning of his body, is also revealed.

The stylistically spare words of the Book of Genesis express quite clearly that everyone finds himself again, in his own way, in this 'knowledge." We know that the constitution of woman is different from that of man, even in the deepest biophysiological determinants. Maternity manifests this constitution internally as the particular potential of the female that, with the help of man, allows for the conception and begetting of a human being.

By means of the body, the human person is "husband" and "wife." But, in the particular act of "knowledge," mediated by personal femininity and masculinity, we also discover the "pure" subjectivity of the gift, so that mutual self-fulfillment seems to be reached. Through procreation, the man and the woman know each other reciprocally in the "third" being that is sprung from them. "Knowledge," consequently, becomes a discovery, a revelation of a new man in whom both man and woman recognize their humanity, their living image. Through this "knowledge," the biological determination of man by his body and sex reaches the specific level and content of self-conscious and self-determining persons, not passive objects. It involves a particular consciousness of the meaning of the body that is bound up with fatherhood and motherhood.

The exterior constitution of woman's body, its power of perennial attractiveness, is at the beginning of the "knowledge" referred to in Genesis 4:1, and is in close union with motherhood. So it is that the Bible and the liturgy, when they honor the "womb that bore you and the breast that you sucked" (Lk 11:27), proclaim a eulogy of motherhood, of femininity, and of the female body and its expression of creative love. The first woman, discovering the maternal maturity of her body, recognizes that she has had the "help of the Lord."

The words, "I have gotten a man with the help of the Lord," express the whole theological depth of the function of begetting, of procreation, in that the woman's body becomes the place of the conception of a new man, and he assumes his specific human aspect before being born. The homogeneity of man and woman—"bone of my bones and flesh of my flesh" (Gn 2:23)—is confirmed by the remark, "I have gotten a man." The first woman is fully aware of the mystery of creation, which is renewed in human generation, and God's participation in human generation. The first parents transmit to all parents the fundamental truth about the birth of man "in the image of God" according to natural laws. This new man—born of the woman-parent, thanks to the man-parent—is reproduced in the very "image of God," who "created man in his own image, male and female he created them" (Gn 1:27).

Even today, that "image of God" constitutes a basis of continuity and unity between, on the one hand, original innocence and, on the other hand, our state of hereditary sinfulness. "Knowledge" speaks of the act in which, in union with the Creator, we give existence to a new person. The first man, in his solitude, and that same "man," as male and female, unite so closely that they become "one flesh" and renew the existence of man as the "image of God," in testimony of the first birth of man on earth. This says everything that can and must be said of the dignity of human generation; what is more, it sets the pattern for every man and woman to take up again this "image of God" in the mystery of creation and transmit it with the "help of the Lord God."

From biblical "knowledge," man realizes what the name "man" expresses as he realizes humanity in the newly generated man. The biblical cycle of "knowledge-generation" is constituted by the union of persons in love—love that enables them to unite so as to become one flesh and, by means of "knowledge," conceive and generate a new being like themselves to whom they can give the name "man." In this act, they take possession of their own humanity. At the same time, as they generate another being of which it can be said "this is bone of my bones and flesh of my flesh," they are taken possession of by humanity, which, in union and mutual "knowledge," they wish to express again through the whole sequence of human conceptions and generations. This "possession," however, is not the possession of an object.

In chapter three of the Book of Genesis, the cycle of knowledge-generation "is subjected, after sin, to the law of suffering and death" (see Gn 3:16,19-21). The horizon of death extends over the whole perspective of human life on earth, and man is detached by God-Yahweh from the tree of life. The life that has been given to man in the mystery of creation is not taken away, but it is restricted by the limit of conceptions, births, and deaths and by the perspective of hereditary sinfulness. Genesis 4:1 shows, however, that, in a way, life is given again in the ever recurring cycle. The "beginning" of man's history on earth is always formed anew in its most fundamental dimensions by means of the "knowledge-generation" of which the Book of Genesis speaks.

Each man bears within himself the mystery of his "beginning" that is bound up with the awareness of the generative meaning of the body. Genesis 4:1-2 describes the threshold of man's history on which man, as male and female, stands with the awareness of the generative meaning of his own body. Masculinity conceals within it the meaning of fatherhood, and femininity conceals the meaning of motherhood, a meaning that Jesus eventually used as the basis of his answer to the Pharisees.

In the "knowledge-generation" cycle, life struggles anew against the inexorable perspective of death and always overcomes it. When man goes beyond the solitude of his own being and affirms this being in an "other," and then both of them affirm it in the new man they generate, biblical "knowledge" acquires an even greater dimension. It takes place in that "vision" of God himself: "It was very good" (Gn 1:31).

The Pope ends his analysis of knowledge and procreation with the observation that man, in spite of all the experiences of his life—the sufferings and disappointments with himself, the sinfulness and, finally, the inevitable prospect of death—puts "knowledge" at "the beginning" of "generation" and participates in that first "vision" of God himself. Thus, man confirms anew the truth of God's words: The Creator "saw everything that he had made and, behold, it was very good."

The following are the points in the Pope's three addresses on knowledge and procreation for a theology and a spirituality of the body and of sexuality.

1. The "knowledge" in Genesis 4:1-2 raises the conjugal relationship to the dimension of persons; man and woman participate in this reciprocal knowledge by means of their body and sex.

2. In Genesis, *datum (knowledge)* and *donum (gift)* are equivalent; Genesis 4:1-2 stresses *datum* because, in conjugal "knowledge," the woman is "given" to the man and he is given to her, revealing a new discovery of the meaning of the body—a unique and unrepeatable identity and concreteness due to the body and sex.

3. In Genesis 4:1, the mystery of femininity is manifested and completely revealed in motherhood, and the mystery of masculinity is revealed in the generative and fatherly meaning of man's body; the biblical "knowledge" of self-conscious and self-determinant persons involves a particular consciousness of the meaning of the human body that is bound up with fatherhood and motherhood.

4. With the "help of the Lord," the first humans transmit to all human parents the basic truth about the birth of man in the image of God; when a man and woman "know" each other as one flesh, they confirm and renew their existence in "the image of God" and transmit this mystery of creation with the help of the Lord.

5. Even after the horizon of death extends over human history, the life that is given to man in the mystery of creation is not taken away, but only restricted by the limit of conceptions, births, and deaths; the knowledge and procreation cycle renews the original revelation of the body from "the beginning" of human history, when humans were aware of the generative meaning of their own bodies.

6. Biblical "knowledge" takes place in the "vision" of God that everything he made was very good; when we continue to put "knowledge" at "the beginning" of "generation," we seem to participate in the same vision and confirm that "it is very good."

Spiritual Reflections

The Pope's analysis of "knowledge" and procreation leads us to reflect more deeply on the significance of parenthood and generativity—two activities that are the subject of much discussion in our contemporary society. Studies of human growth and development indicate that we achieve adult maturity only when we are able to experience concern for the next generation. At the same time, the issue of parenthood, with its corollaries of motherhood and fatherhood, is subject to much scrutiny and, in some circles, is even downgraded as a "not significant" component of a happy life.

When we consider the contemporary situation, we have to say that concerns about generativity are rather ambiguous. In some ways, we have made notable progress in the development of positive concern for our young and for those who will come after us. In general, we do not practice infanticide or subject children to the equivalent of slave labor. Our young are given an opportunity for education and, in most parts of the world, are not starving and, in most instances, are protected from the extremes of child abuse. In our private lives, we might be deeply concerned about the well-being of our own children, perhaps more concerned than it was ever possible for parents of previous generations to be. From a perspective of human history, then, we could say that we are an advanced culture when it comes to concerns about generativity. But when we stop and reflect on the situation of the young in our world today, we also realize that we have a long way to go before we, as a society and even as individuals, can claim that generativity is a controlling factor in our decision-making processes.

Consider the picture that appears on the back cover of Jill Uris' book, *Ireland: A Terrible Beauty.* A little boy, not more than four years old, wears a soldier's cap and carries a weapon in his hand. He is but one of the woeful children of this world. Pictures from the strife-bound countries of the world repeatedly show the innocent young victims of adults' inability to live in peace and harmony. Closer to home, reports of child abuse indicate the continuing cycle of physical violence against the young; in many instances, the parent who is abusing a child had been the object of an abusing parent. Although there are not many instances of attempts at infanticide, even many persons in our society who do not find abortion morally offensive are disturbed by the increased use of abortion as a form of birth regulation. Sexual abuse of children, in the form of incest, kiddie pornography, and teen-age prostitution, is yet another way in which the young are violated. Stories of shelter homes for teen-age prostitutes, and arguments in favor of incest as a way of helping a child develop an understanding of his or her body, make us aware of how the young are often treated as objects.

In addition, the debunking of motherhood by some segments of the women's movement, as well as the obstacles that the working world puts in the way of a woman who seeks to combine motherhood and work, are leading many young women to question whether they want to commit themselves to the tasks of motherhood. If young women make that commitment, they often wonder whether it will be possible to be a "good" mother and, at the same time, be able to exercise their other creative abilities.

The Pope's reflections on knowledge and procreation address an enigmatic situation. We certainly *want* to act with a concern for our children—the next generation and the future of humanity— but we are not always sure how best to act out this concern. We have conflicting needs and often find ourselves responding to the immediate situation without regard for the broader implications of what we do. The Pope's addresses on knowledge and procreation call upon us to reflect on what the experience of parenthood, of motherhood and fatherhood, reveals about the divine plan for human existence. If we can gain a better understanding of the divine plan, perhaps we will be able to order our priorities so that we can be generative people. We might learn to take into consideration how our behavior influences others, first, in our immediate environment, then, in the larger environment of today's world, and lastly, in the overall context of the future of humanity.

Parenthood, and its two components of motherhood and fatherhood, appears to be unique among humans. The papal addresses indicate that the full understanding of femininity and masculinity is only appreciated when we know the meaning of motherhood and fatherhood. So, too, human growth and development theory tells us that the sharing of our identity with another in a relationship of intimacy needs to result in the development of concern for others who are outside that relationship if intimacy is to avoid becoming stagnant. Motherhood and fatherhood would thus seem to be symbols of how intimacy leads to the development of concern for others.

Consider what happens to a man and a woman when they move into the roles of father and mother. Many of us who are parents would have to admit that parenthood makes us more fully aware of our own fallibility. Still, we also know that parenthood has challenged us to behavior that we never would have imagined possible before we actually became parents. Aspects of our personalities that had been dormant before the experience of parenthood have become quite active as a result of following along the development of a child—from the time we were first aware of the conception, to whatever age that child is today. Of course, we are not pleased with all aspects of our parental personalities; none of us, after all, can claim to be always the "perfect" parent. Nevertheless, we know that the experience of parenthood has tapped positive feelings, emotions, and behaviors that have told us things about ourselves we had not previously known.

We are, it appears, genetically programmed for parenthood, a parenthood that requires a strong link between the mother and child over a very extended period of time. *Homo sapiens*, as a species, depended on this commitment of the mother for its survival; the mother, for her part, depended on her sexual attractiveness to the father of her offspring to ensure that he would care for her and, at least indirectly, for the child during the period of its dependence. The genetic roots of parenthood are strongly linked to the powerful sexual attraction toward unity between the male and female.

Richard Leakey, in *People of the Lake,* advances the hypothesis that, very early in human history, the male and the female formed an economic bond, or an economic contract, in which the product was children.[1] It was this economic contract that led to emotional involvement between the mother and the father and also between the parent and the child. The questions for us, as we reflect on the meaning of this contract between a man and a woman in today's society, are the following: What does parenthood do to us? What does parenthood reveal about the divine plan for human relationships? What does our reflection on the experience of parenthood tell us about God and about the meaning of human existence?

Although it is impossible to generalize and say that *every* parent reacts the same way to parenthood, we can consider some of the possible reactions of parents and then add to that story of these reactions our own experiences—either from our own parenthood or from observing others in their role as parents. We need to "unravel" parenthood in its components of motherhood and fatherhood; we need to recognize the role of mother and father in human history and then consider what is going on in the experience of motherhood and fatherhood in contemporary society; we need to formulate an ideal vision of motherhood and fatherhood and seek to discover what this ideal motherhood and fatherhood reveals about femininity and masculinity, about how we are to be "in the image of God," about what it means to be fully human.

Let us begin with motherhood. There is an interesting phenomenon occuring among today's young women; many are exercising their ability to choose whether and when to have a baby. Oftentimes, before the child is born, the young mother experiences a good deal of ambivalence. If she is a career woman, for example, she will often make plans to return to work soon after the child is born. And even those women who do not consider their work to be a career are taking maternity leaves of just three or four months because the family needs two incomes to pay its living expenses.

Quite often, however, an amazing event takes place when the child is born. The mother finds that she has fallen in love again— this time with her child. This helpless little baby, even when it is making extraordinary and exhausting demands on the mother, is such a marvel that many mothers do not want to turn the precious moments of their child's young life over to a baby sitter, a grandmother, or a child-care center.

Nancy Thayer, in her book, *Stepping*, captures some of the feeling that many mothers experience in the following observation:

> When I gave birth to Adam and Lucy, I changed. It was as if when they were inside my body, they had reached up and literally torn off a piece of my heart and my stomach and swallowed them so that now

they carry a part of me everywhere with them. I am linked to them by something more physically real and less scientifically observable than laser beams or remote control. They are small creatures, but I love them hugely, more than I love the earth or myself, more than I love Charlie [her husband]. There it is. My children have become my lovers. I am finally unfaithful to my husband. Their smooth, fresh, rounded plump limbs are juicier and more delicious than Charlie's. I fondle them more. Their eyes are brighter, their breath sweeter. They gave me an understanding of life at their birth that Charlie had never been able to reveal to me; they connected me up to something deep and wide and wild and good in this world. Their births gave me the shocking great knowledge that I could eat grass, dance in trees, fall from roofs, and dissolve into shimmering molecules of sparkling snow. Their births made me know that I was grabbing death and tearing it in half and washing it away with my warm, proud blood. When I took their naked, perfect bodies in my arms, I felt ecstasy and content. Now, four and two years later, that hot, exhausted joy is over, but the strength, the feeling, remains. I press their bodies against mine, kiss them, stroke them more than I do Charlie. They surprise me more than Charlie does; they are more extravagant and lustful and ferocious in their love. After we have known each other for thirteen years, I am sure my children and I will be less hot and vivid in our relations with each other. Undoubtedly I will be more rational. But until then, at least for a few more years, I will continue to wade through this life with my little children as if I were wading through a vat of hot, sticky, sweet chocolate: the chocolate impedes me, slows me down, often irritates me, but I still stay here, happy in the hot, thick, gooey mess, licking sweetness off my fingers and arms and belly.[2]

Although this bonding between mother and child stretches a woman and encourages her to develop hidden aspects of her personality, it is not always an easy task for a mother. Again, as Thayer's heroine observes:

Psychologists write of the importance of *bonding* between mother and child; that word indicated ties, mutual physical entities such as ropes joining the two. A perhaps more suitable word would be *siphoning*. For at least the first seven years of life a child siphons off from its mother everything he can get: love, attention, food, warmth, words, touching, clothes, bouncing, a sense of identity.[3]

Those of us who have children who have moved beyond the age of seven can attest to the fact that, even though the physical needs of our children might not be so demanding as they were when our children were younger, we continue to be strongly linked to them at an emotional and psychological level.

Recent studies in endocrinology indicate that the bond between mother and child is reinforced through hormonal changes. Sociologist Alice Rossi, in an article entitled "A Biosocial Perspective on Parenting," examines the implications of these hormonal influences on parenthood in modern society.[4] If, in fact, there is a genetic character to the bonding of mother and child, this link does not necessarily mean that fathers cannot assume some of the caring role of mothers. It does mean, however, that fathers might need to learn some aspects of parenting that are part of women's genetic makeup.

Mothers who have a close link with their offspring from the time of birth seem to be more attuned than fathers, who have not shared this close bonding, to the physical and emotional needs of their children as the children grow into adult life. Mothers who, of necessity, have learned how to juggle the telephone and their kitchen duties and still know where their two year old and four year old are playing, begin to develop the skill of doing more than one thing at a time, of paying attention to the needs of more than one person at a time, in a way that is not demanded of those who do not spend large amounts of time with small children. How much of the mother's caring tendency is *nature* and how much is *nuture* is still widely debated. The facts of the matter, however, seem to be that, in our contemporary society, women still exercise a more caring role in family relationships, that is in parent-child relationships. If this caring tendency reveals something about femininity, it does not necessarily mean that only women are to be the carers. Rather, motherhood reveals something about what it means to be "in the image of God." Motherhood is a component of human experience that reveals part of God's plan for all humanity.

So, too, when we examine fatherhood, we see the link between the unity of two in one flesh and the concerns about generativity. The biosocial perspective on parenting indicates that, for most of human history, the care a father shows for his offspring has been the care of the one who provides the necessities for physical survival. This does not necessarily lessen the importance of the role of father in the development of the child's personality. Biblical stories, for example, show the importance of the father. During New

Testament times, Jesus referred to God as a father by using the endearing term *Abba*, which describes a father with whom it was possible to have a close emotional relationship. Recent research indicates the importance of a father's influence in the formation of religious values for his offspring—especially for his daughters.[5] It seems that fathers, at least in the past and oftentimes in the present, are the ones who point their children to the world beyond the home. This type of caring is no less important for the development of the child than the emotional caring that arises from the close bonding of the mother and child. And, as the story of the Prodigal Son indicates, today's concern that fathers be caring parents would not result in a condition of fatherhood that would be unique to our time in history.

Motherhood and fatherhood are manifestations of human concerns about generativity. Although they are not the only ways in which human beings express their concern for the world beyond themselves, motherhood and fatherhood, which, "with the help of the Lord," allow us to "get" a new man, nevertheless serve as models for how humans must care for each other in spite of all the "messiness" that might occur. A man and a woman, a husband and a wife, when they are father and mother according to the biblical model, should be able to support each other in meeting the generativity needs of both their family and the world in which they live.

If today's family life calls for a change in emphasis in mother-father roles, then it seems crucial that mother and father share with each other how both of them might meet the strong bonding needs of their child and also serve as models to their child of concern for the world beyond the home. Some observers of the contemporary scene believe that the recent attempts to minimize the importance of the mother's role in parenting have not led to an increased involvement of the father in parenting; instead, these attempts have resulted in less parenting within a family. Fathers, according to these observers, are not furnishing the kinds of caring tasks that mothers provided in the past.

The vision we find in the Genesis story—the vision of a man and a woman joining in a conjugal union and, with the help of the Lord, creating a new man "in the image of God"—emphasizes the importance of shared parenthood. Shared parenthood in a modern, technological society requires that both parents assume new

91

aspects of the human task of parenting; to do this, the parents must be able to look upon parenting and say, along with their Creator, "it is good." Then, the parenting role allows both the man and the woman to participate in the creative act and expand their personalities so that they can assume new dimensions in their roles as parents.

There is a need for much discussion of how it is that we humans can be generative in a society such as ours. We need to investigate what generativity means now that the infant mortality rate is very low and individual life expectancy is very high. We need to consider how we can best meet the emotional needs of the children we generate—both when our offspring are young and when they are in their adult years. We need to understand how we can continue to be generative when we have a so-called "empty nest." We need to look at the model of a man and a woman who beget a child "with the help of the Lord," and then apply that model to our own particular situation.

Obviously, if we wish to be the kind of parent who echoes the Creator and says "it is good," we must do much more than simply produce an offspring. Parenthood that operates at the level of "in the image of God" is both freed from the constraints of the body and committed to generativity. We will be able to say "it is good" about our parenting role only when we, like Adam and Eve, are able to view this role as a cooperation with divine Love. Of course, "putting knowledge at the beginning of procreation"—a knowledge that is the conjugal union described in Genesis 2:23-25—requires a mature consciousness of both the meaning of our body and the meaning of sexuality. We have the model of parenthood in the Genesis story, and this story challenges us to work toward a parenthood that operates at the level of "the image of God."

In the midst of all of the troubles that currently beset our world—war, strife, famine, murder, discrimination, and disunity—men and women continue to "risk" parenthood and, in the process, tell themselves that they *hope* in the future of humankind. Some people in today's world deliberately choose not to be parents; they say that they do not hope, they do not want to bring a child into this world of unparalleled strife and overpowering uncertainty. It seems, then, that only when we are able to hope, with the "help of the Lord," can we confidently allow our conjugal union to lead to the creation of a "new man."

The papal vision that is presented in these three addresses on knowledge and procreation offers us the hope that God does cooperate in our procreative activity. At the same time, it challenges us, both as individuals and as a society, to create an environment in which people feel free to hope in the the future of humankind. Admittedly, the issue of procreation in contemporary society is a complex one. There are no simple solutions to such diverse problems as overpopulation and underpopulation that many cultures face. It seems, then, that we need to evaluate whatever solutions are proposed for population problems in light of the Genesis model, which urges us to seek the "help of the Lord" to determine how we can best fulfill the human need to create a new human.

The union of two in one flesh, if it is to help us uncover the nuptial meaning of our bodies and the divine plan for male-female relationships, challenges a man and a woman to adopt the concerns for the rest of humanity that a father and a mother must have for their children if these children are to grow physically and emotionally. The importance of parenthood in our present world must be a crucial concern for those of us who believe that we are made "in the image of God, male and female."

EIGHT
Shame and Lust

*You have heard that it was said, "You shall
not commit adultery." But I say to you that
everyone that looks at a woman lustfully has
already committed adultery with her in his
heart [or has already made her adulterous in
his heart].* —Matthew 5:27-28

*For all that is in the world, the lust of the
flesh and the lust of the eyes and the pride of
life, is not of the Father but is of the world.
And the world passes away and the lust of it;
but he who does the will of God abides
forever.* —1 John 2:16-17

*Then the eyes of both were opened, and they
knew that they were naked; and they sewed fig
leaves together and made themselves aprons.
And they heard the sound of the Lord God
walking in the garden in the cool of the day,
and the man and his wife hid themselves from
the presence of the Lord God among the trees
of the garden. The Lord God called to the man
and said to him, "Where are you?" And he
said, "I heard the sound of thee in the garden,
and I was afraid, because I was naked; and I
hid myself." Then God, Yahweh, said, "Who
told you that you were naked? Have you eaten
of the tree of which I commanded you not to
eat?"* —Genesis 3:7-11

Summary of the Pope's Addresses

Having followed Jesus' directive to return to "the beginning" in order to understand the remarks Jesus made to the Pharisees (Mt 19:4 and 8), the Pope now wishes to turn to an analysis of Matthew 5:27-28—a passage that he finds to have a key meaning for the theology of the body. Like Jesus' words to the Pharisees, this passage has an immediate context, but also a wider, global context in which we develop a theology of the body. Matthew 5:27-28 is a passage from the Sermon on the Mount. It is part of a fundamental revision of the way of understanding and carrying out the moral law of the old covenant. Jesus declares: "Think not that I have come to abolish the law and the prophets: I have come not to abolish them but to fulfill them" (Mt 5:17). And it will be necessary to "fulfill" the law in order to realize the kingdom of God in its eschatological dimension.

The fulfillment of the law conditions the kingdom in the temporal dimension of human existence and fully corresponds to the meaning of the law, of the Decalog, of the individual commandments; it must, however, also be a fulfillment of that justice that must "superabound" in man himself. Thus, there are two aspects to the "fulfillment."

Here we find ourselves at the heart of the *ethos* of the New Testament. The Sermon on the Mount is a great turning point in the field of *ethos*. A living morality is not formed only by norms found in commandments, precepts, and prohibitions such as, "You shall not commit adultery"; rather, we find in the Sermon on the Mount a living morality in which not only the very meaning of being a man is realized, but also the law is fulfilled by means of the "superabounding" justice. This morality is formed in the interior perception of values in which duty is the expression of one's conscience and of one's ego. This *ethos* makes us enter the depth of the norm itself. Moral value is connected with the dynamic process of man's intimacy; we cannot stop "at the surface" of human actions; it is necessary to penetrate inside.

In Matthew 5:27-28, Jesus connects the two commandments, "You shall not commit adultery" and "You shall not covet your neighbor's wife," not by identifying the scope of these two commandments, but by pointing out the dimension, the interior action,

that is referred to in the words, "You shall not commit adultery"—
an action that finds its visible expression in the "act of the body."
The casuistry of the Old Testament aimed at investigating the exterior criteria that constituted this "act of the body" and sought to
combat adultery. But it had various legal "loopholes" because of
"hardness of heart," thereby distorting the meaning of the original
commandment. People often kept to the legalistic observance but
did not "superabound" with interior justice in their "hearts."

Jesus' words in Matthew 5:27-28 appeal to the interior man
whose "beginning" we traced in the preceding analysis. He speaks
not only to the man who hears the Sermon on the Mount, but also
to every other man in human history—including those of us in our
contemporary age—to "each" of us and to those who have this
commandment only "written on his heart." Jesus' words have an
explicit anthropological content; they concern those perennial
meanings through which an "adequate" anthropology is constituted. They also demand that man should enter into his full image.
To do this, historical man must again find himself interiorly, that is,
in his "heart"—in that dimension of humanity with which both the
sense of the meaning of the human body and the order of this sense
is directly linked.

When considering Matthew 5:27-28, we must consider the relationship between the anthropological and ethical reasons for Jesus'
directive. The desire indicated by the expression, "everyone who
looks at a woman lustfully," has a biblical and a theological dimension that, though not directly manifested here, is deeply rooted in
the global context of the revelation of the body. We must go back to
this context so that Jesus' appeal "to the heart," that is, to the
interior man, will be understood in all the fullness of its truth.

Matthew 5:27-28 has an indicative character; it refers to both
man and woman and illustrates with a concrete example how "the
fulfillment of the law" must be understood according to the meaning intended by God the legislator, and, in addition, how the "superabounding of justice" must be understood. But Jesus does not want
us to dwell on the example itself; rather, we must penetrate the full
ethical and anthropological meaning of the statement. If we follow
its traces, we can arrive at an understanding of the general truth
about "historical" man that will be valid for our theology of the
body.

The words of Jesus in the Sermon on the Mount are in direct

reference to the "lust" that arises in the human heart; they also guide our understanding of a universal truth about man, a truth that is expressed in the biblical doctrine of the three forms of lust mentioned in the first letter of St. John (2:16-17). These words appear in the context of the whole Johannine theology and in the broader context of the whole Bible. Although they do not explain lust in its three forms, they indicate its origin. Lust is "not of the Father" but "of the world," that is, it is the fruit of the tree of the knowledge of good and evil, which is in man's heart, rather than the fruit of the mystery of creation. In the three forms of lust, the covenant with the God-Yahweh is broken in man's heart. As a consequence of this breaking of the covenant with God in the human heart, the "world" of the Book of Genesis becomes the "world" of Johannine theology.

The statement that lust "is not of the Father but of the world" directs us again to the biblical "beginning" where we find what is essential for the theology of the body. We must return once more to that "beginning" and examine the "threshold" of authentic human experiences. Our analysis of this threshold of the revelation of "historical" man will uncover the same fundamental meanings that were found in our analysis of "original" time and will be seen as an essential element of both an adequate anthropology and a theology of the body.

In this process, we are trying to uncover the truth about man that has been revealed and expressed in the general biblical context. We want to understand the man that Jesus addresses when he speaks of the man who "looks" at a woman "lustfully." It appears that this man is also the "man of lust" in St. John's first letter, and that both the man who looks lustfully and the woman who is the object of this look live in the dimension of the three forms of lust, which "is not of the Father but is of the world." Consequently, we need to examine the "lustful man" of the Bible if we want to discover the depth of Jesus' words in Matthew 5:27-28. We can then explain the meaning of his reference to the human "heart"—a meaning that is important for our theology of the body.

When we return again to the Yahwist narrative in Genesis 3, we find that the biblical description highlights the key moment in which the gift is questioned in man's heart. The man who gathers the fruit "of the tree of the knowledge of good and evil" makes a choice against the will of the Creator and accepts the motive of the tempter, which includes the questioning of both the gift and the Love from which creation has its origin. The man who has received the "world" as a gift and is "in the image of God" turns his back on the "Father" and questions in his heart whether love is the specific motive of creation and of the original covenant. Man turns his back on God—on Love; man casts God out of his heart. In so doing, he detaches his heart—almost cuts it off—from what is "of the Father" but keeps within himself what is "of the world." Genesis 3:7 reveals man's "situation" after sin and suggests the beginning of "lust" in man's heart. In this verse, we discover the "frontier" between the state of original innocence (especially in Genesis 2:25) and the state of man's sinfulness. In Genesis 3:7 there is explicit reference to shame in connection with sin, a shame that is the first source of the manifestation in both the man and the woman of what "is not of the Father but of the world."

Genesis 3:7 speaks of the mutual shame of the man and the woman as a symptom of the fall, wherein shame reaches its deepest level and seems to shake the very foundations of human existence. When the man and the woman hide themselves in Genesis 3:8, we discover the depth of the shame that both feel before each other as a result of choosing the tree of the knowledge of good and evil. A fear that had previously been unknown is revealed as we move on to Genesis 3:9-10. Although a certain fear belongs to the very essence of shame, this original shame reveals its character in a particular way: "I was afraid because I was naked." The man's remark indicates that there is something deeper than physical shame bound up with the consciousness of man's nakedness. The man tries to cover the true origin of his fear with the shame of his own nakedness, indicating its effect in order to avoid having to acknowledge the cause of the shame. In Genesis 3:11, Yahweh-God confronts man with the question, "Who told you that you were naked? Have you eaten of the tree of which I commanded you not to eat?"

The Genesis 3 narrative records the surface of man's emotions in such a way that it reveals their depth. "Nakedness" is not the origin of a shame that is related only to the body; rather, through "nakedness," we see man deprived of participation in the gift, alienated from the Love that had been the source of the original gift. Man suffers a loss of what belonged to him in the original fullness "of the image of God." The three forms of lust relate to the loss, the deficiencies, the limitations that appear with sin. Lust is a lack that has its roots in the original depth of the human spirit.

The words of Genesis 3:10 show a radical change in the meaning of original nakedness. In the state of original innocence, nakedness did not express a lack but, rather, a full acceptance of the body in all its human and personal truth. In original innocence, the human body bore in itself the unquestionable sign of "the image of God" and was the specific source of the certainty of that image present in the whole human being. Acceptance of the body was the basis for acceptance of the whole visible world. It was, for man, a guarantee of his dominion over the world, which he was to subdue (see Gn 1:28). But, to be "afraid because I was naked" shows the loss of man's original certainty of "the image of God" that is expressed in his body, and the loss, to some extent, of his right to participate in the perception of the world he enjoyed in the mystery of creation. When man participated in the divine vision of both the world and his own humanity, he was able to appreciate the value of the world, which "God saw was very good" (Gn 1:31).

With the collapse of the acceptance of the body as a sign of the person in the visible world, we find that the acceptance of the material world, in relation to man, is also shaken. The words of God-Yahweh were a forewarning of the hostility of the world, the resistance of nature with regard to man, and the fatigue the human body was to feel in contact with the earth, which had been subdued by man (Gn 3:17-19). Adam's words in Genesis 3:10 express an awareness of being defenseless and an insecurity over his bodily structure before the processes of nature and their inevitable determinism. There seems to be a "cosmic shame" implied in this statement whereby man, created "in the image of God," realizes that he is subject to the earth, particularly in the "part" of his transcendent constitution that is represented by the body.

This "cosmic shame" makes way, in the biblical text, for another form of shame produced in humanity itself, a shame that is at once immanent and relative. This shame is revealed in the depths of human interiority and, at the same time, refers to the "other"—the woman "with regard to the man," the man "with regard to the woman." This mutual shame obliges them to cover their nakedness; they hide their own bodies and remove from their sight the visible sign of femininity and masculinity.

The Yahwist text, especially Genesis 3:7, seems to explicitly indicate the "sexual character" of this shame, which leads us to wonder if this shame might only be a "relative character," that is, shame of one's own sexuality only in reference to a person of the other sex. When we consider the whole immediate context of Genesis 3:7, however, we discover a more immanent background to that shame which is manifested in the "sexual order" and reveals a difficulty of perceiving the meaning of one's own body, a difficulty that was not experienced in original innocence. These words reveal a rupture of man's original spiritual and somatic unity; his body ceases to draw upon the power of the Spirit that has raised him to the level of "the image of God." Original shame bears within it a specific humiliation that is mediated by the body and, in this way, is immanent. The realization of this shame creates a fundamental disquiet in the whole of human existence, not only in the face of the prospect of death but also in the ethical dimension of human life. The original shame of the body ("I am naked") is always fear ("I was afraid") and shows the uneasiness of a conscience troubled by lust.

The body, no longer in the state of original innocence, becomes a constant center of resistance to the Spirit and threatens the unity of the human person, which is rooted in the very constitution of the person. Lust, particularly lust of the body, is a threat to the structure of self-control and self-mastery through which the human person is formed. The man of lust no longer controls his body with simplicity and naturalness. The self-mastery essential for the person is shaken to the very foundations.

Immanent shame is connected with this disruption and has a "sexual" character because human sexuality seems to highlight the imbalance that springs from lust, especially from the "lust of the body." Genesis 3:7 reveals that the "man of lust" (man and woman "in the act of the knowledge of good and evil") realizes that he has stopped being above the world of living beings, especially in the dimension of his body and sex. He feels a specific break of his own body's personal integrity, a break that is connected with the call to unity in which man and woman "become one flesh" (Gn 2:24). At least indirectly, then, immanent shame, that is, sexual shame, is always relative; it is the shame of our own sexuality "with regard" to the other human being. In this first moment, we find shame explained by means of lust, and lust explained by means of shame.

In order to understand the sense of Jesus' words on "adultery" in the heart, it is necessary to understand how the human heart keeps within itself both desire and shame. The birth of shame occurs at that time in which the inner man, "the heart," closes himself to "what comes from the Father." The birth of shame in the human heart is connected with the three-fold forms of lust in Johannine theology. Man is ashamed of his body because of lust; actually, he is more ashamed of the lust and, because of it, he is ashamed of his body. The state of his spirit, overcome by desire or lust, makes him ashamed of his body. We should note here the difference between the biblical and theological meaning of lust and the psychological meaning of lust. Biblical lust, on the one hand, indicates the state of the human spirit that has been removed from original simplicity, from existence "in the dimensions of God." Psychology, on the other hand, views lust as a desire that comes from lack or necessity and can only be satisfied by the value that is desired.

Shame, then, has a double meaning. Although it indicates a threat to the value of the body, it preserves this value interiorly. When the human heart feels shame as well as lust, we find that it is possible and necessary to appeal to the "heart" in order to guarantee those values that have been distorted by lust. The Pope concludes that, because of this, we are able to understand why Jesus, when speaking of lust, appeals to the human "heart."

The following are the main points for a theology of the body and of sexuality that emerge from the Pope's five addresses that explain shame and lust.

1. Morality, according to the *ethos* of the Sermon on the Mount, is connected with the dynamic process of human intimacy; to develop this morality, we must go beyond the surface of human actions and penetrate into the human heart. This morality arrives at "fulfillment" of the law by means of the "superabounding" of justice, which is why Jesus appeals to the interior man, to the heart, in Matthew 5:27-28.

2. There is an ethical and anthropological character to Matthew 5:27-28 that directs us to seek an understanding of the general truth about "historical" man; Jesus addresses all humans in his words to the "interior" man, demanding that

we should enter into our full image while remaining in relationship with each other through our body and sex.

3. The biblical doctrine of the three forms of lust, in 1 John, indicates that the genesis of lust is in the human choice for that which is "of the world" and "not of the Father"; this genesis of lust gives us the general biblical context of the truth about humans that Jesus addresses in Matthew 5:27-28.

4. In Genesis 3:1-5, we find humans turning their backs on God-Love (the Father) and casting him out of their hearts; the shame of Genesis 3 is one of the first manifestations in humans of what is "not of the Father."

5. There is a radical change in the meaning of original nakedness in Genesis 3; "nakedness" reveals man deprived of the gift, and alienated from Love, the source of the gift. Lust in Genesis 3 is a lack that has its roots in the original depth of the human spirit, which is lost through the collapse of the original acceptance of the body as a sign of the person in the visible world, and implies a "cosmic shame" in which we are subjected to earth, particularly in our bodies.

6. The shame in humanity, which is caused by human choice for "the things of the world," is both immanent and relative; immanent shame refers to the interior imbalance that is caused by the rupture of our original bodily unity and springs from lust, especially lust of the body; this shame is indirectly relative because it is the shame of our own sexuality "with regard" to the other human being.

7. The birth of shame in the human heart, revealed in Genesis 3, accompanies the beginning of the three forms of lust, particularly the concupiscence of the body; we are ashamed of our bodies due to lust, to the state of our spirit removed from the simplicity and fullness of values that humans and the world possessed in "the dimension of God."

8. Shame, which indicates the disruption of the original value of the body as "good," at the same time preserves that value interiorly; since the human heart experiences shame, it is possible and necessary to appeal to it when guaranteeing the values that are threatened by lust.

Spiritual Reflections

The Pope's lengthy analysis of the general biblical context of Jesus' words in the Sermon on the Mount regarding "adultery in the heart" calls upon us to consider how it is that we share with Adam and Eve the experience of hiding from the real implications of the choices we make for the "things of the world" rather than for the "things of the Father," especially in the area of our sexuality. We need to understand how our lust "for the things of the world" almost cuts us off from God as we question the possibility of using our sexuality as a way of revealing love in the world. We need to examine how our sense of shame over our choice of "the things of the world" causes an imbalance between our spirit and our body and, at the same time, interferes with our ability to use our sexuality as a basis for meaningful relationships with other human beings.

If we were able to integrate all the dimensions of our sexuality— that is, our bodily self-image, the ways in which we give and receive affection, our expectation for male-female roles, our ability to be sex educators, our family lifestyles, our erotic behavior, and our reproductive ability—so that in each of these areas we would reflect the plan of God, we would have a harmony between our spirit and our bodies. Most probably, we would then be able to enter into intimacy relationships in which we could be gift for the other, in which we would exist *with* and *for* another, and in which we would not use the other as an object for our own satisfaction. Reflection on our experiences in the various areas of sexuality makes us painfully aware of how far we are from the ideal of an integrated sexuality that would allow us to begin to reflect the plan of God. Reflection on our experiences also makes us aware of the many times we feel a sense of shame over the misuse of our sexuality. It is this sense of shame that keeps us conscious of the need to try to be more integrated in the use of our sexuality. This sense of shame also is a source of our search for some broader vision that will help us make sense out of why it is that we come in male and female varieties.

Biblical lust, the Pope tells us, signifies a lack, a lack of harmony between our interior spirit and our exterior bodily behavior. Oftentimes, especially in the area of our sexuality, we are conscious of this imbalance; many times, however, we push the awareness of the imbalance below the level of our consciousness so that we won't have to deal with the shame we feel over the misuse of our masculinity and femininity.

In preparing ourselves so we might develop a living morality that is based on the penetration of our spirit rather than a simple consideration of surface behavior, we must reflect on our present behavior in all the areas of our life that are affected by our masculinity and femininity. We must become conscious of the ways in which our activities indicate our choice for "the things of the world" rather than for "the things of the Father."

Reflecting on various experiences of ourselves as male or female is not an easy task, especially when it means that we have to consider the pervasiveness of our sexuality. We have been so used to compartmentalizing the various dimensions of our sexual identity that the challenge to admit that sexuality is more than sex, more than erotic behavior and reproduction, causes a great deal of confusion and even frustration.

We feel empathy with people who come to a talk on religious aspects of sexuality wanting directions for specific sexual behavior either for themselves or for their children. They voice legitimate concerns about how they might pass on values to their children, but they have a great deal of difficulty expressing just what values they want to pass on. They are looking for a quick set of rules that will guarantee "correct" behavior from their children. They are dismayed over what they consider to be promiscuity among today's teen-agers and would like religion to impose rules for their children. In the process, however, they ignore the fact that the best way to pass on values about sexuality is for the mother and father to have an integrated vision about sexuality that influences their behavior in all areas of relationships that are affected by sexual identity.

Consider, for example, the story a mother tells about her fifteen-year-old son. The young man is unhappy with his geometry teacher, a woman. He complains to his first-year algebra teacher (a man) about the geometry teacher's inability to teach the course. The man counsels the boy to be patient with his new teacher; after all, the former teacher had certainly been patient with the boy in the beginning days of his algebra course. The mother comments on the whole situation: "Oh, he's probably just like his father. He thinks a woman can't possibly teach him anything and so he's sure that this woman can't possibly be a good teacher."

This mother, although she might not have been aware of it, was expressing how we pass on values about sexuality. Our children learn what it means to be a man or a woman and about relationships between men and women, through the example that parents and other adults set for them. No matter how good a sex-education course might be for this young man, a good deal of his "sexuality" education has taken place in his home. His parents' attitudes on male-female identity have established the basis for his appreciation of a woman's ability in certain areas. If adult behavior encourages children to accept stereotypes and apply them to all women and all men, then the stage is set for confusion in later relationships between the sexes.

In a similar manner, parental behavior teaches children about bodily self-image and ways of giving and receiving affection. Parental attitudes contribute to parental behavior that, in turn, will build the foundation for children's attitudes, and these foundations will, for many children, be the basis of later problems in coming to grips with their sexual identity. We begin to see the necessity for integration if we are to succeed as educators in human sexuality.

An area of our behavior that is strongly influenced by our sexual identity and clearly shows the overlap among the various dimensions of our sexuality is the way in which we give and receive affection. Ethnic background often influences how we demonstrate our feelings of affection; even within various cultural differences, however, the influence of sexuality is often evident.

The anti-body, anti-sex attitudes of those who, in the past, strongly influenced the religious and cultural habits of our American society are evidenced in current attitudes about what is the appropriate way to show affection for both members of our own sex and members of the opposite sex. Even today, in a so-called sexually liberated society, public displays of affection are judged by what is considered "appropriate." Public hugging of one male athlete by another, after a winning touchdown has been scored, draws little disapproval. Yet similar displays of affection between two males outside of the athletic arena, although they might be more readily acceptable today than twenty years ago, are still far from the acceptable norm for male interaction. Most men would not feel comfortable in a similar situation, and many of us, both men and women, find ourselves ill at ease when we witness this type of affection between two men.

When we reflect on experiences from our own particular cultural background, we uncover how basic attitudes toward the body and sex have influenced the ways in which people in these cultural groups are able to give and receive affection. Reflecting on the experience of Irish-Americans is but one example of how this influence works. Consider the case of the Irish immigrant woman who is now in her seventies; she was one of ten children and yet she cannot recall ever being hugged, kissed, or held by her mother. Nor was there ever any public display of affection between her parents. Occasionally, her father would bounce a child on his knee but, aside from that, display of affection—indeed, any display of emotion—was tightly controlled. Such control of display of emotion would seem to be tied into a "fear" of some greater evil. There was a need to "hide" from the power of the emotion, to be ashamed of the emotion because of a deeper shame over what the emotion revealed.

We are not surprised, then, when we consider the experience of the young Irish-American women of the next generation, women who were educated in the period captured in John Powers' best seller, *Do Black Patent Leather Shoes Really Reflect Up?* We discover that this tendency to be reticent in displaying emotion is not at all unusual for women who were close friends in high-school days in the late '40s and early '50s. When we meet now, we are uncertain about whether to show affection with an embrace or a kiss. Such was not our habit in the days of our youth and, though we might display our affection with more recent acquaintances, we are uncertain if a similar show of affection is appropriate with these friends from our youth.

Every ethnic group, indeed every family and every individual, has a story about how they developed particular attitudes about displaying affection. Although it is permissible for mothers and daughters to demonstrate their affection throughout their lives, for example, such is often not the case with fathers and their sons. Too much affection is often considered sentimental and unmanly. In many families, once the child reaches a certain age, a display of affection between the child and the parent of the other sex is also discouraged, adding to the impression that affection is dangerous, that affection will somehow stir up unwanted and uncontrollable sexual desires, which we should obviously be ashamed of. Thus, people learn from family behavior to be afraid of any action that might arouse sexual feelings.

The original plan of God called for us to join with him in saying, "it is good" about the body and, consequently, about the ability of our bodies to allow us to express the depth of our warmth and affection for one another. Still, we often find ourselves afraid that this type of affection will lead to our destruction. Like Adam and Eve, we know how easy it is to make a choice "for the things of the world," and rather than admit our fear of that choice, we try to hide from ourselves and from others the challenge of the "nuptial meaning of our body." Whenever we go along with the cultural stereotypes about how to give and receive affection, we are falling back on the "fig-leaf approach" to appreciating the goodness of our bodies—that is to say, we are afraid, so we hide. This approach is learned through the education we have received in sexuality. Unless we take positive steps to avoid this, we pass similar attitudes on to our children.

This negative understanding of how to give and receive affection, which has been passed on through sexuality education in the family, is closely linked to our cultural and religious appreciation of the body, which, in turn, affects our bodily self-image. As we have already observed, few of us have emerged unscathed from the traumas the teen-age years deliver to our bodily self-image. When we couple the almost natural negative feeling that can emerge during those years with religious attitudes about the dangers of the body, we can understand why many Catholics who were educated in the pre-Vatican II era are very uncomfortable with their bodies and are not willing, or at least are not able, to convey to their children a positive attitude toward the body. The body was so

closely linked with sex and sexual desire that it had to be continually protected from its evil possibilities. Immodesty was a sin to be
carefully guarded against. Campaigns to assure modesty in dress
reached the proportions of the so-called S-D-S movement of the
early 1950s. Catholic girls were urged to buy only modest formals—
never a strapless—under the premise that, if all Catholic girls
demanded modest dresses, the supply of modest dresses would
increase. Thus, the motto S-D-S meant Supply-Demand-Supply.
Girls with strapless ball gowns were often sent home from proms
and their parents castigated for allowing their daughters to be
occasions of sin for their prom dates.

There is little wonder that many of the young women who grew
up in a home and school environment that encouraged such views
found it exceedingly difficult to be open about their bodies once
they entered a marital relationship; indeed, it is understandable
that many felt shame. But in all fairness, we cannot blame only the
church for negative attitudes about the body. Even now, in a day
of so-called sexual freedom, we find some of the most "liberated"
people in our society still disparaging the body. Consider the reaction of many feminists to an increase of articles on the sexiness of
many famous women over 40. Such articles are condemned by
feminists because we should not be celebrating the physical attractiveness of women; rather, the feminists argue, we should celebrate
the intellectual attractiveness of women. The roots of this attitude
are not so far removed from the roots of the attitude that led to
the formation of S-D-S. The body is not to be celebrated because
the body cannot possibly be good. The intellect is good, however,
and it should be celebrated. There is something about the body, however,
that will lead us astray if we place too much emphasis on it. Both
the proponents of S-D-S and modern-day feminists are opposed to
the "sexiness" of the female body. The S-D-Sers felt that sexiness
would lead to sin in the form of arousal of the young male who
would observe the young woman in her strapless attire. For the
feminists, emphasis on the sexiness of the female body is only a
way to satisfy the "lust" of the male; bodily attractiveness is a
betrayal of the female desire to advance in the world. Both attitudes are rooted in a fear that the body will destroy us; so we hide
from our fear of destruction by putting a negative emphasis on the
body.

We need to examine our own attitudes toward our bodies, attitudes that have been developed out of sexuality education and have negatively influenced our ability to appreciate our bodies and be able to freely show affection. We continue to pass on these attitudes to the next generation when we fail to recognize how they are a negative interpretation of the meaning of our human sexuality.

The Pope's reflections on shame and lust call us to examine the presence in our lives of shame, shame regarding our sexuality. When we acknowledge the presence of this shame, we discover that (1) we are not living our sexuality according to the plan of the Father, (2) we do not have an integrated sexual identity, and (3) we are not freely able to appreciate the body and its sexuality as part of our personal identity and concreteness. Because we live in the world of the "tree of knowledge of good and evil," we will undoubtedly always have experiences of shame, experiences that cause us to realize that so often we choose the "things of the world" rather than the "things of the Father," especially regarding our sexual identity. We are challenged by the Pope, therefore, to continually recognize the roots of our shame in our inability to live according to the plan of the Father. The body is not the cause of our shame, but rather, our shame is rooted in our failure to appreciate the positive call of our body to a union with another, a union which respects the other as a person created "for himself or herself." We must determine how we can learn to begin to celebrate the "goodness" of our body and sex if we are to participate in the feast that has been planned by God. Our morality must flow from an examination of our "hearts."

NINE

Appropriation

I will greatly multiply your pain in childbearing; in pain you shall bring forth children.
Your desire shall be for your husband, and he shall rule over you. —Genesis 3:16

Summary of the Pope's Addresses

As we seek to penetrate deeper into the mysteries of the human heart, we find that Genesis 3 helps us understand the profound dimensions of human experience of shame, especially as we move beyond the dialog between God-Yahweh and man and woman into the monolog of Genesis 3:16. Although these words seem to speak of a particular "disability" that is unique to woman, this is not a social disability or inequality. Rather, these words refer to another form of inequality that woman will experience as a lack of the unity to which both man and woman were called in Genesis 2:24.

God-Yahweh's words in Genesis 3:16 refer to more than a specific sexual union; they include all aspects of the conjugal union. In the context of the entire Yahwist narrative, these words mean a violation, a fundamental loss of the original community/communion of persons. Both man and woman experience a deep shame after they have broken their original convenant with God. Their original beatifying, conjugal union will now be distorted in their "heart" by lust. Though these words are addressed to the woman, they refer to both of them.

In this new situation, man and woman are no longer united; they are divided and opposed because of their masculinity and femininity; they are estranged from their bodies, the source of their original union; they are each opposed to the other because of the body and sex. Although this opposition does not destroy the possibility of conjugal union that has been planned by the Creator, it does confer on this union the consequences of the "man of lust."

The woman and the man of Genesis 3:16 are the same human couple entering into the same marriage described in Genesis 2:24, but they are now something different; they are threatened by the insatiability of that union and unity to which they are attracted because they have been called from eternity to exist "in communion." The deep meaning of sexual shame is connected with the inability to achieve a mutual communion of persons in the "conjugal union of the body."

Genesis 3:16 indicates that the basis of shame experienced by "historical" man is the three-fold lust of 1 John 2:16. The words "he shall rule over you" indicate a "pride of life" that changes the structure of the communion of the interpersonal relationship, making the human being an object that can be desired by the lust of the eyes.

The explanation of original shame is not sought in the body itself, but goes back to the changes the human spirit has undergone. When the spirit is aware of the impossibility of achieving mutual unity between man and woman, it blames the body, thereby depriving the body of its original simplicity and purity of meaning. Shame, then, is a secondary experience in relation to this awareness; it reveals the moment of lust, but also can protect the man and the woman from the consequences of the three forms of lust. Indeed, through shame, man and woman almost remain in original innocence because shame continually reminds them of the loss of the nuptial meaning of the body, the "sacramental" expression of the "communion of persons" that is distorted in Genesis 3:16.

In historical times, the "body" continues to desire personal union on the basis of masculinity and femininity. Lust, however, directs this desire in its own way, often for the satisfaction of the body and at the cost of a real and full communion of persons.

The man, who says to God-Yahweh in Genesis 3:10, "I was afraid because I was naked and I hid myself," seems to be the one who feels the shame of his own body. He is the one for whom shame, coupled with lust, becomes an impulse to "dominate" the woman. Shame in the woman, however, is seen as an insatiable desire for a different union. What had been "communion of persons" now becomes the possession of the other as the object of one's own desire. Despite the seemingly different results of lust in man and woman, both have become subject to lust, and, consequently, the lot of both is shame that touches the innermost recesses of both, albeit in different ways.

Thus, Genesis 3 demonstrates that the three forms of lust limit the nuptial meaning of the body both in the way in which the human being is aware of the body and also in all the experiences of the body in its masculinity and femininity and its constant predisposition to these experiences. The "meaning of the body" is not simply conceptual; it is, in addition, the attitude, or the way of experiencing the body, that which the "heart" of the Sermon on the Mount applies to the human body and its masculinity and femininity (its sexuality).

The human body and sex have an objective significance that is, in a "historical" sense, outside the system of real and concrete interpersonal relationships between man and woman. The "meaning of the body" of which we speak, however, is an interior dimension that can be considered "historical." When we speak of lust as an infraction, or distortion, of the nuptial meaning of the body, we refer to our preceding analysis of the body in original innocence (see chapter 6). We also refer to "historical" man in the meaning that he, "in his heart," applies to his own body and its masculinity and femininity, and how he determines his attitudes and decides his way of living in the body.

In this way, we are able to link the words from Matthew 5:27-28 to the threshold of man's theological history. Lust as limitation, infraction, and distortion of the nuptial meaning of the body becomes more clearly understood in light of our examination of "the beginning." From Adam and Eve's story, we have been able to discover the nuptial meaning of the body and how this meaning both is a measure of the human "heart" and leads to the "communion of persons." Since the personal experience of Adam and Eve has undergone imbalance and distortion, we realize that the nuptial meaning of the body also must have undergone a distortion. We must determine the nature of this distortion in order to answer the questions, What is lust of the flesh?, and What is its theological and anthropological character?

Concupiscence that "comes from the world" limits and distorts the body's objective way of existing. The human "heart" experiences this limitation especially in the sphere of man-woman mutual relations. Femininity and masculinity no longer are the expression of the spirit that is aimed at personal communion, but remain merely an object of attraction akin to that of other living beings.

When we say that the human body in its masculinity-femininity has "almost" lost the capacity of expressing the love in which the man-person becomes a gift, it is because the dimension of the gift continues, to some extent, to permeate and mold the love in the human "heart." The "nuptial meaning of the body" is not completely suffocated by concupiscence but it is habitually threatened. We find that the "heart" becomes a battlefield between love and lust; the more that lust dominates the heart, the less the heart realizes the nuptial meaning of the body. This is not always obvious because when lust has the upper hand, it often passes itself off as "love." This does not mean that we should distrust the human heart, only that we should keep it under control.

Lust attacks the "sincere giving" in which man "can fully discover his true self." It deprives man of the dignity of giving that is expressed by his body through sexuality, depersonalizing him and making him an *"object for* the other" instead of *"together with* the other." In the sacramental unity "of the body," the female becomes an object for the male, and the male becomes an object for the female; this situation calls into question the fact that each of them was willed by the Creator "for his own sake." The subjectivity of the person gives way to the objectivity of the body. The personal relations of men and women are unilaterally and reductively linked with the body and sex, and these relations become almost incapable of accepting the mutual gift of the person.

Concupiscence entails the loss of the interior freedom of the gift; the man and the woman can exist in the relationship of self-giving only if each one controls himself. Concupiscence, however, reduces self-control and, to a certain degree, makes impossible an interior freedom of giving. At the same time, concupiscence obscures the beauty that the human body possesses in its sexuality as an expression of its spirit.

The body becomes an object of lust and a "field of appropriation" of the other human being. Concupiscence appropriates; consequently, a relationship of *gift* becomes a relationship of mutual appropriation. When man considers woman only as an object to be possessed and not as a gift, he condemns himself to become, for her, only an object of appropriation and not a gift. So it is that the structure of communion between persons disappears.

Genesis 3:16 seems to suggest that this happens at the expense of the woman, and she feels it more than the man. Perhaps this is because, from "the beginning," man was to have been the guardian of the reciprocity of the gift. When we analyzed Genesis 2:23-25, we saw man's responsibility in accepting femininity as a gift in a mutual, bilateral exchange. To take this gift by means of concupiscence, however, is in direct contrast to Genesis 2:23-25. The responsibility of maintaining the balance, or reciprocity, of the gift has been entrusted to the man and the woman; but a special responsibility rests on the man, as if it depended more on him whether the balance is maintained or broken or re-established.

Obviously, the diversity of roles that was highlighted in Genesis was dictated by the social emargination of women of that time; the Old and the New Testament provide sufficient evidence for this view. Still, there is some truth to the diversity of roles that is independent of this particular historical situation.

Because of lust, the body becomes almost a "ground" of appropriation of the other; there is also a consequent loss of the nuptial meaning of the body and the mutual "belonging of persons" who unite in order to "become one flesh." This dimension of the personal union of man and woman through love is expressed by the pronoun *my,* which has always belonged to the language of human love but which, in its strictly "material" connotations, signifies a relationship of possession. In reference to love, the pronoun *my* indicates the personal analogy of the relationship, that is, the mutual belonging of man and woman "in unity of the body." We can speak of persons *belonging* only if we do so analogically, in its specific meaning, because *belonging* presupposes the relationship of subject to object, possession and ownership. In the language of love, however, *my* indicates reciprocity of the donation in which the mutual communion of persons is established by the gift of masculinity and femininity and the nuptial meaning of the body is preserved. In the language of love, *my* is a radical negation of the relationship of subject to object.

Triple lust takes away the specific dimension of the personal analogy and leads to an attitude of possession; what I possess, then, has a meaning for me and my enjoyment because it is at my disposal. This enjoyment of the object that I possess, however, negates the "nuptial meaning of the body." "Disinterested giving" is excluded from selfish "enjoyment." In 1 John 2:16, we find that lust shows itself, above all, in the state of the human spirit. So, too, the lust of the flesh gives witness to the state of the human spirit. Sin creates in the human heart an opposition between the spirit and the body; its consequences are felt in the mutual relationship of persons whose unity has been determined from "the beginning" by the fact that they are man and woman. As Romans 7:23 indicates, another law, which is at war with the law of my mind, has been installed in man. In order to understand the appeal that Christ makes to the human heart in the Sermon on the Mount, we must remember the possibility that our way of seeing, evaluating, and loving will respond "to the desire of the body" because it is more powerful than "the desire of the mind."

These reflections on the consequences of the three forms of lust conclude the Pope's analysis of "the beginning" and prepare the way for our understanding of the New Testament *ethos*.

The following six important points for a theology and a spirituality of the body emerge from the Pope's four addresses on appropriation.

1. The words of Genesis 3:16 refer to a violation, a fundamental loss, a distortion of the original communion of persons that is caused by lust; the words refer to both man and woman, who are now divided—even opposed—because of their masculinity and femininity. This opposition does not destroy the conjugal union that has been willed by the Creator, but does threaten it as a result of the three forms of lust.

2. The desire for personal union that is directed by lust becomes, in man, the impulse to "dominate" the woman and, in the woman, the insatiable "desire" for a different kind of union; both the man and the woman have become human beings who are subject to lust in the innermost recesses of their personalities and are afflicted by shame.

3. The three forms of lust limit the "nuptial meaning of the body" and affect not only the full awareness of that meaning, but also all experience of the body's masculinity

and femininity and the constant predisposition to this experience; the human "heart" experiences this limitation especially in the sphere of man-woman mutual relations, which no longer seem to be the expression of the spirit aiming at personal communion.

4. The "nuptial meaning of the body" has not been completely suffocated by lust, only habitually threatened; our "heart" has become a battlefield between love and lust on which the more lust dominates our heart, the less our heart experiences the nuptial meaning of the body.

5. The relationship of mutual gift, which is described in Genesis 2:23-25, becomes a relationship of mutual appropriation in Genesis 3:16; the personal union of man and woman through love, which is expressed in the word *my*, becomes a relationship of the possession of the subject by the object rather than an indication of the reciprocity of the gift which establishes the communion of persons.

6. The diversity of roles that is found in Genesis 3:16 is somewhat dictated by the social emargination of women; this view is sufficiently demonstrated in an analysis of the Old and New Testament. It often seems that relationships of appropriation are at the expense of the woman.

Spiritual Reflections

When we reflect on the changing role of women in American society over the last twenty years, we realize that it is virtually impossible to ignore the presence of radical changes in the societal understanding of woman's role. Nor can we ignore the fact that these changes have caused a great upheaval in the area of male-female relationships. Both those who favor change—and even push for more radical change—and those who oppose change must agree that, a scant twenty-five years ago, neither men nor women would have predicted women's new role.

Twenty-five year reunions—whether for grammar school or high school or college—as well as silver wedding celebrations are occasions for remembering our expectations of twenty-five years ago. In the early 1950s, educational and marriage plans were made with an unhesitatingly firm belief in the divine origin of the myth that it was a "man's world" and "woman's place was in the home." For the most part, men and women alike unquestioningly believed that such was the way things had always been and were always meant to be. Even women who exercised their minds by attending college during these years generally did so with a double intention; they wanted to both find a well-educated husband and acquire skills that would be useful in the event that this husband met an untimely death. Nursing and teaching were both considered "acceptable" areas of interest for young women.

A woman graduating from college in the mid-50s reflected the attitude of most of her peers when she proclaimed, "I will work until I have my first baby. After that, the only thing that would get me back to work would be some dire financial need. I'll probably do some volunteer work, but, after all, it's my husband's responsibility to support our family." Somehow, in that era of togetherness which followed the Second World War, we lost sight of the economic contribution to the family that women had made in the past, even when they bore the major responsibility of childrearing.

During that period of togetherness—and probably during most previous eras of human history—little thought was given to the problems that could arise from too heavy an emphasis on role differentiation. Throughout most of human history, the survival needs of the species—and later of the family, the tribe, the community, the nation—made it imperative that women dedicate the major portion of their adult life to childbearing and childrearing activities, and that men be responsible for protecting the family and providing for its economic survival. Just as our strong sexual desire had to be subjugated to the survival needs of the society, the same survival need also determined what behaviors were to be considered appropriate for men and for women. This survival need oftentimes fostered relationships of appropriation in which a man would dominate, or "lord it over," his wife, and a woman might hope for another kind of relationship.

For most of human history, however, there simply was not an opportunity for very many people to begin to realize the possibility of a relationship of gift. This is not to say that many husbands and wives did not discover the possibility of giftedness in their conjugal union. Literature that extends as far back as biblical days indicates that, in some instances, the three forms of lust were not so predominant as to completely wipe out the possibility of love in a relationship.

Still, the polarization of men and women seems to have resulted from the societal need to emphasize specific sex roles. The similarities between man and woman—similarities that had led Adam to proclaim, "this is bone of my bones and flesh of my flesh," and had allowed their conjugal union to be a "communion of persons" who were united "in the image of God"—are overlooked when there is a heavy emphasis on specific sex-role behavior. The body then ceases to be vehicle of unity and becomes, instead, the sign of difference and, oftentimes, opposition.

We observed earlier that the possibility of two different bodies forming a unity of one flesh is a sign of the possibility of unity despite differences, a sign of the contribution that differences make to an enriching unity, a sign of the possibilities of pluralism, a sign of a unity that most of us long for but seldom experience for any length of time. Our experience of the difference between the male body and the female body has led to a stereotyping of man and woman that seems to polarize the sexes in most areas of our relationships.

We can maintain with a high degree of certitude, however, that it has been difficult for both sexes to learn from each other about the full meaning of being human. Men have not been free to put into practice what they have learned about humanity from their encounter with the femininity of woman. Women, in their interaction with the masculinity of man, were not allowed to enrich themselves with the deeper understanding of human nature that they uncovered in these encounters. We have not been encouraged to exist as mutual gift for each other. Specific sex roles and stereotypes of sexual behavior have encouraged relationships of appropriation, in which we have simply used the masculinity or femininity of the other for the satisfaction of a particular need rather than for the formation of a communion of persons.

Although different cultures in "historical" time have developed diverse models for male and female behavior, some degree of sexual stereotyping nevertheless appears to be universal. Anthropologists tell us that the patriarchal model—the male "lording" it over the female—appears to have developed when meat became the medium of economic exchange. Women, who were physically so closely bonded to their offspring, were able to contribute to the economic well-being of the community when survival depended on food gathering, and when meat was a luxury to be enjoyed only when the men were successful in their hunting. Babies could be carried along while women went about gathering food; but women were, of course, unable to hunt and care for their young at the same time. So, as soon as commerce between tribes had increased and the fruits of hunting had increased the prestige of the community, the hunter—the male—acquired the power to "lord" it over his wife.

The emotional bonding between the man and the woman, which directed them toward the possibility of an awareness of the nuptial meaning of the body, became subject to certain "appropriate" behavior, which was determined for the man and the woman by the *ethos* of their particular culture. Masculinity and femininity then became the basis for a division between man and woman. Our bodies are a constant reminder of the pluralism of the human condition; from the vantage point of today's perspective, it seems that sexual pluralism in most cultures has been especially harsh for women.

Twenty-five years ago, when our present-day jubilarians were in school and getting married, male-female relationships were not so obviously ones in which the man dominated the woman as they were in many past cultures, or as they are in some contemporary societies. Twenty-five years ago, American women had begun to acquire a degree of economic and political independence; American men, home from the wars, were being encouraged to develop a family togetherness and to consider their spouse as a friend and a lover as well as a wife. But these women, who were gaining independence, and these men, who were being encouraged to enjoy family intimacy, were still creatures of cultural stereotypes that continued to limit how "acceptable" independence was for a woman and intimacy was for a man. It is little wonder, then, that the advent of the pill, which increased the opportunities for independence for women and marital intimacy for men, caused both individual and societal upheaval.

Betty Friedan's book, *The Feminine Mystique*, and the women's movement—specifically the National Organization for Women (NOW)—are not totally responsible for the widespread change in public attitude about what is "appropriate" behavior for women; there had, of course, been other, earlier movements of women seeking change. Yet, even though one movement had succeeded in obtaining suffrage for women, it had not been able to break the powerhold of the myths that have supported the stereotype of "a man's world" and "woman's place in the home." Friedan's book and the National Organization for Women, however, have been more successful at calling into question the myths and the stereotypes because the cultural situation of our advanced technological society, in the second half of the twentieth century, is such that women and men experience in their own lives some of the fallacies of the stereotypes.

Medical and technological advances have lengthened the individual life spans so that marriages now last for as long as fifty years. Infant mortality has decreased so that most children now survive birth and early infancy and grow to maturity. There is now an almost foolproof means of birth regulation. There is decreased dependence on mere physical strength for economic and physical survival of both society and the individual. Television and other recent advances in telecommunications have put us in close contact with peoples from the far-flung corners of the world. And, too, the current economic situation increasingly requires that families have two incomes or, in some situations, that women function as the sole support of a family. All these conditions have contributed to a reality of life that has caused people to deny, based on their own experiences, the validity of earlier myths.

Friedan's book and the National Organization for Women have given some focus to how some individual women and society as a whole respond to this reality. The division—even opposition—between the sexes, which, for too long, had not been acknowledged as a distortion of a relationship of gift, is more readily visible to our conscious reflection. All of us, no matter how ardently we might embrace even the most radical feminist position, are still influenced by the powerful hold that the myths and stereotypes consciously exercised on previous generations and continue to exercise, often unconsciously, on today's culture and on individuals within the culture. Even the most committed conservative cannot ignore the challenge that is being issued by changing roles.

The woman who graduated from college twenty-five years ago and disparaged the thought of ever returning to work most probably is now gainfully employed, or back in school "retooling," or developing new career interests. Her husband, it is hoped, is supportive of her change in attitude. (It is quite possible, of course, that the husband's support was given on the condition that his wife would always "have my dinner ready when I get home from work." These are not the easiest of times for men or women.)

When we examine our own feelings and behavior regarding "appropriate" conduct for men and women, we can't help realizing that our heart is a "battlefield between love and lust." A sense of shame, which we experience in the depth of our personality— either masculine or feminine—accompanies the confusion and uncertainty and contradiction that we feel over attempts to shatter the myths and stereotypes about men and women. Of course we believe that women should have the opportunity to develop their potential, to be well educated, to be employed in jobs that make use of their talents and abilities. We also believe that women should receive equal pay for equal work and be judged on their ability, not on sex-related expectations. Yet, however much we may support this view and try to live it out in our own lives, we periodically find ourselves clinging, at least emotionally, to some aspect of the stereotypes.

Perhaps someone gives our two-year-old son a doll, for example, and we feel uncomfortable when he plays with it. Or perhaps a very attractive young woman is rapidly promoted within the ranks of our company, and we find ourselves assuming that she has used sex as a means of currying favors from her bosses. Or perhaps our fifteen-year-old son, who has enjoyed performing in school plays, discovers that he is good at ballet and begins to talk about concentrating on dance as a career. Or perhaps our daughter decides to break another barrier and secures a job on a construction crew.

Or maybe we count ourselves among the ranks of those who believe that the myths have their roots in the plan of God and that male-female stereotypes are essential for the good of society. If we reflect on the full implications of those stereotypes, however, we soon discover that it is next to impossible for them to remain intact, even in our own lives, unless we are willing to revert to a society in which power is related to physical strength and women spend all their adult life bearing and rearing children.

Today's cultural situation calls into question myths and stereotypes about masculinity and femininity and makes us realize that relationships between men and women that are based on these stereotypes are a distortion of God's original plan for a communion of persons. Our new societal understanding of male-female relationships, however, will not necessarily contribute to an increased appreciation of the nuptial meaning of the body. The confusion we all experience over the lack of a clearly defined sexual identity certainly highlights the need to respect the person of the other in any intimacy relationship. Unfortunately, in any period of transition such as the one we are experiencing today, it is possible for new stereotypes to develop that are as detrimental to our quest for unity as the previous ones had been. As the Pope observes, it often seems that women have suffered more in scriptural stories from relationships of appropriation than they probably have in the recent past—or even at present in cultures where those relationships are still the norm. In this context, a relationship of appropriation involves more than the man simply "lording it over the woman"; in a relationship of appropriation, one or both of the parties considers the other to be *my* possession. There is ample evidence today to suggest that the liberation of women has not necessarily decreased the tendency toward this type of relationship; on the contrary, it seems that these relationships of possession now allow both men and women to ignore their responsibilities for maintaining the balance of the gift of the nuptial meaning of their bodies. If a stereotype of the so-called sexually liberated woman becomes a norm, we, both men and women, will continue to find our desire for conjugal union habitually threatened.

Another consequence of this relationship of appropriation has been the loss of an appreciation of the feminine side of God in whose image we are made. As we recall, the image reflects the model; we study the image in order to speak analogically about the model that we are imaging. In the course of human history, and particularly for us who understand our God from the biblical perspective, the fundamental loss of the original communion of persons in the "image of God," and the consequent distortion of the "nuptial meaning of the body," have resulted in a lack of appreciation for the feminine dimension of God. As we reread our Scriptures today, we do find evidence that at certain periods this feminine dimension had once been acknowledged. For the most part, however, the history of our religion shows that the femininity of God has never received much attention. Some scholars feel the emphasis on Mary in the Christian tradition was an attempt to fill that void.[1] Mary certainly was instrumental in revealing God to us. So, too, we find that at certain periods in church history, especially those times when women religious wielded power, there was a tendency, at least among the mystics, to acknowledge the feminine dimension of God. Juliana of Norwich referred to "Jesus my Mother" because she believed the loving aspects of Jesus were representative of the womanly dimension of God.

Unfortunately, our religious tradition and the development of our doctrines, creeds, and theologies have been the work of many men who were steeped in a belief in the divine origins of male dominance. The experiences of these men consciously or unconsciously affected the direction of their work and eventually led to an organization of the church that continued to reflect a patriarchal view of God. And because religion, by relying on a patriarchal image of God, reinforced the societal need for women to bear children and for men to protect the needs of women and children, the church helped contribute to the idea of the superiority of the male. Like the Old and New Testament communities, the church often supported relationships of appropriation that seemed to affect women more adversely than men.

Admittedly, there is a great deal of chaos in our culture today regarding male and female roles. The spirituality we seek in these reflections—a spirituality that will keep in our consciousness the fact that we are made male and female in the image of God, that we are to exist *with* and *for* another person in the relationship of *gift*—challenges us to carefully evaluate new lifestyles for men and women from the perspective of God's original plan. It also requires that women become more actively involved in articulating how their experiences reveal God. The following poem, which was written to commemorate the fifteenth anniversary of the founding of a women's theology study group, expresses how women can contribute to a broader understanding of God:

Appropriation

Fifteen Years

Tornado Spirit flew through open windows,
Uprooted solid walls around our faith,
While women, newly free, were whirling through space.
Like Dorothys blown to Oz, we searched for home.
No easy answers. Church and role alike
In need of calming breeze. Our enterprise
Became a double quest for God. We looked,
But found confusion rampant everywhere.

Until one day, like women drawing water,
Mary weeping for a stolen Lord, disciples
In flight, we met a most amazing stranger.
This Water of Life and Risen Lord did stop
With us along our journey's way and soothe
Our anxious hearts with words that told of God
Alive today and found within our midst.

We came to know the stranger better, thanks
To many teachers. Sharing their wisdom,
They peeled away the masks we placed upon
Our God, till soon we recognized the Lord.

We hurried back with joy to spread the news,
Our words describing God in feminine hues.
A gentle Spirit blows away the cares
Of all who hear the message brought by us.

Today we meet the Lord again, now friend,
Not a stranger, and seek new ways to speak of God.
Our hearts, our minds, our lives, our Church explored,
Reveal our shattered expectations. Now,
The Lord plumbs our very depths, transforms
The chaos hidden there and bids us spread
The story of the womanly side of God.

The Church and world, the parish, family, workplace
Await the tender touch of God who speaks
Through woman's care, concern, mercy, and love
Inviting all to hope that Love prevails.

Our task continues long after this day
For now we know our God as Mother, too,
And such good news cannot remain suppressed.
We envoys of God will shout it far and wide,
Merrily proclaiming the wonder of our God.

No wizard or red slippers for us today,
But a motherly God to bless us on our way.
We ask you, God, please sanctify this day.

We are "historical" people. The three forms of lust limit the "nuptial meaning of the body," and our hearts are a battlefield between love and lust, between our desire for a "communion of persons" and the shame we feel when we realize that we have turned a relationship of gift into a relationship of appropriation. And, too, the realization of how our actions threaten our quest for conjugal union and support relationships of appropriation causes us to feel shame. This shame in our "heart" can be viewed as a reminder of the possibilities for communion that our lust has threatened. We now need to know if there is any way to overcome or diminish our lust for the things of the world. Perhaps we will then be able to appreciate the feast dimension of our sexuality.

TEN
Adultery in the Body

You have heard it said: You shall not commit adultery. —Matthew 5:27

Summary of the Pope's Addresses

In this series of three addresses, the Pope again takes up Jesus' appeal to the human "heart." "Hardness of heart" caused the people of the Old Testament to end up in a situation that was contrary to the original plan of God-Yahweh in Genesis 2:24; they then developed their extensive legislation regarding marriage and relationships between men and women. When Jesus speaks of "hardness of heart," he talks of the whole interior subject who distorts the law; when he refers to the "heart" in the Sermon on the Mount, then, he seems to do more than just accuse the heart.

The Sermon on the Mount is part of the Gospel proclamation of the new *ethos;* it is connected with an awareness of the mystery of creation in its original simplicity and richness. This *ethos* that Christ proclaims in the Sermon on the Mount is also addressed to "historical" man, who has inherited lust in its three forms. So it is that the words of Matthew 5:27-28 are not an accusation or judgment on the human heart, but have an ethical character that is constitutive for the *ethos* of the Gospel.

Although Jesus addresses the people of his times in the Sermon on the Mount, he also addresses, in an indirect way, every "historical" man ("historical" mainly in a theological sense). This man, the "man of lust," has existed at every geographical latitude and longitude, in all ages, and in different social and cultural conditions. He, as well as the man of our own time, feels called by Jesus' remark in Matthew 5:27; he feels called in an adequate, concrete, unrepeatable way because Jesus appeals to the human "heart," which cannot

127

be subject to any generalization. Everyone is addressed *individually* with a call to the "heart;" the "heart" determines each person in a unique and unrepeatable way—it is part of each person's humanity "from within."

When we speak of the man of lust, we speak of his inner being, of his "heart," which, after original sin, was affected by the pressure of the three forms of lust. This inner being is the force that decides both "exterior" human behavior and the formation of the various structures and institutions of our social life. When we examine these structures and institutions in their various "historical" contexts in order to deduce the content of *ethos*, we always encounter this interior aspect of man, which is the most essential element. We cannot study human *ethos* and disregard this interior "heart." With this background, we realize the importance of analyzing Jesus' words in Matthew 5:27-28. We must initially analyze its single parts in order to obtain a broader view; we must also keep in mind not only those who heard the original Sermon on the Mount, but those men of our own time.

Consider, then, the first part of Jesus' statement—that is, "You have heard that it was said: You shall not commit adultery" (Mt 5:27). We realize that Jesus is referring to the commandment that each of his listeners knew well and by which they felt bound. It was a commandment of God-Yahweh, even though both the life of the covenant people and the lives of each individual in the Old Testament demonstrate how often the people wandered away from the commandment. The legislation of the Old Testament also shows this.

The law of the Old Testament was very severe and prescribed rules that supervised the smallest details of the daily life of the people. It seems that the more the law legalized polygamy, the more necessary it became to exercise juridical control over this dispensation in order to protect its legal limits. As we study the great number of Old Testament precepts in light of Jesus' reference to the "beginning," we see that he clearly found a basic contradiction in the Old Testament matrimonial law accepting actual polygamy through concubines and cohabitation with slaves. Even though this polygamy was meant to combat sin, it protected the social dimension of sin, which it thereby legalized. For these reason, it was necessary for Jesus to go beyond the traditional and legal restrictions of Old Testament law.

In the Old Testament, when the prohibition of adultery is balanced by the compromise regarding bodily concupiscence, the position regarding sexual deviation becomes more clearly determined, and punishment for this deviation is severe. Matrimonial law of the Old Testament put the procreative end of marriage in the foreground and, in certain cases, tried to be juridically equitable in the treatment of women and men. Nevertheless, on the whole, the law judged the woman with greater severity.

The terminology of Old Testament Law objectified the sexuality of that time. This terminology helps us understand the necessity for reflecting on the theology of the body. What is sexual is, in a certain way, "impure," especially in regard to physiological manifestations of human sexuality. When the "discovery of nudity" is branded as the equivalent of an illicit and completed sexual act (Lv 20:11;17-21), it seems that the legislator uses terminology that relates to the conscience and customs of the contemporary society and, thus, confirms our conviction that the physiology of sex and the bodily manifestation of sexual life known to the legislator are evaluated in a specific, negative way.

This "negative" judgment is not so much a type of Manicheism but, rather, an objectivism that is motivated by a desire to put order into this area of human life. The concern is not with putting "order" into the "heart" of man, but with putting order into man's *entire social life*, especially marriage and the family. In the Sermon on the Mount, when Jesus says, "But I say to you . . . ," it is clear that he wants to dissociate himself from the interpretation of the so-called doctors of the law and challenge the conscience of his audience to consider the ethical significance of the commandment against adultery.

But the law is not the only Old Testament tradition that concerns itself with adultery. The Prophets also speak of adultery; they use the language of analogy, however, rather than speak about it directly. Still, this analogy helps us understand the interpretation of the commandment, "Do not commit adultery," which is part of the experience of those who listened to the Sermon on the Mount.

The Prophets, particularly Isaiah, Hosea, and Ezekiel, represent God-Yahweh as a spouse; the love that joined God-Yahweh to Israel is identified with the nuptial love of a married couple. Israel, when it abandons its God-Spouse, commits "adultery" in the same way that a woman, in similar circumstances, would be guilty of adultery with regard to her husband.

Jesus says to his listeners during the Sermon on the Mount: "Think not that I have come to abolish the law and the Prophets; I have come not to abolish them but to fulfill them" (Mt 5:17). In the course of the sermon, he addresses the commandment, "You shall not commit adultery" the content of which, because it had been obscured by the number of compromises in the legislation of Israel, is more clearly understood in the Prophets. When we look at the Prophets in some detail, therefore, we see the difference between the two Old Testament understandings.

In Hosea, both his words and his behavior reveal to us that Israel's betrayal is similar to a betrayal in a marriage or, more precisely, to adultery practiced as prostitution (Ho 1:2;2:4-5,13, 16,19-20;3:1). In Ezekiel, the unfaithful Israel-spouse is reminded of the humiliating nudity of its birth (Ezk 16:5-8,12-15,30-32). Ezekiel expresses the analogy between adultery and idolatry in a particularly strong way; out of love, God settles the covenant with unworthy Israel and acts toward Israel as an affectionate, attentive, and generous spouse-consort. In return for this love, Yahweh-Spouse receives numerous betrayals in which "adultery" is committed by Israel-Spouse. This concept of adultery, which is described by Ezekiel, tells of a situation that is not a mutual choice made by husband and wife and born from mutual love, but is, rather, a choice made by the husband and deriving from the love as an act of pure mercy. This choice refers to the part of the analogy that defines the covenant of Yahweh with Israel, but does not give a good definition of the nature of marriage. For the Israelites, marriage was the result of a unilateral choice that was often made by the parents; consequently, the mentality of that time was not sensitive to a marriage of mutual choice.

Still, we find that the text of the Prophets shows a different meaning of adultery than the one found in the text of the law. In the Prophets, adultery is a sin because it constitutes the breakdown of the personal covenant between the man and the woman, whereas, in the law, adultery involves a violation of the right of ownership, particularly the man's right of ownership over the woman who is his legal wife, often one of many.

In the Prophets, the background of legalized polygamy does not alter the ethical meaning of adultery. In many texts, monogamy is the only correct analogy for monotheism in the covenant relationship of God-Yahweh, the Spouse of Israel. Adultery is the antithesis of a monogamous marriage that, within itself, forms an interpersonal alliance of a man and woman—an alliance born of love in which bodily union is the regular sign of the communion of the two people. Adultery committed by either one of them is, therefore, a violation of this right and a radical falsification of the sign of their union. The Prophets clearly express this aspect of adultery.

When we say that adultery is a falsification of that sign which has its simple interior truth in marriage, in a certain sense we again refer to the basic statements that we have made concerning the body that are essential for our theology of the body both from an ethical and an anthropological point of view. Adultery is a sin of the body; in this context, the body is considered in the conceptual bond of the words of Genesis 2:24 that speak of the man and the woman who, as husband and wife, are united in order to form one body.

In all the tradition of the Old Testament, there is witness to adultery as a "sin of the body," and Jesus confirms this. When we analyze Jesus' words in the Sermon on the Mount, we are able to establish the exact reason for the "sinfulness" of adultery. We base our reason on the opposition between the moral goodness of faithfulness in marriage and the moral evil of adultery; the goodness of faithfulness in marriage can be achieved only in an exclusive relationship of both partners that needs nuptial love, the interpersonal structure of which is governed by the interior "communion of persons." This is what gives basic significance to the Covenant (either in the marriage of a man and a woman or, analagously, in the relationship of Yahweh to Israel). Adultery indicates an act through which a man and a woman who are not husband and wife in a monogamous sense, as was originally established, unite as "one body"; the "sin" of the body regards the relationship between the people who are concerned.

We can speak of moral good and evil if there is a true "union of the body" in this relationship, and if it has the character of a truthful sign. When we do this, we can judge adultery as a sin according to the objective content of the act.

The Pope concludes his reflection on Jesus' words, "You have heard it was said: You shall not commit adultery," with the observation that Jesus was considering the objective content of the act of adultery in the reference to the commandment. Jesus, however, does not dwell on this aspect of the problem.

The following main points for a theology and a spirituality of sexuality of the body were developed by the Pope in his three addresses on adultery in the body.

1. Jesus' words in Matthew 5:27-28 call all humans in all times and in all places because he appeals to the human "heart—" in other words, to that which is "from within"; the "historical" man addressed by Jesus is the "man of lust" whose human "heart" has been under the pressure of lust in its three forms and whose "exterior" human behavior and the form of his social institutions have been determined by his inner being.

2. Old Testament law viewed adultery as a sin because it violated the right of ownership, primarily the right of the man's ownership over the woman who was his legal wife. Old Testament matrimonial law is marked by an objectivism that is motivated by a desire to put order into the entire social life of the community; it puts the procreative end of marriage in the foreground and, on the whole, judges women with greater severity.

3. The tradition of the Prophets offers another interpretation of adultery when it uses the analogy of adultery to speak of the love of Yahweh-Spouse and the betrayal of Israel-Spouse; Isaiah, Hosea, and Ezekiel, in particular, present adultery as a sin because it constitutes the breakdown of the personal covenant between a man and a woman.

4. According to the Prophets, adultery is a violation of the bilateral right to a bodily union that is the regular sign of a communion of two people; it is also a falsification of the sign of the various dimensions of the "communion of persons" that were uncovered in our analysis of the original situation.

5. Both the law and the Prophets consider adultery a "sin of the body," the "body" being a conceptual bond of Genesis 2:24 in which the husband and wife unite so closely that they form "one body"; when a man and a woman who are not husband and wife unite as "one body," the "sin" of the body

is identified because of the relationship between the two people who are concerned.

6. In the Old Testament understanding, adultery is a sin on the basis of the objective content of the act. Jesus has this content in mind when he reminds us, "You shall not commit adultery"; however, Jesus does not dwell on this understanding of adultery.

Spiritual Reflections

Again, when Jesus speaks to the crowd in the Sermon on the Mount, we find ourselves part of the group, very much at home, knowing that adultery is a sin of the body. Our religious and cultural background, like that of Jesus' listeners, is filled with warnings about "sexual sins." Just as Old Testament law sought to keep order in the social life of the community with its many regulations, our rulemakers want to control the human sexual drive and subject it to the needs of society. In both Old Testament days and in our most recent past, the proliferation of rules supposedly rooted in the sixth and ninth commandments has emphasized a compartmentalizing of sexuality and has concentrated on the exterior acts that are related to the use of our bodies.

Every society has a need for laws that will protect the common good and deter the powerful from exploiting the weak. Nevertheless, laws, whether they are church laws or civil laws, often keep us from engaging in behavior out of fear of the consequences. These laws do not necessarily lead us to appreciate the reasons for the laws. We might stay within the 55 mile per hour speed limit on an empty stretch of an expressway, for example, because we know that this area is a speed trap; in areas where we expect no interference from radar patrols, however, we might ordinarily drive at 70 miles per hour. We might not drive at high speeds in heavily traveled areas because we want to avoid accidents; but on the open road, the fear of being ticketed for a traffic violation deters us, not the belief that fast driving is evil.

So, too, those of us who were raised in a pre-Vatican II church might have avoided sexual sins out of a fear of hell, but we did not necessarily learn to appreciate God's positive plan for the use of our bodies. Few of us learned how to relate to the other sex in a mature, healthy way that would reveal God for us. We were given the "rules," but we were never encouraged to look for the real meaning of the body or sex or sexuality. The rules told us what we should do to avoid sin. This often led to the belief that the body was an occasion of sin because "sexual sins" were related either to the use of our body or to thoughts about the use of our body.

When we remember the historical picture that led to the formulation of many church and social rules about sexual behavior, we can appreciate how they were actually a response to the needs of society. In the earliest days of the church, marital laws were controlled by the civil domain; they eventually came under church control after the barbarian invasions, because the church was the only stable institution in society. Both civil and church marital rules encouraged those unions that had procreation as their primary aim; consequently, prohibitions against certain kinds of sexual behavior were generally based on the belief that such sexual behavior was destructive to procreative potential. Many church laws, which sought to apply the sixth and ninth commandments to the everyday life of society, often objectified the sexuality of the time—a sexuality that needed to be "controlled" if the society were to survive.

Just as in Old Testament times, many of the official and quasi-official rules for sexual behavior (interpretations of church law by local religious leaders, nuns, and cultural traditions nurtured in the home) evaluated physical manifestations of sexuality in a negative way. Even in the early part of the century, women in some ethnic groups were taught that they could not receive communion after they had engaged in an act of marital intercourse without first going to confession. "Never on Saturday night" was a reality for many of these women. So, too, although the blessing of a new mother is now seen as a positive way of celebrating maternity, the so-called "churching" of a new mother was mandatory for many of our mothers and grandmothers before they could receive communion. Although procreation was seen as the primary aim of human sexuality, the physical activities that were necessarily related to procreation were often negatively evaluated.

This inconsistent approach to evaluating sexuality was largely responsible for many of the "horror stories" which those of us who grew up in the pre-Vatican II church heard about the punishments for sexual sins. Oftentimes, however, our dread of the punishments in the afterlife did not deter us from activities that had been labeled sinful. As teen-agers, many of us were told that the only "non-sinful" kiss was one that caused feelings similar to what we would experience if we were to kiss a lamppost; necking and petting were obviously evils to be avoided. Much attention was given during high school days-of-recollection, retreats, religion classes, and counselling sessions to the evils of "passionate feelings"; any action that resulted in the arousal of passion was evil and, therefore, must be avoided. Given this obviously impossible demand on teen-agers to never allow themselves to feel passion, it is not surprising that many of us made weekly visits to the confessional, others of us lived in fear of damnation, and most of us developed a distorted sense of the significance of the human body and of the divine plan for salvation. Church and societal opposition to premarital sex probably was accepted more out of fear of pregnancy than out of lack of desire on the part of young people; other activities condemned by our "teachers," however, were not so readily avoided, especially when the consequences would not be evident. Instead, we developed guilt.

Even today, some religious leaders, who are disturbed over societal problems with sexuality, are attempting to pass laws that they hope will remedy the abuses. The extreme example of this concern is found in some of the activities of the Moral Majority and other groups that have decided to rid our society of distorted media images of human sexuality. If the Moral Majority is successful in its campaign against the media, we might find ourselves less subjected to distorted presentations of human sexuality. This does not guarantee, however, that a Moral Majority-influenced media will provide an image of human sexuality that reflects the original divine plan. Concern about rules often covers up the lack of a vision that will encourage in us a positive moral behavior.

When laws regarding marriage and sexual behavior were rooted in the societal need to emphasize the procreative aspects of human sexuality, adultery and all sexual sins were somehow related to the body. The influence of this emphasis on the body continues to prevail, though often unacknowledged, in our contemporary society. Some contemporary secular "visions" of human sexuality, for example, emphasize satisfaction of the body as the sole aim of human sexuality. Consider the advice offered in a sophisticated women's magazine to young working women who are interested in having a summer romance; a good prospect for a summer affair, according to this magazine, is the husband whose family is away at a summer cottage while he spends the week nights in the city. It's only going to be a fling, the reasoning goes, so no one will be hurt; and, besides, some of these wives are probably happy to have their husbands occupied while they are away. Just don't let yourself get too involved because once your summer "lover's" wife is back in the city he won't have time for you. And, too, there are stories in this magazine of women who are unfaithful not because "they" are dissatisfied with their marriages, but just because their "bodies" don't seem to be satisfied. As one woman says: "I started having affairs when I realized I wasn't getting as much from my marriage as I should have and that I have only one life to live."

Although new "rules" are pressuring us to experience our bodies to the fullest, they often ignore any attempt to uncover more than the surface meaning to the use of our bodies. Concentration on the body without an appreciation of its deep significance in our lives could result in a lack of dignity that is as destructive for relationships as the rigid objective legal interpretations of the sixth and ninth commandments that we have already encountered.

The Old Testament Prophets certainly guide us to broaden our understanding of the significance of the body in forming a relationship in a marital union. Adultery in the prophetic understanding reminds us that sharing our body with someone other than our spouse is bound to be destructive to our marital relationship. Ironically, now that society has come to accept divorce, adultery is often the forerunner of divorce. One 37-year-old woman observed that she had no intention of ending her marriage. It was only after three years of an affair—which, she said, was with a man that she didn't especially care for—that she realized that the lying, the guilt, and the shame weren't worth it, and that divorce would be a "more honorable solution." Eventually, most women who engage in extramarital affairs, once they have faced up to the reason for their affair, often begin to feel that it would be better if they left their spouses. Bodily union, for many of us, continues to have significance for our relationships. Adultery with our bodies falsifies this sign and runs the risk of destroying the union. The Prophets remind us that we need to be conscious of the way in which our bodies and our bodily union express the depth of our relationship in marriage.

As we hear Jesus' words reminding us of the sixth and ninth commandments, we are reminded of the need to evaluate "rules" about our bodies. If we are to be able to use our bodies as a sign of our gift to another, then we certainly need to develop an appreciation of how the body serves as a medium for the union of two in one flesh. We need to reflect on our own experiences of the use of our body as a sign of our desire for union, and then evaluate these experiences in light of the original plan of God and the law of the Decalog, which Jesus came to fulfill. We need to keep in mind that fulfillment of the law requires both that we "superabound" in justice and that we appreciate the basis of the law in the original plan of God, which respected the dignity of each individual person. Fulfilling the law requires that we understand the depth of the prohibition against adultery as a falsification of the sign of the possibility of union. We must also keep in mind that Jesus' words in the Sermon on the Mount do not allow us to limit adultery only to those situations in which two people who are not married to each other join their bodies so as to be "only one flesh." Although this joining is contrary to the covenant relationship of a marital union, adultery in the body is not the only falsification of a marital relationship.

Like those who were gathered for the Sermon on the Mount, we long for the transformative power of Jesus' presence in our lives; we know that neither the rules of the old law of the church nor the new "rules" of sexuality help us to come to grips, in the modern world, with our femininity and masculinity. We know that adultery in the body is wrong, but we sense that there is more to our sexuality than what is generally understood by the term adultery in the body. We need to listen to the rest of Jesus' words concerning adultery.

ELEVEN

Desire

"But I say to you, everyone who looks at a woman lustfully . . ."—Matthew 5:28

Turn away your eyes from a shapely woman, / And do not look intently at beauty belonging to another; / Many have been misled by a woman's beauty, / And by it passion is kindled like a fire. —Sirach 9:8-9

The soul heated like a burning fire / Will not be quenched until it is consumed: / A man who commits fornication, / Will never cease until fire burns him up; / To a fornicator all bread tastes sweet, / He will never cease until he dies. / A man who breaks his marriage vows / Says to himself: "Who sees me? / Darkness surrounds me, and the walls hide me; / No one sees me. Why should I fear? / The most high will not take notice of my sins." / His fear is confined to the eyes of men; / He does not realize that the eyes of the Lord / Are ten thousand times brighter than the sun; / They look upon all the ways of men, / And perceive even the hidden places . . . / So it is with a woman who leaves her husband, / And provides an heir by a stranger. —Sirach 23:19,22

Summary of the Pope's Addresses

During the Sermon on the Mount, Jesus recalled the commandment against adultery and, in so doing, implied the evaluation of the behavior of his listeners just considered in the preceding chapter. When Jesus moves on to the second part of the statement, "But I say to you . . . ," he does more than dispute the interpretations of the law and the morality of the Torah; he offers a direct transition to the new *ethos*. When he speaks of "adultery committed in the heart," he contrasts this with "adultery committed in the body." "Adultery," in its fundamental sense, can only be a sin of the body. Jesus' question boldly asks how can an "act" that a man commits in his heart also be called adultery? If we examine the phrase, "But I say to you that everyone who looks at a woman lustfully," we will find that these words concerning desire affect the shifting of the significance of adultery from the "body" to the "heart."

Whoever "looks lustfully" is the concupiscent man, the man who "desires." In order to understand Jesus' words in Matthew 5:27-28, we need not only a psychological interpretation of this person, but also a theological interpretation; these two contexts are superimposed upon each other and have significance for both the entire *ethos* of the Gospel and our understanding of the content of the word "lust" or "looking lustfully."

Jesus is speaking directly to his listeners in this passage, but he is also addressing the experience and conscience of the man of every time and place. For those directly listening to him, whose consciences were formed by the Bible, "lust" is linked to the precepts and warnings in the Wisdom Books, which contain repeated admonitions about concupiscence of the body and how to avoid it. The Wisdom tradition, which had a special interest in the ethics and morality of the Israelite society, presented a certain one-sidedness in its admonitions that are, for the most part, addressed to men. Woman most frequently appears as an occasion of sin or as a seducer to be avoided, though both the Book of Proverbs and The Book of Sirach praise the woman who is the "perfect life companion of her own husband" (see Pr 31:10ff). Still, a frequent Wisdom admonition refers to the beauty and graciousness of the woman who is not one's own wife as the cause of temptation and occasion for adultery (Pr 6:25).

The pedagogical significance of the Wisdom texts is found in the fact that they teach virtue and seek to protect the moral order by appealing back to God's law and widely understood experience. In addition, they have a special knowledge of the human "heart" and develop a specific moral psychology. In this way, the Wisdom texts are close to Jesus' call to the "heart," even though they make no attempt to change *ethos* in a fundamental way. Their authors use the conscience of human inner life to teach morals that are related to the *ethos* of the time. An actual transformation of the fundamental structure of ethical evaluation does not come about until Jesus' Sermon on the Mount.

The knowledge of human psychology that was present in the Wisdom tradition, however, had nevertheless prepared Jesus' listeners to understand his words when he referred to the "lustful look" and to "adultery committed in the heart." Sirach 23:17-22 analyzes the state of the soul of the man who is dominated by the concupiscence of the flesh and provides a background for understanding how Jesus' listeners would interpret his words concerning the man who "lusts."

The biblical description of the man of lust that is found in Sirach compares concupiscence of the flesh with fire; it flares up in man, invades his senses, excites his body, involves his feelings, takes possession of his "heart," and suffocates the most profound voice of conscience—his sense of responsibility before God. External modesty with respect to man does persist; at least there is an appearance of decency shown in the fear of the consequences of the evil rather than in the fear of the evil itself.

When the voice of conscience is suffocated, passion causes restlessness in the "external" man, and the "internal" man is reduced to silence. Passion then exhibits itself in insistent tendencies to satisfy the sense and the body. Gratification of both the senses and the body, however, does not put out the fire because it does not reach the source of internal peace. Thus, the man is "consumed."

Passion aims at satisfaction and thereby blunts reflective activity and ignores the voice of conscience, which tends to "wear itself out." When passion enters into the whole of the human spirit it can be a creative force, but it must undergo a radical transformation.

When it suppresses the deepest forces of the heart and conscience (Sir 23:17-22), man is consumed. In the Sermon on the Mount, Jesus seems to presuppose that his listeners, both present and potential, understand his meaning of "looks lustfully." He does not penetrate this experience in all the breadth of its interior dynamism but, rather, considers "lust" before it has been changed into an exterior action, that is, an "act of the heart" that expresses itself in a look but reveals its content nevertheless because a look expresses what is in the heart, that is to say, it expresses the man within. By his look man reveals himself to the outside and to others by showing what he perceives on the "inside."

For Jesus, a look is almost like the threshold of inner truth, and in this look we can single out the understanding of concupiscence. "Looking lustfully" indicates an experience of value to the body in which the "nuptial" significance is lost because of concupiscence. The man who is "looking lustfully" is attempting to distort the meaning of the body that is at the basis of the communion of persons, both outside of marriage and, in a special way, when men and women are united "in the body." Jesus indicates that concupiscence, like adultery, affects "the nuptial meaning of the body." He refers his listeners to their internal experiences of this loss of appreciation.

When concupiscence of the flesh is coupled with the inner act of "lust," a human being feels separation from the matrimonial significance of the body and experiences conflict with his personal dignity. We find, then, that the biblical and theological meaning of "lust" are different from the purely psychological meaning, which describes lust as an intense inclination toward the object because of its particular value—in this case, "sexual" value. The biblical interpretation goes beyond this psychological meaning and sees "lust" as a deception of the human heart in the perennial call of man and woman to communion by means of mutual giving. When Jesus refers to the "heart," he is reverting, as he did in his response to the Pharisees (Mt 19:8), to the whole problem of man, woman, and marriage.

The perennial call that we have analyzed in our discussions of the Book of Genesis—that is, the perennial mutual attraction of man to femininity and of woman to masculinity—is an indirect invitation of the body, but it is not "lust" in the biblical sense. "Lust" that leads to concupiscence of the flesh diminishes the significance of the invitation that is inherent in the reciprocal attraction. Jesus' words in the Sermon on the Mount indicate that "lust" is a real part of the human heart, a "reduction" of the original mutual attraction of masculinity and femininity. Although we must be conscious of the value of sex as part of the rich storehouse of values with which the female appears to the man, we must not "reduce" all the personal riches of femininity to that single value by considering sex a suitable object for the gratification of sexuality itself. Even though Matthew 5:27-28 refers only to the man who looks lustfully, the same reasoning can equally be applied to women.

The eternal attraction of man toward femininity (see Gn 2:23) frees in him a gamut of spiritual-corporal desire that is of a personal and "sharing" nature and then leads to a pyramid of values regarding sexuality, "Lust," however, limits this gamut and obscures the pyramid of values in the interior horizon of man and woman. In "lust" femininity loses its character of being a sign; it ceases to bear the matrimonial significance of the body and to correlate this significance in the context of conscience and experience. "Lust" that arises from concupiscence of the flesh aims only to satisfy the sexual need of the body as its precise object.

According to Jesus this reduction takes place through a "look," that is to say, through a purely interior act that is expressed by the look. When concupiscence enters the inner structure, the look becomes one of "lustful knowledge." The biblical expression "to look at lustfully" indicates both a cognitive act that the lustful man "makes use of" and a cognitive act that arouses lust in the "will and heart" of the other object. We are called upon by Jesus' words, therefore, to discern the intention of the very existence of man in relation to the other. Consequently, when a man is "looking at a woman lustfully," the woman at whom the man "looks" ceases to exist as an object of eternal attraction and begins to be only an object of carnal concupiscence. When we analyze the situation that Jesus outlined stressing that "looking lustfully" is a "purely interior" act hidden in the heart, then we can uncover what happens to the woman as a result of this act. The woman, who, in her personal subjectivity, exists perennially "for man" and waits for him to exist "for her," is deprived of the meaning of her attraction as a person and becomes only an object for the man—that is, an object for the potential satisfaction of the sexual need inherent in his masculinity. Even though the act is completely interior and expressed only by the "look," it changes the very intentionality of its existence.

This change of intentionality of existence is carried out in the "heart" because it is carried out in the will. When the intentional reduction sweeps the will into its narrow objective, and brings forth a decision for a relationship with another human being according to the values of "lust," then it can be said that the "desire" has gained possession of the "heart." When "lust" can gain possession of the will, it is dominant over the subjectivity of the person and is at the basis of the will, establishing the very way of existing with regard to another person.

When we speak of "desire" as the transformation of the intentionality of existence whereby woman becomes merely the object for the potential satisfaction of the sexual need, we are not questioning that need as an objective dimension of human nature with the procreative finality that is characteristic of it. Jesus' words are not Manichean; rather, they address man's and woman's way of existing as persons—as mutually "for" each other—in which "sexual need" serves the building up of communion in their mutual relations. Indeed, this building up of unity is the fundamental meaning of the perennial and reciprocal attraction of masculinity and femininity that is contained in our constitution as person, body, and sex.

The possibility of one person in a relationship existing only as the subject of the satisfaction of sexual need, and the other person becoming exclusively the object of this satisfaction, is in conflict with the plan of "the beginning." When both man and woman exist simultaneously as the object and subject of satisfaction of sexual need, there is still a reduction of the reciprocal and perennial attraction of human persons and their masculinity and femininity. This reduction does not correspond to the "nature" of that attraction because it extinguishes the personal meaning of communion through which "a man . . . cleaves to his wife and they become one flesh" (Gn 2:24). "Lust" reduces the perennial attraction to its utilitarian dimensions in which one human being "uses" the other human being merely to satisfy his own "needs."

Jesus addressed his words in the Sermon on the Mount to man's "interiority," that is, to his "heart," which is at the core of the transformation of the *ethos* toward which he aims.

The following main points for a theology and a spirituality of the body and sexuality were developed by the Pope in his four addresses on desire.

1. The transitional phrase in Matthew 5:28—"But I say to you that everyone who looks at a woman lustfully . . ."— shifts the meaning of adultery from "body" to "heart"; these words are addressed to the concupiscent man, the man who "desires" and "looks lustfully"—a man who was familiar to Jesus' audience because of the warnings of the Wisdom literature.

2. The Wisdom texts teach virtue and seek to protect the moral order on the basis of God's law and human experience, but they do not attempt to change the fundamental structure of the ethical evaluation of the day; they are a preparation, however, for understanding "adultery in the heart," a transformation of *ethos* that comes from the Sermon on the Mount.

3. When passion suppresses the deepest forces of our heart and conscience (Sr 23:17-22), it "wears out" and consumes us; but "looking lustfully" is an interior act of the heart in which the nuptial meaning of the body is lost because the concupiscence of the flesh is coupled with the inner act of "lust."

4. The perennial mutual attraction of man to femininity and of woman to masculinity is an indirect invitation to the body, but it is not lust; sex is part of the rich storehouse of values with which men and women appear to each other, whereas "lust" reduces all the personal values of masculinity and femininity to sex as a suitable object for the gratification of sexuality, thereby obscuring the significance of the body and of the person.

5. Jesus addresses the purely "interior" act of the heart in which we are deprived of our attraction as a person and, through our sexuality, become an object for the potential satisfaction of the other's sexual need, thus changing the very meaning of existence; when this reduction of the meaning of the body results in decision for a relationship to another human being according to the values of lust, then desire has gained possession of our heart and is at the basis

of our will, dictating our very way of existing with regard to another person, as in Sirach 23:17-22.

6. Jesus' words are not Manichean, nor is the true Christian tradition; the reduction of the meaning of the perennial attraction of masculinity and femininity does not reduce the "nature" of the attraction, but extinguishes the personal meaning of "communion" that is characteristic of man and woman cleaving and becoming "one flesh."

Spiritual Reflections

When we hear Jesus' words about the man who "looks lustfully," we, like Jesus' original audience, connect them with the misuse of our strong sexual drive. We are reminded of the many times when we have "desired" another simply on the basis of his or her ability to satisfy our sexual needs. The power of the sexual drive is such that, at various times in our lives, we have experienced this "desire" to such a degree that is has been disruptive of our ability to enter into or maintain a commitment to one particular person; our thoughts have been constantly distracted by our sense of desire.

When we read that a presidential candidate has admitted to having "lusted after women in his heart," we might have considered that his admission was a very foolish statement. Yet none of us could deny that we, too, have had erotic fantasies. We know that we "desire," and that this desire sometimes seems like a good and positive thing. But we also know that, at times, our "desiring" gets carried away. Like Dolores in Marilyn French's novel *The Bleeding Heart,* we are not sure what we can do about this.

Obviously, it is impossible to deny the powerful sexual attraction of the human body. Indeed, the whole focus of these spiritual reflections has been to help us appreciate the revelatory power of this attraction; we are also confronted, however, with the fact that we, and others, often turn this attraction into a destructive force for ourselves and for others. It is this paradox in our sexual attraction—its possibility for good and evil—that causes such a quandary for us as we strive to attain sexual maturity and an integrated sexual identity.

Ironically, many of the past attempts by religious leaders and groups to "control" the power of the sexual attraction have led to a denial of its positive potential. The attraction was viewed as the source of sin and something to be "controlled." Erotic thoughts came to minds that were "the devil's workshop." The bodily inclination that influenced much of human behavior was evil and somehow had to be subdued. The end result of these attitudes has been a failure to respond to the human need to transform this experience and use it as a positive force for unity and for discovering God.

While churches have been busy trying to "control" the misuse of our sexual drive, secular society has been busy exploiting this sexual drive for a variety of purposes. Advertisers, movie and television producers, and magazine editors recognize the value of an attractive male or female body in promoting their particular endeavors. Certainly the promise that we might be as desirable as a particular model, if only we use the same product that she does, is a sign that we also want our bodies to be desired by others. The promoters who use the attractiveness of physical sexuality to sell their products recognize the pervasive power of the human sexual drive. They remind us of the "extraordinary" power of physical sexuality and of the fact that we are not immune to "desire." Though we might resent the manipulation—especially of women (although, indirectly, it is a manipulation of a man who would "desire" a woman)—we cannot help recognizing that the "sex sells" approach is a response to a powerful human drive. The fact that this approach might, at times, distort our use of our sexual drive does not, however, diminish the perceptiveness of those promoters who use it.

At another level, certain societal practices are blatant reminders of how we humans allow "desire" to be the overriding factor in our sexual relationships. Pornography and prostitution, certainly not newcomers in human culture, continue to remind us that even in this era of "sexual freedom" many people suffer from others' exploitation of the human sexual drive. Articles on kiddie porn and teen-age prostitution remind us that, when sexual attraction is reduced to the satisfaction of one person's bodily needs, the weakest people in a society are bound to suffer. A recent article on teen-age runaways who had been forced into prostitution—often with middle-age men whose children were the same age as the prostitute—makes us think of the man consumed by fire in Sirach. It seems difficult to imagine that the teen-age prostitute would be able to discover the revelatory possibilities of his or her sexuality. And, certainly, those who make use of the prostitute's services are reducing the revelatory possibility of sexual attraction.

It is ironic in a society such as ours, which has developed an advanced understanding of sexuality, that exploitation of people through their sexual drives seems to be increasing rather than diminishing. Although we might feel a certain sense of satisfaction if we are not among those who blatantly exploit others through prostitution and pornography, we also know that there are times when we allow our own bodily needs to dictate the basis of our relationship with another. Perhaps, for example, we are afraid of committing ourselves to one person, so we use "sexual freedom" as the rationale for a variety of bed partners and, in the process, claim that "no one gets hurt." Or we continue being sexually intimate with our spouse, but only in a very routine way, because we are afraid he or she might want more depth in our relationship than we are willing to give. Or we might encourage attention from someone who finds us sexually attractive, even though we know that there is no possibility of a long-term relationship, because it satisfies our need to feel physically attractive. Or we might be in the midst of our "middle-years" crisis, and we might need sexual acceptance from a younger person to ward off this encounter with the aging process.

Reflecting on the times in our own lives when "desire" has dictated our relationship to another, as well as examining the personal consequences of societal practices that focus solely on bodily satisfaction, makes us, like Jesus' audience, conscious of the consequences of "lust." We think we know what Jesus means when he uses the words "look lustfully." We know from the "wisdom literature" of our own day—scientific analyses of human sexuality—that when lust suppresses the deepest forces of our heart and conscience, it "wears out our passion and indirectly consumes us." Neither the playboy nor the prostitute stands much chance of forming deep emotional bonds on a permanent basis. And, although a particular relationship, in which we might have allowed "desire" to be the criteria, might have been initially satisfying, eventually this relationship becomes unsatisfactory for one or both persons.

Or else we, like the presidential candidate, think we know what "looking lustfully" means; it means having erotic fantasies. Jesus seems to be telling us that not only is acting upon our desires sinful, merely having them is likewise sinful and to be avoided. Yet, this interpretation of Jesus' words, according to the Pope's analysis, is limited to a psychological understanding of lust. If we consider lust in the broader theological context that we have maintained throughout our considerations of the Pope's addresses, we discover that perhaps our original understanding of the words "looks lustfully" needs to be expanded to include the idea that lust is a choosing "the things of the world" rather than "the things of the Father."

Jesus is not telling us that passion, the response to our strong sex drive, is bad. Indeed, as the Pope has emphasized in his previous analysis and will reiterate in later addresses, if the Christian tradition is true to its roots, it cannot consider sexuality, sex, or passion to be evil because this attraction is part of the creation upon which God looked and said, "it is very good." The Pope is emphasizing, however, the tendency of all of us who live in the world of the knowledge of good and evil to lose sight of the divine plan for human sexuality. "Looking lustfully," which a man is not to do (nor is a woman to "look lustfully," for that matter), is a purely interior act of the heart that changes the very meaning of human existence each time we allow it to happen, because it reduces the meaning of the body. Most of us would have to admit that at those times when we have allowed the values of lust to dictate the basis of a relationship, the "desire" of Sirach has been dominant and destructive of our ability to follow God's plan for the use of human sexuality.

But as we reflect on the Pope's analysis of these words and consider it in the larger context of the understanding of lust that he has developed in his earlier talks, we begin to understand that "looking lustfully," when it is a preliminary to an act of "adultery in the heart," means more than what Jesus' audience knew about desire from the Old Testament Wisdom literature. It also means much more than what we know as abuse of our powerful physical sexual attraction in a relationship that is based solely on our own bodily needs. Jesus seems to be calling on us to broaden our understanding of adultery. Like Jesus' audience, we who have focused our attention on the sins of the body as the only misuse of human sexuality are being called to appreciate the theological understanding of lust—that is, lust is a disregard for the divine plan, a plan that is written in our hearts, a plan that understands the various dimensions of human sexuality and its pervasiveness in human experience.

We end our reflections on these papal addresses reminded that the physical attraction of our masculinity and femininity was seen by God as "good," but, as a result of our choice for the "things of the world," we often "look lustfully" and abuse the possibilities of this attractiveness. To understand how "looking lustfully" applies to all aspects of the male-female relationship, we must now turn to the Pope's analysis of "adultery in the heart." Even the words, adultery in the heart, present a challenge to those of us who have limited all sexual sins to either sins of the body or sins of thoughts about the body.

TWELVE

Adultery in the Heart

"Everyone who looks at a woman lustfully has already committed adultery with her in his heart."—Matthew 5:28

Summary of the Pope's Addresses

The splitting of Jesus' words regarding adultery in the Sermon on the Mount into three parts is useful for those who are seeking the ethical meaning of the whole text when it is done in a conjunctive way. The Pope divides the text in order to stress the specific content and connotation of each part, which is, at the same time, directly related to the other parts. There are four principal semantic elements in the text as a whole: (1) to commit adultery, (2) to desire, (3) to commit adultery in the body, and (4) to commit adultery in the heart. As we noted in chapter 11, the ethical sense of "desiring" is more fully established when it is related to the element of "adultery in the heart." Although we touched upon this final element in the previous analysis, it is now necessary to do a special analysis of the phrase "to commit adultery in the heart" in order to more fully understand it. We do this analysis because we need to establish the ethical sense of Jesus' words, which expand on the commandment, "Do not commit adultery." We seek to understand how to put this commandment into practice so that the "justice" willed by God-Yahweh may abound to a greater extent than it did in the casuistry of the Old Testament.

Jesus' words, which aim at constructing a new *ethos* on the basis of the same commandment, seek a deeper clarification of the meaning of "adultery." Immediately after mentioning the well-known prohibition, "do not commit adultery," Jesus changes his style and logical structure from the normative to the narrative-affirmative and describes an interior fact whose reality was easily understood by his listeners, a fact that indicates how the commandment must be understood and put into practice if "justice" is to abound.

The expression, "has committed adultery in the heart," is key to understanding the correct ethical meaning of the commandment, which reveals, at the same time, the essential value of the new *ethos* of the Sermon on the Mount. The paradox of the exterior act of "adultery" not being forbidden by the law causes us to wonder if perhaps this is only a metaphorical expression used to highlight the sinfulness of lust. As we reflect on the ethical consequences that would derive from this metaphorical interpretation, however, we discover grounds for doubting whether this takes into account all the aspects of both revelation and the theology of the body that must be considered when we wish to understand the full import of Jesus' words.

We need to re-examine the paradox connected with Jesus' words "adultery in the heart." As we have seen, adultery takes place when the man and the woman who unite with each other so as to become one flesh are not legal spouses. Adultery as a sin "in the body," which is connected with the "exterior" act, also refers to the "status of the acting persons," which is recognized by society. If Jesus' expression, "everyone who looks at a woman lustfully," refers only to those who according to their legal status are not husband and wife, then we must ask ourselves if Jesus admits and approves of such a look—an interior act of lust—directed toward the wife of the man who so looks at her.

A reasoning that employs objective correctness and accuracy seems to indicate that only the man who is the potential subject of "adultery in the flesh" can commit "adultery in the heart." Consequently, a man-husband cannot commit "adultery in the heart" with regard to his own wife; he alone has the exclusive right to "desire" or "look lustfully" at the woman who is his wife without being accused of "adultery in the heart." If he has the right to unite with his own wife so as to become one flesh, this act can never be alled "adultery." Such an interpretation, however, ignores the rich anthropological and theological implications of Jesus' reference "to the beginning" (Mt 19:8). Jesus' words in the Sermon on the

Mount that refer to the human heart contain a specific "weight" on the enunciation that, at the same time, determines its consistency with the whole evangelical teaching. This reference to the human heart, which is expressed in a paradoxical way, comes from a man who "knew what was in man" (Jn 2:25). Although he confirms the Decalog, he also expresses that knowledge of man which, in our previous analysis, enabled us to unite awareness of human sinfulness with the perspective of the "redemption of the body"; it is this knowledge that lies at the basis of the new *ethos* that emerges from the Sermon on the Mount.

Just as Jesus had criticized the erroneous and one-sided interpretation of adultery that had derived from the failure to observe monogamy, so here, by "adultery in the heart," Jesus not only takes into consideration the real juridical status of the man and the woman in question, but he makes any moral evaluation of "desire" specifically depend on the personal dignity of the man and the woman. This dignity is important both when it is a question of persons who are not married and, perhaps even more, when it is a question of persons who *are* married.

Our analysis of Matthew 5:27-28 has indicated the need to amplify and deepen our interpretation of the ethical meaning of this enunciation. Jesus describes the situation in which a man "commits adultery in his heart" by means of an interior act of lust. Jesus does not stress that the situation involves "another man's wife" or a woman who is not the man's own wife, but uses the generic description "a woman." The inner, personal relationship that makes it possible to determine if somebody has "committed adultery in the body" does not exclusively and essentially decide if one commits "adultery in the heart." Rather, "adultery in the heart" is committed not only because man "looks" this way at a woman who is not his wife, but also precisely because he "looks" in this way at a woman. If the woman he looks at is his wife, he could also commit adultery "in his heart."

This interpretation takes into consideration what has already been said about lust, especially lust of the flesh, in preceding chapters. When lust as an interior act results in the reduction of the riches of the perennial call to the communion of persons and allows the person to become merely the object of the potential satisfaction of the other's own sexual "needs," the mutual *for* is distorted. The man who "looks" in this way, "uses" the woman to satisfy his own instincts, even though he does not do so with an exterior act. If he has already inwardly assumed this attitude with regard to a given woman, he has committed adultery "in his heart." A man can commit this adultery in the heart with regard to his own wife if he treats her only as on object to satisfy his instinct.

We arrive at this interpretation of Matthew 5:27-28 when we take into consideration the theological character of lust, that is, the organic relationship between lust (as an act) and the lust of the flesh, which is a permanent disposition derived from man's sinfulness. The theological interpretation points toward the ethical meaning of Matthew 5:27-28. Jesus has not come to abolish the Law and the Prophets, but to fulfill them (Mt 5:17). He shows how deep an analysis of the human heart is necessary if the heart is to become a place of "fulfillment of the law." "Adultery in the heart" points out, by contrast, the right way to fulfill the sixth and ninth commandments because it refers to the sphere in which "purity of heart" (Mt 5:8) is necessary to avoid the univocal and severe prohibition against adultery. The severity of the prohibition is highlighted by Jesus' figurative call to "pluck out one's eye" and "cut off one's hand" (Mt 5:29-30).

The Old Testament legislation did not contribute to fulfillment of the law because its casuistry was marked by compromises with the lust of the flesh. Jesus teaches, however, that the commandment is carried out through "purity of heart," which requires that man firmly resist that which springs from the lust of the flesh.

The commandment, "do not commit adultery," is rooted in the indissolubility of marriage in which man and woman unite, according to the original plan of the Creator, so as to become one flesh. Adultery is in conflict with this unity and with the dignity of persons that is affirmed in this unity. Jesus confirms this essential ethical meaning of the commandment, but also seeks to strengthen it in the very depth of the human person, which is called "heart." Jesus calls for a liberation of the "heart" from "lust" in order that man and woman, in the interior truth of their mutual *for,* may shine forth more fully in that heart. Lust of the flesh brings a constraint of the spirit; when freed from this constraint, however, the husband and wife form the sacramental unity that has been willed by the

Creator himself. In the Sermon on the Mount, Jesus has in mind above all, the indissolubility of marriage, but he also refers to ever other form of the common life of men and women that constitute the pure and simple fabric of human existence. By its nature human life, is "coeducative," and its dignity, its balance, depend, ir every moment of history and at every point of geographical longitude and latitude, on "who" she will be for him and "who" he will be for her.

Jesus' words in the Sermon on the Mount had this universal and profound significance, and they call on all of Jesus' actual and potential listeners to perceive anew the lost fullness of humanity and want to regain it. When we understand that Jesus, who knew "what was in man" (Jn 2:25), also bore within himself the mystery of the "redemption of the body," we see that our analysis of his words in the Sermon on the Mount leads to further indispensable reflections if we are to reach a full awareness of both "historical" man and modern man, as well as "who" she will be for him and "who" he will be for her.

The following are the main points for a theology and a spirituality of the body and of sexuality that the Pope developed in his two addresses on adultery in the heart.

1. The splitting of the text in Matthew 5:27-28 leads to an understanding of the ethical sense of the text when it is carried out in a conjunctive way that requires that "adultery in the heart" be seen as an indication of how the values of justice, which have willed by God-Yahweh, have been lost in the usual Old Testament understanding and application of this commandment; Jesus indicates, through his description of an interior fact, how the commandment must be understood and put into practice if it is to lead to "justice."

2. "Adultery in the heart" is not merely a metaphorical expression that would logically rule out the possibility of a man committing it against his own wife; instead, Jesus makes the moral evaluation of "desire" depend on the personal dignity of the man and the woman, regardless of their marital status.

3. Adultery in the heart is committed because a man looks at a woman (even if that woman is his own wife) only as an

object to satisfy an instinct (or if a woman looks at any man in the same way); thus, a theological understanding of lust, that is, choosing the things of the world rather than the things of God, helps us understand the ethical meaning of Matthew 5:27-28.

4. Prohibition against "adultery in the heart" teaches us that we must perceive anew, in our hearts, the lost fullness of our humanity and seek to regain it if we hope to fulfill the law; the new *ethos* which Jesus brings is connected with the revelation of that depth that is called "heart," in which we must discover "who" woman will be for man and "who" man will be for woman if we want human life to retain its dignity and balance.

Spiritual Reflections

When the world press gathered in Rome for the 1980 Synod on the Family, they heard the Pope declare that it was possible for a man to commit adultery against his wife. An uproar was heard around the world; the Pope's comments, taken out of their context, were the cause of much confusion and ridicule. It seemed that the Pope was condemning the man who had erotic fantasies about his wife (and, indirectly, the woman who had erotic fantasies about her husband). Because most married people would maintain that such fantasies are a natural result of their sexual intimacy and are, indeed, important for the enrichment of their sexual intimacy, it seemed to many observers that this was just another indication of the church's condemnation of the body and sex.

Having followed the Pope's analysis of sexuality thus far, we have come to a theological understanding of "looking lustfully" that makes it possible for us to realize that the Pope is not condemning erotic fantasies about one's spouse or erotic behavior.

Still, our reflections have nevertheless helped us to appreciate the paradox of Jesus' words. We know that, at times, we have been guilty of sins of the body. We also know that we expend much of our energy in our search for sexual maturity on trying to control the body. We evaluate how we are progressing in this search based on how we use our bodies. We tend to judge the level of societal morality in terms of how well its members avoid "sins of the body." And we often consider marriages successful as long as both partners are physically faithful. (Physical infidelity is often the straw that breaks the back of a troubled marital relationship; it is not, however, the first sign of marital difficulties.)

The rule-oriented mentality, which served as the basis for sexual morality in previous generations, still influences what we perceive to be sins against our sexuality. If we only reflected on the first two parts of Jesus' words in Matthew 5:27-28, we could easily see "looks lustfully" as referring to fantasies about sins of the body, sins that are forbidden by the rule-oriented approach to sexual morality. At this point, we might have enlarged our understanding of sins against our sexuality to include sins of the mind, but we still would have considered these to be fantasies about erotic behavior.

When the Pope reminds us that our reflections on the separate elements in the biblical text are to be conjunctive and related to the broader theological understanding of lust that has been covered in previous analyses, we recognize that in this text, as in so many of the parables, Jesus is trying to shatter our expectations in order to open us to a call for transformation. Jesus' listeners, with their Old Testament background, appreciated the shattering nature of his pronouncement on "adultery in the heart" more readily than we do. Centuries of analysis of Jesus' words have unfortunately led to a watering down of the powerful impact they must have had on his listeners.

Adultery in the heart has been relegated to the realm of erotic fantasies with little appreciation for the paradox that Jesus presented to his audience. How could adultery—a sin in which two people who are not married to each other join their bodies in a union that was, according to divine law, reserved only for those who had left father and mother in order to cleave to each other— be committed in the "heart?" The Jewish audience must have wondered about this in the same way that we have wondered about the seeming contradiction in the Pope's claim that a man could commit "adultery in the heart" with regard to his own wife.

But those people gathered for the Sermon on the Mount were able to perceive that Jesus was calling for the "fulfillment of the law and justice" when he joined the phrases "looks lustfully" and "adultery in the heart." They saw this as a call to move beyond the narrow interpretation of both the meaning of the body and the commandment against adultery that had been fostered by the legalistic approach to interpreting the commandment. We, too, find that our analysis of "looks lustfully," when we consider lust in the broader perspective, as a choice for "things of the world" rather than the "things of the Father," makes the Pope's claim that a husband can commit adultery against his wife (and a wife against her husband) a real possibility.

The Pope's clarification of Jesus' words shatters any self-satisfaction we might have about not being adulterous. When the Pope indicates that a husband who reduces the femininity (the sexuality) of his wife to that of an object for the satisfaction of his sexual needs is guilty of "adultery in the heart," in effect, he interprets Jesus' words as a challenge to our attempt to limit sins against sexuality to sins of the body. Husband and wife commit "adultery in their heart" when they "look lustfully" at each other, that is, when they fail to recognize the personal dignity of each other, a dignity that is manifested in their bodies—in their masculinity and femininity—when their relationship is a relationship of appropriation rather than a relationship of gift, when they use their bodies only to satisfy an instinctual need rather than as a way of cleaving to each other so as to become one flesh.

Once we recognize that the commandment forbidding adultery applies to actions committed in our "hearts" wherein we choose, as Adam and Eve chose, either to fulfill the divine plan for human sexuality or to go the "way of the world," we realize that sins against our sexuality are not merely the sins of the body. When spouses commit adultery by "looking lustfully" at each other, we know that fulfillment of the law forbidding adultery requires that we appreciate the pervasiveness of human sexuality, the way in which the fact of human maleness and femaleness influences our relationships even when they are not relationships "of the body." When we limit sins against sexuality to sins of the body, we can often excuse our breaking of the commandment on the basis of the power of the sexual drive that overcame the decisions of our mind, much as the heroine of *The Bleeding Heart* bemoans the problems caused by her body. But, when we come to realize that we break the commandment against adultery when we reduce all of sexuality to sex, we discover that, no matter how carefully we have avoided the "sins of the body," we have a long way to go if we wish to fulfill the commandment so that justice will abound, that is, if we hope that our sexuality will reflect the divine plan for human existence.

The Pope reminds us that, although Jesus is specifically referring to the marital relationship, his words apply equally to all those areas of our lives that are affected by our masculinity and femininity. In light of our previous reflections on how sexuality affects various aspects of our lives, we come to see that we commit "adultery in the heart" when we depend on stereotypes for our understanding of what is proper masculinity and femininity, when we fail to offer young people positive models of sexuality, when we nurse a negative bodily self-image, when we are apathetic about the need to grow in intimacy in a marriage (including apathy toward sexual intimacy), and when we neglect the generative needs of our society. Sometimes we commit this "adultery in the heart" within the context of our marital relationship; at other times, we are guilty of "adultery in the heart" even though we are not married or, if we are married, in our relationship with people other than our spouse. Jesus' words, and the Pope's interpretations of these words, remind us that none of us could have cast the first stone against the adulterous woman. In one way or another, all of us have failed to follow the divine plan for human sexuality. We have "looked lustfully" even when we have not been engaged in erotic fantasies. Indeed, for most of us, our most serious sins of "looking lustfully" probably have been unrelated to erotic fantasies; more likely, they have resulted from our failure to realize that sins against sexuality are more than simply "sins of the body."

Each of us, in our own reflections, knows in which areas of sexually related behavior we are most guilty of "looking lustfully," that is, failing to choose the plan of the Father. For most of us, our failure to have an integrated sexual identity—to be mature and spontaneous in our appreciation of the depth of our sexuality—is largely attributable to the fact that we have limited both sexuality and sins against sexuality to the "body." In this way, we have failed to appreciate the body and the possibility of bodily unity as the sign of how we are to have relationships of gift, rather than relationships of appropriation, with our fellow human beings.

We end our reflections on the Pope's analysis of this particular element of Matthew 5:27-28 deeply aware of how the commandment against adultery speaks to all areas of male-female relationships. We know that we have sinned against this commandment even though we might never have physically joined our body with the body of one to whom we are not married. We recognize that, in the Sermon on the Mount, Jesus tried to break down the barriers we erect which not only make it difficult for us to appreciate the pervasiveness of sexuality, but also allow us to limit sexuality to sex and thereby limit our sins against sexuality to sins of the flesh. Jesus is telling us that we can no longer accept the narrow interpretation of the sixth (and the ninth) commandment. Although we are not to commit sins of the body, simply avoiding sins of the body does not mean that we will have fulfilled the law so that justice will abound. Jesus has shattered our illusions about the meaning of the commandment. When we are confronted with the realization of the innumerable ways in which we commit "adultery in the heart," we are left to wonder how we are to fulfill the law so that justice will abound. We must return to the Pope's analyses for some further insights that will assist us as we seek an answer to this question.

THIRTEEN
Appeal to Goodness

You have heard that it was said, "You shall not commit adultery." But I say to you that everyone who looks at a woman lustfully has already committed adultery with her in his heart. —Matthew 5:27-28

Summary of the Pope's Addresses

Several questions come to mind as we reflect on Jesus' words in Matthew 5:27-28. The first: Is the heart accused, or is it called to good? The second: How "can" and "must" the person who accepts Jesus' *ethos* in the Sermon on the Mount act in the area of sexuality, that is, on what can he rely in his "inner self," which is the source of his interior and exterior acts? In addition: How "should" the values that are known according to the "scale" of the Sermon on the Mount constitute a duty of his will and his "heart"? In what way are these values binding on him in action and behavior if they already "commit" him in thinking and "feeling"? We ask these questions because they are significant for human "praxis"; lived morality is always the *ethos* of human practice.

Various answers have been given to these questions; ample literature from the past and from our own day confirms this. It is also necessary to consider the many answers that concrete man gives to these questions that are repeatedly presented to him by his conscience, his awareness, and his moral sensitivity. It is at this level that an *interpenetration* of *ethos* and *practice* is carried out; at this level, individual principles that have been worked out and made known by moralists meet the principles that have been worked out by individuals—linked somehow, with the work of moralists and scientists—who are the authors and direct subjects of real morality and on whom the level of morality itself depends.

"Historical" man always evaluates his own "heart" in his own way and judges his own "body," passing from pessimism to optimism, from puritanical severity to modern permissiveness. If we are to hear the *ethos* of the Sermon on the Mount, which is concise in comparison with everything in secular literature that has been written on sexuality, it is important that we understand this tendency of "historical" man.

If we analyze the reactions to Matthew 5:27-28 throughout history, we find that Jesus' words have been stripped of their simplicity and depth and given a meaning that is far removed from the one that is actually expressed in them, a meaning that is, in fact, a contradiction to them. The influence of Manicheism on the Christian theology and *ethos* of the body led to a condemnation of the body, sex, marriage, conjugal life, and other spheres of human behavior in which corporeity is expressed. The severity of Manicheism might seem to some to be in harmony with the severity of Matthew 5:29-30, which advises "plucking out" one's eye and so forth. Consequently, an attempt was made to see this as a condemnation, whereas the Gospel was only addressing a particular requirement to the human spirit.

Interpreting Matthew 5:27-28 as a condemnation of the body could be a loophole to avoid the requirements of Jesus' words, requirements that are really based on an affirmation—rather than a denial or condemnation—of the femininity and masculinity of the human being as the personal dimension of "being a body."

If the words of Matthew 5:27-28 are an accusation, the charge is directed at the man of lust. The heart is not accused but, rather, is subjected to a judgment, that is, called to a self-critical examination. The judgment about desire as an act of "lust of the flesh" contains an affirmation of the body as that which, together with the spirit, determines man's ontological subjectivity and shares in his dignity as a person. In this way, the judgment is essentially different from the one that springs from Manicheism.

The body—its sexuality—is called, from "the beginning," to become the manifestation of the spirit. Our previous analysis of this beginning and of Jesus' warnings against the lust of the flesh, coupled with his defense of the inviolable rights of the conjugal union in which the body and its sexuality assume the value of a sacramental sign, indicate that the ethical meaning found in Jesus' teaching has nothing in common with the Manichean condemnation of the body. Rather, Jesus' comments are linked to the "redemption of the body" that is necessary because, through man's sinfulness, he has, among other things, lost a clear sense of the nuptial meaning of the body. This is a "partial," potential loss in which the sense of the "nuptial meaning of the body" is confused with lust.

The Manichean attitude toward Jesus' words would lead to an "annihilation of the body" and a negation of the value of both human sex and the masculinity and femininity of the human person; sexuality would be tolerated merely because of the "need" of procreation. The Christian *ethos* calls for a transformation of the conscience and attitudes of both men and women so that they might realize the value of the body and sex according to the original divine plan. For the Manichean, the body and sexuality constitute an "anti-value"; for the Christian, the body and sexuality remain a "value not sufficiently appreciated." Because man lives in the state of fallen but, at the same time, redeemed nature, a new *ethos* is necessary.

Thus, we see that Jesus' words in the Sermon on the Mount, even if they seem to contain a certain accusation against the human heart, are more deeply an appeal to it. The accusation of the moral evil that is concealed within desire is actually a call to overcome this evil. It is a question of detaching one's self from the evil of the act, rather than transferring the negative character of this act to its object. Such a transfer would not constitute a victory over the evil of the act but would conceal within it the danger of justifying the act to the detriment of the object. Clearly, Jesus demands detachment from the evil of "lust," but he does not in any way allow that the object of that desire—the woman who is "looked at lustfully"—is an evil, which sometimes seems to be the case in some Wisdom texts.

The difference between the "accusation" and the "appeal" lies in the fact that the accusation that is leveled at the evil of lust is, at the same time, an appeal to overcome it and a call to discover the true values of the object, an object that, as a result of the evil of "lust," is a "value not sufficiently appreciated." Although the human heart is "accused" of lust, it is also called upon to discover the full sense of what, in the act of lust, constitutes a "value that is not sufficiently appreciated." "Adultery in the heart" can and must be understood as a "devaluation;" that is, an intentional depravation of the dignity to which the complete value of femininity corresponds in the person in question. Matthew 5:27-28 calls for a discovery of this value. The appeal to master the "lust of the flesh" springs from the affirmation of the personal dignity of the body and sex and serves only this dignity. The Manichean interpretation of the body and sexuality is therefore essentially alien to the Gospel.

The Pope also finds it necessary to examine the significant convergence and the fundamental divergence that exists between Jesus' affirmation of the personal dignity of the body and sexuality, which is found in the Gospel, and the Freudian-Marxist-Nietzschean interpretation of the meaning of man and morality, which is, according to one commentator, based on suspicion. Freud, Marx, and Nietzsche, who have exercised a great influence on the culture and beliefs of our time but who have nevertheless been called "masters of suspicion" by Paul Ricoeur, seem to judge and accuse man's "heart" because of what is called, in biblical language, the three forms of lust. Nietzsche seems to be judging and accusing the "pride of life"; Marx is concerned with the "lust of the eyes"; and Freud deals with "the lust of the flesh." The divergence occurs because the Bible does not allow us to keep the heart in a state of continual suspicion.

Jesus' words in Matthew 5:27-28 acknowledge the reality of desire and lust but do not permit us to make lust the absolute criterion of anthropology and ethics; it is however, an important coefficient for our understanding of man, his actions, and his moral behavior. Jesus' words are an expression of a completely different *ethos*—one that differs not only from the Manichean *ethos*, but also from the *ethos* of the so-called masters of suspicion—because Jesus' words are an appeal to the human heart rather than only an accusation or a condemnation of it. We see this when we consider these words in the context of the *ethos* of redemption in which a man must feel called and "called with efficacy." When we reread Jesus' words in the context of the redemption of the body, we see that we cannot stop at putting the human "heart" in a state of continual and irreversible suspicion because of the lust of the flesh. Instead, we must feel called to realize the nuptial meaning of the body and then express the interior freedom of the gift of the spiritual state and spiritual power that are derived from a mastery of the lust of the flesh.

Jesus' words in the Sermon on the Mount, which are "outside" man in the appeal to the "heart," are also a call from "inside." If man lets these words act in him, he will be able to hear within himself the echo of that good "beginning" which Jesus uses to remind his listeners who man is, who woman is, and who we are for each other in the work of creation. Jesus' words in the Sermon on the Mount are not addressed to the man who is completely absorbed in the lust of the flesh and therefore unable to seek another form of relationship with a woman. Rather, Jesus' words bear witness to the fact that the original power (grace) of the mystery of creation becomes, for each person, the power (grace) of the mystery of redemption. Interiorly, man feels, along with lust, a deep need to preserve the dignity of the mutual relations that, thanks to sexuality, find their expression in the body.

Our rereading of Jesus' appeal must always be related to the context of concrete existence. The appeal always means the rediscovery of the meaning of the whole of existence, which contains the nuptial meaning of the body. These words reveal a vision of man's possibility that is different from the meaning found in the Freudian libido. Man, in his "heart," should feel not only irrevocably accused and given as a prey to the lust of the flesh, but also called in the truth of his humanity, his sexuality, and his body, which have been his heritage from "the beginning"—the heritage of his heart, which is deeper than his sinfulness and deeper than lust in its three forms. Jesus' words, understood in the context of creation and redemption, reactivate this heritage and give it power in man's life.

The following are the main points for a theology and a spirituality of the body that are found in the Pope's three addresses on an appeal to goodness.

1. We must ask ourselves if Jesus' words in Matthew 5:27-28 are an accusation of the human heart or a call to goodness; we also must ask what Jesus' words say regarding how we can and should act in relation to our sexuality. We must

ask these questions because we are the authors and direct subjects of a real morality, the co-authors of its history who determine the level of morality itself.

2. Jesus' words, which are a call for transformation, have been misinterpreted as a condemnation of the body and sex, as a "loophole" with which to avoid the need for an affirmation of human sexuality as the personal dimension of "being a body"; those who use the Manichean condemnation of the body, sex, marriage, and conjugal life in an attempt to influence the Christian theology and *ethos* of the body have contributed to this misinterpretation of Matthew 5:27-28 throughout history.

3. Jesus' words call for a transformation of the conscience and attitude of men and women so that we might express the value of the body and sex that is found in the original divine plan, a value not sufficiently appreciated as a result of the evil of lust; the appeal to overcome this evil can in no way be equated with a condemnation of the object of desire, that is, the woman who is looked at lustfully.

4. Any view of sexuality that holds the human heart in continual mistrust, considering lust the criterion of anthropology and ethics, does not appreciate the real meaning of the Gospel *ethos*; the man of lust (every one of us) is called by Jesus' word in Matthew 5:27-28 to realize the nuptial meaning of the body and is assured that he can respond to this call because of the promise "of the redemption of the body."

5. In our hearts, we feel both irrevocably accused and prey to the lust of the flesh *and* forcefully called as persons, in the truth of our sexuality and our bodies, to that supreme value of love; this heritage of our hearts, which is deeper than the heritage of both sinfulness and the three forms of lust, is reactivated by Jesus' words which give it real power in our life because the power (grace) of the mystery of creation has become for us the power (grace) of the mystery of redemption.

Spiritual Reflections

It is, perhaps, not so surprising that Jesus' words are frequently misinterpreted as a condemnation of the body, sex, the conjugal union, and, (often) of women. The power of the sexual attraction and our numerous experiences of "desire," which lead to behavior that often causes us to feel shame, are indications of how very difficult it is for us to deal with the mystery of our human sexuality. The attraction that has such powerful potential for good, for unity, and for the revelation of God and the divine plan, so often causes us and others anxiety, pain, disruption, and loss of self-worth. At times, we all wonder about the strange power our bodies seem to exercise over the direction of our lives; we feel that a certain demon is leading us away from our goal of sexual maturity, and, at these times, we rather easily view the body and sex as the source of our troubles.

At the same time, however, the body of the other, so "different" from ours, holds both an appeal and a threat to our sense of self. She is attractive to us, for example, but she also exercises some influence on our life, an influence that we might not be ready to accept. She represents a call to commitment, for example, that challenges our self-centeredness; our bodies threaten to break down the barriers that we have set up in order avoid the call to intimacy.

In addition, the body of the other is mysteriously "different" from ours. Although this difference can be the source of great satisfaction in physical unity, it represents a difference that can also be threatening because it both calls us out of ourselves and represents a different way of being human. It is not so surprising that a woman's body, which was able to bleed for extended periods of time with no apparent consequences, was mysterious and perhaps threatening to the primitive male who would weaken considerably and perhaps even face death if he were to suffer the loss of a similar quantity of blood. And the fact that this female body was the first resting place for the next generation greatly added to its sense of mystery, a sense that undoubtedly caused both awe and fear in the males of primitive societies. Whether Freud was correct in claiming that the female experiences penis envy is a much-debated topic today; but the idea that both men and women nevertheless find each other's bodies attractive and threatening certainly seems to be nondebatable. For all of us, the perennial attraction of our sexuality is, at times, a cause for great celebration and, at other times, a cause for intense confusion. It is not surprising that, at various times in history, there have been forms of Manicheism.

Nor is it surprising that Jesus' call for all of us who have "looked lustfully" to realize the nuptial meaning of the body has been misinterpreted as a condemnation of the body or as a judgment against the body. Jesus is calling us to appreciate the heritage of our hearts, a heritage in which we can uncover God's original plan for our sexuality and, with this discovery, work out how we can and should act regarding that sexuality. In short, Jesus puts the responsibility for sexual morality on us.

Although we might work in conjunction with moralists, we are not free, after hearing Jesus' words, to simply follow "rules" about sexual behavior. Now we must transform our conscience and attitudes in light of the value of our bodies and of sex that has been uncovered in the original divine plan. We can no longer be content with interpretations of the body and sex that consider them evils to be controlled through rules about erotic behavior and reproduction; nor can we accept an interpretation that sees the body only as an object for the satisfaction of a sexual need. Jesus' judgment in Matthew 5:27-28 is, in fact, a judgment against the second interpretation, which ignores the sacramental value of our bodies and our sexuality. At the same time, however, Jesus' judgment is a call to realize that the attraction of human sexuality calls for an affirmation of the dignity of the person. Sex should be a reminder of the value of the "communion of persons" that has been planned by God.

But it is difficult for those of us who have looked lustfully, who have desired, who have committed sins of the body, and who have ignored the other dimensions of sexuality by concentrating only on sexual sins, to hear Jesus' words about "adultery in the heart" and not feel condemned. We know that we are guilty—if not of adultery in the body, than certainly of "adultery in the heart"—and it becomes difficult for us to see beyond the accusatory aspect of Jesus' words. We do not readily recognize that they are addressed to those of us who "look lustfully," who "desire." We fail to recognize that the appeal to our "hearts" is like Jesus' directive to the Pharisees regarding "the beginning," an appeal to examine our hearts and uncover in them the value of the body and sex that we do not sufficiently appreciate when we "look lustfully."

When we become reflective about our sexuality, we are forced to admit that we do not adequately appreciate the value of the body and sex. We must remember, however, that Jesus' words in Matthew 5:27-28 are spoken within the larger context of the promise of the redemption of the body. Jesus is calling on us to rediscover the nuptial meaning of the body that has been lost to us because we have "looked lustfully." Jesus challenges us to transform our understanding of masculinity and femininity and rediscover the dignity of each person in his or her body and sex. But those of us who have lived according to the rules of correct sexual behavior, and those of us who have limited the meaning of sexuality to sex, find ourselves at a loss in trying to respond to the Lord's call to transformation. If sexuality is meant to lead us to Love, to be lovers as God is a lover, how are we who "look lustfully" and "commit adultery in the heart" to discover and reveal this meaning in our own lives?

Jesus' emphasis on *heart* is key for those of us who want to hear his words as an appeal to goodness rather than a condemnation or judgment. If we will reflect, if we will examine our hearts, if we will return to "the beginning" and God's plan for sexuality, we can reread Jesus' words in the Sermon on the Mount as an appeal to transform our attitudes toward sexuality. We do this in light of the answers that God's plan gives to the confusion that we experience in our hearts over our inability to achieve a mature sexual identity.

We know, when we reflect on our experiences of our own masculinity and femininity, that we have not fully integrated our sexuality; we do not have a sense of the meaning of sexuality that permeates our behavior in all the areas of our lives that are affected by our masculinity and femininity. If we have lived our lives according to the "rules," we might have controlled our erotic behavior; but this does not necessarily mean that we have come to an appreciation of the nuptial meaning of the body. In fact, in many circumstances, those who grew up in the pre-Vatican II Manichean-tinged atmosphere have kept the rules but have never developed a sufficient appreciation of the value of the body and sex. Those who, in keeping with the new sexual freedom, have developed a greater ease about the body have not necessarily seen the relationship between that appreciation of the body and the appreciation of the dignity of the person who is represented by the body.

These difficulties with our sexuality, which become apparent when we reflect in our hearts, urge us to look for some way to overcome the lust of our hearts and reassert the dignity of our sexuality. Jesus' call in the Sermon on the Mount is a call to transformation that is issued in the context of the "redemption of the body." We who want to move beyond lust and rediscover the dignity of our sexuality are promised that the grace of redemption will assist us as we seek to rediscover the innocence (grace) of original time. When Jesus appeals to us to move beyond the stage of limiting sins against sexuality to sins of the body, he indirectly (in the context of the redemption of the body) promises us the grace that will make this transformation possible.

Our preconceived notions have been shattered. We know that we look lustfully, that we desire, and that we tend to feel "condemned." But these reflections on Jesus' words make it obvious that neither the body and sex nor the person who lusts is condemned. Rather, we who lust are promised the grace to transform our experiences of sexuality so that we might realize the "nuptial meaning of the body."

Jesus, who came to fulfill the law so that creation might superabound with justice, is calling upon us to transform our limited understanding of sexuality. He assures us that we can respond to this call. We begin our response when we seriously examine our hearts and reflect upon our own reactions to masculinity or femininity. Although we lust, this lust does not need to be the criterion of our response to our sexuality. We are free, through the grace of redemption, to uncover in our hearts the divine plan. We are called to love and promised that our bodies, our sexuality, can help us respond to this call.

We turn now to the Pope's further reflections on how the body and sex assist us as we seek to fulfill the divine plan.

FOURTEEN
Eros, Ethos, and Spontaneity

You have heard that it was said, "You shall not commit adultery." But I say to you that everyone who looks at a woman lustfully has already committed adultery with her in his heart. —Matthew 5:27-28

Summary of the Pope's Addresses

These words in Matthew 5:27-28 are an appeal to the human heart, an appeal with an ethical character that is important and essential to the very *ethos* of the Gospel. In order that this appeal might be heard by the conscience of contemporary man, it is necessary to consider the meaning of *eros*, an alien term that is unknown to biblical language. The term *ethos*, however, which we also use in our analysis, is known in both the Old and the New Testament: according to the general meaning that it has acquired in philosophy and theology, *ethos* refers to the complex spheres of good and evil; it depends on the human will and is subject to the laws of conscience and the sensitivity of the human "heart."

The Greek word *eros* passed from mythology to philosophy to literary language and to spoken language, and has a philosophical meaning in Plato that is different from both the common meaning and the meaning that has been attributed to it in literature. According to Plato, the word *eros* refers to the interior force that draws man to everything good, true, and beautiful; it is an attraction that has the intensity of a subjective act of the human spirit. The common meaning of *eros*, however, refers to its sensual nature; *eros* arouses the mutual tendency of both the man and the woman to draw closer to each other to a union of bodies. We must ask ourselves if this common understanding of *eros* describes what we find in the biblical narrative, especially in Genesis 2:23-25, and how it influences the way in which we understand the "lust" referred to in Matthew 5:27-28.

The common defintion of *eros* seems to refer to the psychological meaning of lust; lust indicates the objective intensity of straining toward the object because of its sexual character or sexual value. In the Sermon on the Mount, we hear of the concupiscence of the man who "looks lustfully." To understand these words in their psychological meaning, we refer to what is commonly described as "erotic." Even though Matthew 5:27-28 refers to an interior act, and "erotic" usually refers to external manifestation of interior acts, it seems that we could equate "erotic" with what "derives from desire." If this were the case, Jesus' words would be a negative judgment about what is "erotic," and the human heart would receive a severe warning against *eros*.

But if we take into account the Platonic meaning of *eros*, there is then room for *ethos*, the ethical, and, indirectly, theological content, which we have seen in Jesus' appeal to the human "heart." If we are to understand the riches of the "heart" to which Jesus appeals, then we must take into consideration the multiple semantic nuances of *eros* and the various types of behavior that are considered to be erotic in different human cultures.

Within the sphere of the Platonic understanding of the concept of *eros*, we must find a way to understand Jesus' call in the Sermon on the Mount. The call to what is good, true, and beautiful in the *ethos* of redemption is also the call to overcome the results of the three forms of lust. In addition, the call points to the possibility—indeed, the necessity—of transforming what has been drawn down by the lust of the flesh. We find, from this perspective, that *eros* and *ethos* do not differ and are not opposed to each other but, rather, are called to meet in the human heart and bear fruit. The form of what is considered to be "erotic" should be, at the same time, the form of *ethos*, that is, what is "ethical."

The relationship between *eros* and *ethos* is very important to an understanding of *ethos* and ethics, especially because ethics, with its norms, commands, and prohibitions, is often considered "negative." For this very reason, we are inclined to consider Jesus' words on "looking lustfully" to be a prohibition that applies exclusively to the "erotic" sphere. Content with this understanding, we do not try to uncover the deep and essential values that this prohibition ensures, values that the prohibition also liberates and makes accessible if we learn to open our "heart" to them.

Reflections on the mutual relationship between what is ethical and what is erotic demonstrate that it is necessary that *ethos* should become a constituent form of *eros*. If the human spirit does not continually rediscover the nuptial meaning of the body "in the erotic," the attraction of the senses and the passion of the body may stop at mere lust, void of any ethical value, and thereby deprive us of the fullness of *eros* in which the erotic becomes true, good, and beautiful.

From this perspective, we can see that it is erroneous to consider *ethos* a hindrance to spontaneity in the erotic sphere. Those who think *ethos* is detrimental to spontaneity not only demand that *eros* be detached from *ethos*, but also see the words in the Sermon on the Mount as a hindrance to the good of *eros*. In fact, however, the person who accepts the *ethos* of Matthew 5:27-28 must know that he is also called to full and mature spontaneity in the relations that spring from the perennial attraction of masculinity and femininity. Spontaneity is the gradual fruit of the discernment of the impulses of our heart.

Jesus' words are severe in that they demand that, in the sphere of relations with persons of the other sex, we should have a full and deep consciousness of our own acts, including interior acts. We should be aware of the internal impulses of our own "heart" so that we can distinguish them and maturely qualify them. Jesus' words about the erotic, which seems to belong exclusively to the body and the senses, call for reflection by the interior man who should be able to (1) obey conscience, (2) be true master of his own deep impulses, and (3) draw from all those impulses that which is fitting for "purity of heart," building through conscience and consistency a personal sense of the nuptial meaning of the body.

The man who wishes to respond to Matthew 5:27-28 must learn with perseverance and consistency the true meaning of the body, that is, femininity and masculinity, not only through objectifying abstraction, but, above all, in the interior reactions of his own "heart." This "science" cannot be learned only from books; man must learn to distinguish between the riches of masculinity and femininity that are found in the perennial attraction of the sexes and what comes from lust. Although these two inclinations of the heart can be confused, the interior man has been called by Jesus to discern and judge in his own heart. This is a task that *can* be done and is worthy of man; and, what is more, it has an essential relationship with spontaneity. We know, for example, that when sexual desire is linked with noble gratification, it differs from desire pure and simple. So, too, in the immediate reactions of the "heart," sexual excitement is quite different from the deep emotion with which interior sensitivity and sexuality itself react to the total expression of masculinity and femininity. Jesus' words are severe in that they contain in them profound requirements concerning human spontaneity.

We know that there is no spontaneity in the movements and impulses that arise from mere carnal lust. Through self-control, however, man reaches the deeper and more mature spontaneity with which his "heart" resists his instincts and allows him to rediscover the spiritual beauty of the sign of the human body and its sexuality. His discovery becomes enhanced in his conscience as conviction and in his will as guidance of possible choices and mere desire. The human heart then becomes a participant in man's spontaneity in a way that is unknown to carnal man. Jesus' words in Matthew 5:27-28 call for this type of spontaneity and directly indicate the way toward a mature spontaneity of the human heart that does not suffocate its noble desires and aspirations, but frees them and, in a way, facilitates them. A relationship between the ethical and the erotic, according to the *ethos* of the Sermon on the Mount, points the way toward a "praxis" that gradually prepares the way for such spontaneity.

The following are the main points for a theology and a spirituality of the body and sexuality that are found in the Pope's addresses on *eros*, *ethos*, and spontaneity.

1. When we think of "erotic" in the context of the Platonic description of *eros* as that which drives us toward everything good, true, and beautiful, we see that in the *ethos* of redemption we must overcome the three forms of lust; the form of what is erotic should be the form of what is ethical.

2. When *eros* and *ethos* meet in the human heart, we must

give up our inclination to see Jesus' words about lust as a prohibition against the erotic sphere; actually, Jesus' words are meant to reveal the deep and essential values that are found in the heart and thereby make them accessible to us if we open our "hearts" to them.

3. Jesus's words in Matthew 5:27-28 are a call to full and mature spontaneity in the relationships that spring from the attraction of our sexuality; *ethos,* when is it joined to *eros,* does not take away the spontaneity of *eros* but makes us aware of the impulses of our heart so that we will be consistent in our search for an appreciation of the nuptial meaning of the body.

4. If we wish to respond to the call of Matthew 5:27-28, we must learn to discern and judge in our "hearts" the meaning of the body and sexuality, for in this meaning we learn the difference between sexual excitement and the deep emotion with which the interior sensitivity and sexuality itself react to the total expression of femininity and masculinity; in this way, we achieve a mature spontaneity by which we master our instincts and rediscover the spiritual beauty of sexuality, thereby creating and facilitating our noble desires and aspirations in a way that is unknown to "carnal man."

Spiritual Reflections

For many people, the idea that Jesus' words in the Sermon on the Mount are actually the call to use our erotic inclinations in our search for the meaning of life—for that which is true, good, and beautiful, for God—is startling and, perhaps, even upsetting. This reaffirmation of the importance of the body and of sex and passion seems contrary to all the prohibitions we have been used to from most religious commentaries on sexuality. In fact, celebrating the erotic as one of the avenues for discovering the meaning of life according to the plan of God seems to be tantamount to giving license to all kinds of bizarre behavior. Members of the Moral Majority point to pornography, prostitution, "girlie" magazines, adult book stores, and sex and violence on TV as signs of what happens when people are not warned against the dangers that are present in the erotic sphere of our life.

Fear of that which is erotic sets up barriers to an appreciation of Jesus' call to discover the divine plan for human sexuality. A man who is actively involved in the Christian Family Movement, for example, was vehemently opposed to a parish program on the Pope's vision of sexuality because, as he put it: "Maybe I am part of the new swing to the Right, but I am sick and tired of hearing about sex, sick and tired of being told that if you're having a problem with your marriage you should run to the local sex therapist and everything will be straightened out. I don't need the church on my back telling me that sex is the answer to all my problems."

A similar attitude was displayed by a married lay woman who, as a member of a parish staff, was opposed to having sexuality included as the theme of the Holy Week liturgy (we die to the abuse of our sexuality in order to rise to a fuller appreciation of God's plan) on the grounds that we would insult people if we referred to sex during Holy Week. She was apparently unaware of the symbolism of plunging the Easter candle into water during the Holy Saturday vigil services.

These are just two of the many examples of the resistance that is encountered in attempts to maintain that the erotic offers an opportunity for discovery of the good, the true, and the beautiful. People do not want to hear that the erotic is, or can be, of assistance in revealing the divine presence in the experiences of our life; people do not want to hear that there is an extraordinary dimension to life that can be perceived when the erotic sphere is joined with the ethical, not in such a way as to prohibit the possibilities for good in the erotic, but in a way that reminds us of the nuptial meaning of the body.

Perhaps it is not so surprising that, in earlier periods of human history, the need to control erotic behavior for reproduction led to prohibitions that eventually encouraged a Manichean perspective or the tendency to be suspicious about an attraction to another's body. Indeed, our own current experiences of the numerous ways in which sexual exploitation is destructive of human relationships leads us to wonder how it might ever be possible for the erotic sphere to be a source of the revelation of God.

On the one hand are those who have held that the erotic is an evil to be tolerated for the reproductive needs of a society; on the other hand are those who have limited the erotic to the ordinary satisfaction of bodily sexual needs. Neither of these perspectives, however, leads to an appreciation of the erotic and of the body as a means for discovering the meaning of life. Our fear of the power of sexual attraction, which we considered in our earlier reflections, often leads us to embrace one of these two positions; we want either to control the erotic, or to enjoy it with a no-strings-attached attitude. In both instances, however, we limit the erotic to the sensual needs of the body and, thus, ignore its role in our search for the good, the true, and the beautiful.

In an age of sexual freedom, our uncertainty about activity in the erotic sphere is even more apparent. The freedom to do pretty much what we want, unencumbered by civil laws, means that we have to discern and judge in our own hearts how we are to act. Consequently, even though we are not always conscious of it, we do develop a level of personal morality in this area of our life. Jesus' challenge in the Sermon on the Mount is a call to remember God's plan for human sexuality when we are developing our code of personal morality. Jesus' words do not prohibit us from responding to the attraction of the body of another. Instead, Jesus calls us to appreciate the way in which erotic activity can assist us in our search for a unity, a communion of persons, that allows us to be "in the image of God."

When our ethical behavior in the erotic sphere is influenced by the fact that we have "discerned and judged in our hearts" the divine plan for human sexuality—that is, when *eros* and *ethos* have met in the human heart—we discover that the ethical is not primarily a system of prohibitions that inhibits spontaneity; we find, rather, that the ethical assists us in finding a deeper appreciation of the meaning of sexuality, freeing us from a slavery to the body and enriching our appreciation of the sign value of the physical attraction of human sexuality.

Those persons in our society who reject an acknowledged ethical perspective regarding sexuality because, they claim, it interferes with a spontaneity that is essential for the full enjoyment of the erotic sphere of our life, put a different interpretation on both "ethical" and "spontaneity." When we subscribe to this position, we generally find ourselves, at some time or other, confused over our inability to be sexually mature. Most of us are turned off by adults who are obviously sexually immature. A married woman who flirts with everyone else's husband, for example, or the man in the office who cannot keep his hands to himself, or the successful businessman who always makes off-color jokes and lewd comments, or the movie star who is on her fourth, fifth, or sixth husband—all of these persons lead us to eventually wonder if they will ever grow up; if these people are being spontaneous, then perhaps we do not want to be the object of such a person's desire to be "spontaneous."

When we begin to identify exactly what we mean by spontaneity in the area of sexuality, we find that we tend to admire the person who seems to have a good bodily self-image, who does not manipulate persons of the other sex, who relates to others as individuals rather than stereotypes, and who has a strong sense of personal sexual identity. In recent surveys, the most popular male actors were men who gave the impression that they were faithful spouses, non-manipulative of female acquaintances and fans, supportive of equality for women, and comfortable with their own image as male sex symbols. If these male actors' public image should change, many who admire their spontaneity would be truly disappointed.

When we examine our own lives and try to determine how we can have a spontaneity about our sexuality—in other words, how we can have a mature sexual identity—we realize how essential it is to appreciate the sign value of the erotic. If we, like the Manicheans, have rigidly controlled the erotic because we have considered it to be evil, we will never achieve spontaneity because we have failed to recognize that the call of the human body is a call to "communion of persons," a call to recognize the personal dignity of the other; we will feel that, so long as we do not sin in our bodies, we are following the commandments. If, however, we think that spontaneity in the erotic sphere is exemplified by an appreciation of soft-core and hard-core pornography, adult bookstores, X-rated movie theatres and cable TV, and concentration during our sexual intimacy on the mechanics of sex, then we miss out on the opportunity that the erotic offers us for discovering that we are "in the image of God."

The sexual feast that is described in Genesis 2:23-24 sees the joining of two bodies as a good that has been created by God, a good that is to be enjoyed and, at the same time, is a means of salvation. The sexual union of two in one flesh who become "in the image of God" requires a continuity between our interior disposition and our external behavior. Our bodily activity in the erotic sphere must be related to a deeper appreciation of the possibilities for salvation that are present in the experience, possibilities that challenge us to be mature and spontaneous adults who respect the dignity of the unique and unrepeatable person with whom we are linked.

So we see that spontaneity in our sexuality means more than an uninhibited response to "the desire" of the moment that is devoid of any concern for the consequences of our behavior. When *eros* and *ethos* meet in the human heart—that is, when we have discerned and judged the meaning of human sexuality and seek to behave in a way that deepens our appreciation of this meaning—we begin to develop the spontaneity of the sexually mature adult, we begin to deepen our awareness of the possibilities of discovering the good, the true, and the beautiful through our erotic behavior. We no longer need fear the evil of the body, of sex, and of erotic activity. When we reflect on our own experiences, however, we wonder whether will we ever achieve this kind of spontaneity. Perhaps we can successfully give up the influence of Manichean dualism, but our experiences remind us that we often fail to use the erotic as a way to the good, the true, and the beautiful. We still tend to be suspicious about the positive possibilities of our bodies.

We end our reflections on these two papal addresses aware of Jesus' call to be reflective about the meaning of human sexuality and to develop a personal code of behavior that will reflect this meaning. Our reflections on "the beginning" have helped us discover that we are male and female in order to bring love into the world, so that we might be lovers as God is a Lover. Our reflections on the Sermon on the Mount remind us that, as Christians, we are called to rediscover, to reveal, to reaffirm this divine plan. But our reflections on human experience, including our own experiences, remind us that spontaneity—mature sexual identity—is not easily achieved by "historical" men and women. We must return to the Scriptures and the Pope's analyses as we seek to find ways to allow *eros* and *ethos* to meet in our heart, so that we can respond to the call to spontaneity that Jesus uttered in Matthew 5:27-28.

FIFTEEN
Redemption of the Body

*It was not for any fault on the part of crea-
tion that it was made unable to attain its purpose; it was made so by God. But the whole of
creation still waits with eager longing to be set
free from its bondage to decay and obtain the
glorious liberty of the children of God. From the
beginning till now the entire creation, as we know,
has been groaning in one great act of giving birth;
and not only creation, but all of us who possess
the first fruits of the Spirit, we, too, groan
inwardly as we wait for the redemption of the
body.* —Romans 8:20-23

Summary of the Pope's Address

Jesus' words in Matthew 5:27-28 are addressed to the "heart," to
the interior man who is the specific subject of the new *ethos* of the
body that Jesus Christ wishes to imbue on the conscience and will
of his followers. This new *ethos* is new compared to the *ethos* of the
Old Testament and also with regard to the state of "historical"
man— the man of lust, that is, man independent of any geographical
and historical longitude and latitude.

This "new" *ethos* is the *ethos* of the redemption of the body of
which St. Paul speaks in Romans 8:20-23. All of creation, but particularly man who has sinned and is now an "adopted son," strives
toward "the redemption of the body," which is the eschatological
and mature fruit of man's redemption in the world that has been
brought by Jesus. Although this redemption of the body is not
specified in the Sermon on the Mount, there is no doubt that Jesus

181

speaks from the perspective of the redemption of both man and the world because this is the perspective of the whole Gospel teaching and mission of Jesus.

Even though the immediate context of the Sermon on the Mount is the historical reference point of the Law and the Prophets, we must not forget that in Jesus' teaching about marriage and male-female relationships, he refers to "the beginning"; this reference can only be justified by the reality of the redemption because, without it, there would only be the "bondage to decay" of the three forms of lust. Only the perspective of redemption justifies the reference to the mystery of creation in Jesus' teaching on sexuality. We must see the words of Matthew 5:27-28 in the same theological perspective.

Jesus does not invite us to return to the state of original innocence; he does, however, call on man to rediscover, on the basis of the perennial meanings of what is "human," the way of the "new man," and thereby establishes a continuity between "the beginning" and the perspective of redemption. In the *ethos* of the redemption of the body, the original *ethos* of the creation is again taken up. Jesus does not change the law but, rather, confirms the commandment against adultery and, at the same time, leads the intellect and heart of his listeners toward that "fullness of justice" that has been willed by God and is contained in the commandment. This fullness is discovered through an interior examination "of the heart" and then through an adequate way of being and acting in which the "new man" can emerge to the degree that the *ethos* of the redemption of the body dominates both the lust of the flesh and the whole man of lust.

The way in which the *ethos* of the redemption of the body succeeds in dominating the lust of the flesh must be the way of temperance and mastery of desires. The *ethos* of redemption points to the imperative of self-control and the necessity of immediate continence and habitual temperance, a temperance and continence that are not suspended in emptiness but are, rather, self-mastery in which the human heart remains bound to the value from which desire would have moved toward pure lust, which is deprived of ethical value. The value that is called for by the *ethos* of redemption is the nuptial meaning of the body—a transparent sign by means of which the Creator, through the perennial, mutual sexual attraction of man and woman, writes in the heart of both the gift of communion, that is, the mysterious reality of his image and likeness.

Although the call for self-mastery may give the impression of suspension and emptiness—especially the first time it is necessary to make up one's mind to respond to it, or when one has been accustomed to yielding to the lust of the flesh—by actually responding to it, man gradually experiences his own dignity. By means of temperance, man bears witness to his own self-mastery and shows that what he is carrying out is essentially personal in him; gradually, he experiences the freedom of the gift that is both the condition and the response of the subject, that is, the nuptial value of the human body in its sexuality. Thus, the *ethos* of the redemption of the body is realized through self-mastery when the human heart enters into an alliance with this *ethos,* when the deepest and most real possibilities and disposition of the person, which are manifested in the innermost layers of his potentiality and which the lust of the flesh would not permit to be shown, acquire a voice. These layers cannot emerge when the human heart is held in suspicion or when Manichean "anti-value" is dominant in consciousness.

The Pope concludes his analysis of Matthew 5:27-28 by maintaining that Jesus' words are a call to the human heart and that, in "historical" man, the consciousness of sinfulness is the necessary starting point and indispensable condition of this aspiration to virtue, that is, to "purity of heart" and perfection. In a most concrete way, Jesus claims that man is unique because, above all, his "heart" decides his being "from within." The "heart" is the equivalent of personal subjectivity, and the appeal to the heart in the Sermon on the Mount is reminiscent of original solitude from which the male "man" is liberated through opening to the other human being, the woman. Purity of heart, which is a requirement of love, is ultimately explained as regard for the other subject who is originally and perennially "co-called." The Pope presents a detailed analysis of purity in subsequent addresses.

The following are the main points for a theology and a spirituality of sexuality and the body that emerge from the Pope's one address on the redemption of the body.

1. Jesus' call in the Sermon on the Mount can only be fully understood from the perspective of the redemption of the

body, in which we can again take up the original *ethos* of creation; the fullness of justice that is willed by God, called for in the commandment, and reiterated in Jesus' words in the Sermon on the Mount is discovered, first, in the "heart" and, then, through an adequate way of being and acting.

2. The *ethos* of redemption contains the imperative of self-control, the necessity of immediate continence and habitual temperance in which the human heart remains bound to the value of the nuptial meaning of the body; self-mastery—not as a suspension in emptiness or based on suspicion of the heart or the anti-value perspective of Manicheism—allows the real possibilities and dispositions of our sexuality to emerge.

3. The *ethos* of the redemption of the body reveals that we are unique, above all, because of our "heart," which, when it responds to the call to purity, reminds us of original solitude from which we were liberated through love, through opening ourselves to the other human being.

Spiritual Reflections

The Pope's brief comments on the redemption of the body serve to tie together the loose ends of various previous reflections. We began with a certain skepticism about the possibility of our sexuality having the dimension of a feast. Although we have experienced, at certain times, the positive possibilities of our masculinity and femininity, we are also aware of the potential for self-destruction or destruction of another in our use of our sexuality. With mixed feelings as well as uncertainty about the real meaning of human sexuality, we listened to Jesus' words directing us to "the beginning"; we found, when we analyzed the creation story in the Book of Genesis, a divine plan for human sexuality. In that same story, however, we were reminded that we so often choose the things of this world rather than the things of God. This is especially true in the area of human sexuality because our strong sexual drive seems, at times, to control both our understanding of sexuality and our behavior.

Yet, reflection on our own experiences also makes us aware that we feel the "groans of the whole creation" while we "wait with eager longing" to "be set free from its bondage to decay and obtain the glorious liberty of the children of God." After all, we would have to admit that Americans are looking for ways to be sexy; some of us want to be sexy looking, and others are concerned about all areas of our sexuality. We all want a better body image even though we drink too much, eat too much, smoke too much, and exercise too little. We want to be affectionate people who are comfortable with our sexual potential and confident that we can pass on to our children a good appreciation of sex. We want intimacy in our marriages and self-fulfillment in our careers and parenthood. We want to be competent, organized women and caring, loving men. In short, we want an integrated sexual identity even when we continually fall short of obtaining this ideal.

It is with a certain sense of "eager longing," then, that we buy magazines and books that promise to tell us how to be successful in achieving sexual maturity. Some commentators believe that we are a "sex obsessed" culture; they point to the increase in pornography, especially the introduction of X-rated shows to the home via cable TV, as one further indication of our degradation in this area. But it is also possible to view the American preoccupation with sex as part of an attempt to understand the best way to respond to a powerful sexual drive. Even in those instances when we or others have used sexuality in a destructive way, we cannot deny the powerful force of sexual attraction, though we might well condemn the choice of behavior.

Those of us who call ourselves Christian—who understand the meaning of life that is offered to us by Jesus through his life, death, and resurrection and see him as the revelation of God's plan—are reminded by the challenge in the Sermon on the Mount that in the *ethos* of the redemption of the body we can, and must, again take up the *ethos* of creation. We *can* do this because Jesus has regained for us the glories of the children of God; we *must* do this—that is, we must understand our sexuality in light of the original divine plan—if we are to both appreciate the value of the "nuptial meaning of the body" and continue God's revelation in our own world.

Our reflections on our experience of human sexuality have forced us to admit that all is not right with our world—and, indeed, probably never has been right—in the area of human sexuality. Yet Jesus is calling upon us to allow the real possibilities of sexuality to emerge; this would be possible only if we would be willing to discern and judge in our hearts the real meaning of sexuality and then develop an adequate way of behaving and acting that is based on this understanding. When we are able to allow the vision of human sexuality that is uncovered in the creation story to speak to our hearts we will recognize how we "commit adultery in the heart;" only then will we know that we are called by Jesus to both accept the "redemption of the body" and live according to the divine plan.

The Pope reminds us that the *ethos* of redemption calls for a self-mastery that is based on neither disdain for nor mistrust of the body and sex, but one that seeks, rather, to allow the real possibilities of sexuality to emerge. Through the redemption of the body, we have obtained the glorious liberty of the children of God; we have been set free from the bondage to the three forms of lust and have been promised the grace of redemption. What is more, we are reminded that we have been liberated from our solitude by love, by an opening to another human being who is, like us, unique because of our "heart."

Although the vision of human sexuality that is found, first, in the creation story and then taken up again in the *ethos* of the redemption of the body does not identify one specific way of behaving in regard to each sexual situation that we encounter, we do seem called in this vision to a sexual maturity. At the same time, when we hear this call within the whole perspective of redemption, we can begin to hope in a way that might not seem possible if we rely solely on the wisdom of the secular world. Jesus has called us to sexual maturity and, at the same time, has promised us the grace to achieve this maturity. With this grace, the call becomes a call with efficacy and invites us to deepen our appreciation of the extraordinary dimensions of our sexuality, dimensions that require that we have a spirituality of sexuality—that is, that we reflect on, discern, and judge "in our hearts" our experience of sexuality in light of the vision of sexuality that we find in both the Scriptures and our tradition. Just as Adam and Eve were free to choose to follow either the plan of God or the plan of the world, we are free to accept or reject the grace of creation that is represented to us as the grace of redemption.

The fact that we, like all of creation, groan inwardly as we wait with eager longing for the glorious liberty of the children of God (for, in other words, the redemption of the body) is a challenge to the religious leadership of our church. The fact that people are looking for ways to be sexy, ways to achieve sexual maturity, ways to discover the possibilities of sexuality highlights the extraordinary dimension of sexuality—its possibility for an encounter with God and its potential as a religious experience. Such a powerful and persistent extraordinary experience seems to demand a religious vision if it is to achieve its positive potential. Jesus' call to goodness, which is a call to take up again the *ethos* of creation, is a call that should be continually echoed by the church, which understands its role as the continuation of his transforming presence to each generation. It is difficult to imagine continuing Jesus' call in our contemporary age with little or no reference to the experience of masculinity and femininity. And the church, which seeks to remind us of the wonderful gift of redemption, cannot ignore that this is a "redemption of the body."

Because organized religion has for so long been associated with a "rules" approach to sexuality, it will be difficult for both church leaders and the general faithful to change their expectations of the relationship between religion and sexuality. In the final analysis, a spirituality of sexuality will, however, have a more significant influence on ethical behavior than the previous "rules" approach had because it will assist individuals as they seek to fulfill the law so that divine justice will superabound. When individuals, working in conjunction with their religious community, reflect on their own experiences of sexuality and relate these to the community's understanding of the divine plan, *eros* and *ethos* meet in the human heart, and Jesus' gift of the redemption of the body becomes operative in our lives. Placing the stories of our own experiences of sexuality into the framework of God's plan for sexuality creates a situation that is quite different from the one we experienced when, with disdain for and distrust of the body and sex, we may have followed the rules but never developed an appreciation of the nuptial meaning of the body.

We conclude this part of our reflection filled with the hope that we *can* experience the redemption of the body in such a way that we will again take up the *ethos* of creation and live with a greater appreciation of the nuptial meaning of the body.

We turn now to the Pope's reflections on how we become people who have "purity of heart" rather than practice "adultery in the heart."

SIXTEEN

The Flesh and the Spirit

Blessed are the pure in heart, for they shall see God. —Matthew 5:8

Not what goes into the mouth defiles a man, but what comes out of the mouth, this defiles a man. —Matthew 15:11

What comes out of the mouth proceeds from the heart, and this defiles a man. For out of the heart come evil thoughts, murder, adultery, fornication, theft, false witness, slander. These are what defile a man; but to eat with unwashed hands does not defile a man. —Matthew 15:18-20

For you were called to freedom, brothers; only do not use your freedom as an opportunity for the flesh, but through love be servants of one another. For the whole law is fulfilled in one word, "You shall love your neighbor as yourself." —Galatians 5:13-14

But I say, walk by the Spirit, and do not gratify the desires of the flesh. For the desires of the flesh are against the Spirit, and the desires of the Spirit are against the flesh; for these are opposed to each other, to prevent you from doing what you would. —Galatians 5:16-17

Now the works of the flesh are plain: fornica-
tion, impurity, licentiousness, idolatry, sorcery,
enmity, strife, jealousy, anger, selfishness, dis-
sension, party spirit, envy, drunkenness, carous-
ing, and the like . . . But the fruit of the Spirit
is love, joy, peace, patience, kindness, goodness,
faithfulness, gentleness, and self-control . . .
—Galatians 5:19-23

Those who live according to the flesh set their
minds on the things of the flesh, but those who
live according to the Spirit set their minds on
the things of the Spirit. To set the mind on the
flesh is death, but to set the mind on the Spirit
is life and peace. For the mind that is set on the
flesh is hostile to God; it does not submit to
God's law, indeed it cannot; and those who are
in the flesh cannot please God. But you are not
in the flesh, you are in the Spirit, if in fact the
Spirit of God dwells in you. Anyone who does
not have the Spirit of Christ does not belong to
him. But if Christ is in you, although your
bodies are dead because of sin, your spirits are
alive because of righteousness. He who raised
Jesus Christ from the dead will give life to your
mortal bodies also through his Spirit which
dwells in you. So then, brothers, we are debtors,
not to the flesh, to live according to the flesh;
for if you live according to the flesh, you will
die; but if by the Spirit you put to death the
needs of the body, you will live.
—Romans 8:5-13

Summary of the Pope's Addresses

A generic meaning of purity is present in St. Paul's letters. It is to these letters that the Pope now turns, gradually examining those contexts in which the meaning of purity is explicitly limited to the "bodily" and "sexual" sphere ; this limitation is similar to the one that Jesus referred to when he spoke of "adultery in the heart" and also recalls the passage in the first letter of John that mentions the opposition between what comes "from the Father" and what comes "from the world." In both Galatians 5:16-17 and Romans 8:5, Paul speaks of another contradiction for the Christian, namely, the opposition and tension between the "flesh" and the "Spirit" (meaning the Holy Spirit). The Pope hopes to show that, in this process, the purity of heart that Jesus spoke of in the Sermon on the Mount is realized in life "according to the Spirit."

As we read Galatians 5:17, it appears that the Pauline terminology refers not only to the essentially different anthropological elements of body and spirit that form the essence of man, but also to the way in which "life according to the flesh" coincides with the three forms of lust. In this context, *flesh* refers to both the "exterior" man and the "interior" man who is subjected to the world and its values. The man who lives "according to the flesh" is the man of the "senses" searching only for what is "of the world."

This man of the three forms of lust lives at the opposite pole to what "the Spirit wants." The Spirit of God aspires to a reality that is different from what is desired by the flesh. The tension between the "flesh" and the "Spirit" is manifested in the heart as a "fight" between good and evil. So, the *desire* that is mentioned in the Sermon on the Mount, although it is an "interior" act, is, in Pauline language, a sign of life "according to the flesh." Our analysis of desire allows us to see that, within man, life "according to the flesh" is opposed to life "according to the Spirit"; in our present state of sinfulness, the "life according to the Spirit" is constantly exposed to the weakness of "life according to the flesh," a weakness to which it yields if it is not strengthened interiorly to do what "the Spirit wants." Paul's words are both a synthesis and a program and must be understood in this way.

The same opposition between life "according to the flesh" and life "according to the Spirit" is found in Paul's letter to the Romans wherein it is placed in the context of the doctrine of justification by faith, by the power of Jesus operating within man by means of the Holy Spirit. In Romans 8:5-10, Paul goes back to "the beginning," to the first sin from which life "according to the flesh" originated, the sin that is the cause of our previous, inherited position to live such a life with its legacy of death. Then, Paul goes on to anticipate the final victory over sin and death in Romans 8:11, in which eschatological perspective he stresses the justification in Jesus that is already intended for "historical man." This justification is essential for interior man and destined for that "heart" to which Jesus appealed in the Sermon on the Mount. This justification is a real power that operates in man and is revealed and asserts itself in our activities.

As Galatians 5:19-23 clearly shows, life "according to the flesh" is opposed to life "according to the Spirit" in man's "heart," but it also expresses itself in works. Works spring from the "flesh" and manifest the man who lives "according to the flesh." But the "fruit of the Spirit" is action, that is, the ways of behaving, the virtues that manifest the man who lives "according to the Spirit." The man who lives "according to the flesh" is a man who has been abandoned to the three forms of lust, and the man who lives "according to the Spirit" is the man who lives according to the *ethos* of redemption, which is expressed and affirmed through what, in man, is the fruit of his dominion over the three forms of lust—lust of the flesh, lust of the eyes, and lust of the pride of life.

Mastery in the sphere of *ethos* is both manifested and realized by the fruit of the Spirit described in Galatians. Behind each of these ways of behaving there is a specific choice; the fruit of the human spirit which is permeated by the Spirit of God is revealed in choosing good. As Paul says, in the struggle between the desires of "the spirit" and "the flesh," man proves himself stronger thanks to the power of the Holy Spirit that is operating within man's spirit and causing his desires to bear fruit and good. These good activities are not so much "works" of man as they are the "fruit" of the "Spirit" in man, that is, the effect of the action of the Spirit in man. In Galatians, the opposition and distinction of "the flesh" and "the Spirit" focuses on not only those sins that are of a carnal nature, but also those that we would not consider carnal and sensual. We would be inclined to call the following sins—"idolatry, sorcery, enmity, jealousy, strife, anger, selfishness, dissension, party spirit, and envy"—sins of the spirit of man rather than sins of the flesh. They seem more related to "lust of the eyes" or "pride of life" rather than "lust of the flesh"; these sins show us the wider meaning of the term "flesh" in the Pauline letters, a meaning in which it is opposed not only to the human "spirit," but also to the Holy Spirit who works in man's soul (spirit).

In this way, we see how the "works of the flesh" are analogous to the understanding that we have developed from Jesus' words regarding real purity, which comes "from the heart" of man (Mt 15:2-20). In both instances, all sins are an expression of life "according to the flesh," which is opposed to life "according to the Spirit." What we consider a "sin of the flesh" is but one of the many manifestations of what Paul calls "works of the flesh."

Again, in Romans 8:12-13, Paul refers to the different meanings that the words "body" and "Spirit" convey to him. His words have an advisory and exhortative meaning that is valid for the evangelical *ethos*, in which he express precisely what Jesus spoke about in Matthew 5:27-28. The mastery that Paul urges—"putting to death the works of the body with the help of the Spirit"—is indispensable for life "according to the Spirit," which is, in other words, a life that is the antithesis of death. Life "according to the flesh" has, as its effect, a "death" of the Spirit. In this context, *death* means not only physical death of the body, but also sin. In Romans and Galatians, Paul widens the perspective of "sin-death" by pointing back to "the beginning" of man's history and forward toward its end, and by affirming that "those who do such things shall not inherit the kingdom of God" (Gal 5:21).

Paul completes the picture of the opposition between the "body" and the "fruit of the Spirit" by showing that everything that is a manifestation of life and behavior according to the Spirit is also the manifestation of that freedom for which "Christ has set us free" (Gal 5:1). As he writes in Galatians 5:13-14, man's justification is carried out in and through Jesus; we are justified in "faith" working through "love" (Gal 5:6), not only by means of observance of Old Testament law. Justification comes "from the Spirit" (of God) and not "from the flesh." Consequently, Paul exhorts those to whom he is writing to free themselves of the false, "carnal" concept of justification so that they might follow the true, "spiritual" concept of justification. They are free according to the freedom with which Jesus "has set free."

Although it might seem that in Galatians 5:13-14 Paul is merely contrasting "freedom" with the "law," a deeper analysis shows that he is emphasizing the ethical subordination of freedom to that love in which the whole law is fulfilled. We are set free by Jesus in the sense that he revealed to us the ethical subordination of freedom to charity, linking freedom with the commandment of love. Understanding freedom in this way leads to an understanding of *ethos* in which life "according to the Spirit" is realized.

It is possible, however, to misunderstand and misuse our freedom. Paul makes us aware of this possibility, which is in opposition to the liberation of the human spirit that has been carried out by Jesus; the misuse of freedom takes place when freedom becomes a pretext to live according to the flesh, for freedom is, then, the source of "works" and is of "life according to the flesh." One who lives according to the flesh submits, even when he is not quite conscious of it, to the three forms of lust, particularly to the lust of the flesh, and ceases to be capable of that freedom by which "Christ has set us free." At the same time, this person ceases to appreciate the real gift of himself, which is the fruit and expression of this freedom. He no longer appreciates the "nuptial meaning of the body."

Thus, the Pauline doctrine of purity, which echoes the Sermon on the Mount, shows "purity of heart" in a wider perspective and permits us to link it with the charity in which the "law is fulfilled." Paul knows both the generic and the specific meaning of purity (and impurity). The "works of the flesh" are all those things that are morally bad, whereas life "according to the Spirit" is linked with every moral good. One of the manifestations of life "according to the Spirit" is behavior and conformity with the more specific meaning of purity that Paul discusses in the First Letter to the Thessalonians.

In the passages of the Letter to the Galatians that we have analyzed, included among the "works of the flesh" are fornication, impurity, and licentiousness. When Paul contrasts these with the "fruit of the Spirit," however, he names only self-control and does not speak directly of "purity." This "control" is a virtue that concerns continence in the area of all the desires of the senses, especially in the sexual sphere. It is, consequently, in opposition to "fornication, impurity, and licentiousness" as well as "drunkenness" and "carousing." Pauline "self-control" refers to continence or temperance; but, in these passages, he is not speaking of purity as the correct way of treating the sexual sphere according to one's personal state (that is, he is not necessarily urging abstention from sexual life), although this concept of purity is undoubtedly included in the Pauline notion of "self-control." But, as our further analysis of the First Letter to the Thessalonians will indicate, Paul is more explicit about how the specific meaning of purity fits into its generic sense.

The following are the main points for a theology and a spirituality of sexuality and the body that the Pope developed in his four audience addresses on the flesh and the Spirit.

1. St. Paul finds a contradiction for the Christian in the opposition and tension between the "flesh" and the "Spirit" that is similar to the opposition found in the First Letter of John in which lust is a choice for that which comes "from the world" and is opposed to that which comes "from the Father," and demonstrates once again that "purity of heart" has both a general and a specific sense; the man who lives "according to the flesh" is the man "of the world," of the "three forms of lust," who is almost at the opposite pole of the reality desired by the Spirit of God.

2. Both in the Letter to the Romans and in the Letter to the Galatians, the opposition between the "flesh" and the "Spirit" is placed in the context of the Pauline doctrine of justification by faith, that is, by means of the power of Jesus operating within man through the Holy Spirit; this justification is a real power that operates in man revealing and asserting itself in his actions so that in the struggle between good and evil the power of the Holy Spirit causes man's desire to bear "fruit" in *good* rather than in the "works" of the man who lives according to the flesh."

3. According to Paul, the "works of the flesh" are not only "carnal sins"—that is, sins of the "body"—but also what we might call "sins of the spirit"; Paul, thus, gives the term "flesh" the wider meaning of that which is opposed to the Holy Spirit who works in man's soul (spirit), and indicates that all sins are an expression of "life according to the flesh."

4. Romans 8:12-13 reiterates Jesus' appeal to the human heart when it indicates that "putting to death the works of the body with the help of the Spirit" is an indispensable condition of "life according to the Spirit," of that "life"

which is the antithesis of life that has "death"—the death of the Spirit—as its fruit; because everything that is a manifestation of life and behavior according to the Spirit is also a manifestation of the freedom for which Jesus has "set us free," we are to free ourself from the erroneous "carnal" concept of justification and follow the true "spiritual" one.

5. The *ethos* of the Gospel is a call to the fuller implementation of human freedom and to a fuller utilization of the potential of the human spirit when this freedom has been subordinated to charity and linked with the commandment of love; it is possible to misuse freedom, that is, to use it as a pretext to live "according to the flesh," thereby causing us to be incapable of the freedom for which Jesus has "set us free" and making it impossible for us to appreciate the gift of the nuptial meaning of the body.

6. The Pauline concept of self-control undoubtedly includes the correct way of treating the sexual sphere according to one's personal state, but it is still more generic in that it considers everything that is morally good as pure and everything that is morally bad as impure; according to Paul, the "works of the flesh" are linked with what is morally bad and life "according to the Spirit" is linked with every moral good.

Spiritual Reflections

Jesus emphasizes that moral purity is more than ritual purity and reminds us once again that we will not come to appreciate the positive dimensions of our sexuality simply by following prescribed rituals or rules. In addition, Jesus' words highlight the fact that a spirituality of sexuality is one aspect of a broader spirituality that has been made possible for us by the redemption he has gained for us.

We ended our previous reflection aware of the appeal of Jesus' words in Matthew 5:27-28 and buoyed up by the promise of the redemption of the body, but still uncertain of our own ability to respond to Jesus' call. Reflection on our own experiences continually reminds us of the fact that we do commit "adultery in the heart." Perhaps we refuse to celebrate the erotic in our sexual intimacy because, for example, our own negative body image has led us to believe that our bodies are unattractive and that the erotic, because it is so closely connected with our body, cannot possibly lead us to God. Or, as women, we have found that adhering to stereotypes for women's behavior gives us an advantage in manipulating the men we encounter so that we can achieve certain goals without having to risk developing our own personal identity. Or we not only fail to educate our children in the "facts of life," but also fail to realize how our own attitudes toward our bodies, toward male-female roles, and toward giving affection in our marital relationship contribute toward our children's developing sexual identity. Or we are the businessman away from home, somewhat lonely, who goes out searching for an available prostitute. Or we are the bored suburban housewife who decides to have an affair to get even with our husband for some real or imagined neglect that he has inflicted on us. The list of the ways in which we commit adultery in the heart goes on and on, leading us to wonder how this "redemption of the body" will possibly help us to gain an integrated sexual identity, to be the sexually mature adult who experiences joy and spontaneity in our relationships with others.

As we consider the Pope's analysis of both Jesus' words on moral purity and St. Paul's reflections on life according to either the flesh or the Spirit, and consider as well the fact that we have been "set free" to live this life "according to the Spirit," we begin to appreciate the link between the *ethos* of sexuality and the *ethos* of redemption as they are applied to all areas of our lives. We see not only that a spirituality of sexuality fits within the broader spirituality required of all Christians, but also that it is an essential component of such a spirituality. We see that the good Christian life can be lived only by someone who has gained an appreciation of the nuptial meaning of the body. And, at the same time, we realize that this appreciation of the nuptial meaning of the body develops out of a response to live as followers of Jesus.

It seems appropriate, therefore, as we wonder how we might respond to Jesus' call for spontaneity in our sexuality, that we stop and reflect on how it might even be possible for us to live lives that somehow continue the transforming presence of Jesus in our midst—not only in the area of our sexuality, but in all areas of our lives.

When we who call ourselves Christians are asked what we believe, we would most probably include the various parts of a creedal statement in some form or another. We would affirm belief in a Creator God who redeemed fallen humankind through an Incarnate Son who continually graces us with the presence of the Holy Spirit. Although we might not use doctrinal language, we probably would also speak of the risen Lord, of our own hope for the resurrection of the body and immortality, and of how we understand the community of believers, the church, to be the continuing presence of God in the world. These are the components of the creed that we affirm when we join in liturgical functions with our fellow Christians.

How we interpret the meaning of these doctrines for our experience of life tells us something about our own spirituality. The way in which we might tell someone about what our beliefs mean to us during a particular crisis situation, or a time of great joy, indicates the way in which we begin to translate creedal statements into an understanding of the mysteries of life, how we begin to interpret the meaning of the extraordinary experiences of life, how we are able to uncover the presence of the extraordinary things that often seem merely ordinary to a nonbeliever. The way in which this process of applying doctrines and creeds to experiences of mystery in our life takes place points toward a way in which we might develop a more conscious spirituality.

A recent study of young adult Catholics indicates the importance of the religious imagination to a linking of life and faith.[1] We are, it appears, better able to fit our experiences of life into the framework of our Christian faith when our imagination has been captured by the symbols and stories of our faith rather than when we rely solely on an intellectual understanding of doctrines and creeds. Although it is important that we who are rational creatures appreciate a rational component to our faith, it is equally important that our imagination be aware of experiences of grace in our lives and interact with the creed and doctrines of our faith through the medium of symbols, images, and stories. When Jesus addresses our hearts, he is speaking to that religious-imagination dimension of our intellect and urging us to link, through reflection, our experiences of sexuality with the divine plan that can best be understood not by following rules, but by rereading the story of "the beginning." As we read the excerpts from Paul's Letters to the Galatians and to the Romans, we begin to see how a spirituality that aims at a death to "life according to the flesh" can allow the Holy Spirit to work through our spirit and manifest what we have been set free to do. We are familiar with the "works of the flesh," with the many ways in which we choose the "things of the world" rather than the "things of the Father," not only in matters related to sexuality, but in all areas of life. Although many of us grew up with the notion that sins related to sexuality (especially sins of the body) were the worst sins we would ever commit, we see, as we read over Paul's list of the works of the flesh, that there are many ways in which we fail to choose the "things of the Father." Although we are capable of choosing "the Father" rather than "the world," reflection on our own experiences makes us consciously aware of how seldom we actually do choose "the Father" rather than "the world." St. Paul is telling us that the times during which we experience the "fruit of the Spirit" are those times during which we have allowed the grace of redemption to permeate our own spirit, those times during which we have allowed the Holy Spirit to operate in our lives and manifest through us the possibilities for human existence. These are the times during which the grace of redemption recaptures for us the grace of creation and moves us away from the three forms of lust that influence all areas of our behavior.

The Christian, then, seems to be called by St. Paul to a spiritual maturity in which we allow the Holy Spirit to influence our spirit in such a way that, with the freedom of choice Jesus has regained for us, we will choose the things of the Father and live a life that bears the fruit of the Spirit.

We who believe in a "justification by faith" are able to appreciate that all sins are an expression of "life according to the flesh." St. Paul calls upon us in Romans to put to death this "life according to the flesh," to give up all those things that we do because of lust in its three forms, because we choose to go the "way of the world." An important part of this process of putting to death the "life according to the flesh" is coming to know "in our hearts" what we personally do with the freedom that Jesus has won for us. Reflection in some form seems to be a mandatory part of the process of developing a spirituality, of putting to death the three forms of lust, the things of the world, and the life according to the flesh. A reflective spirituality increases the possibilities for the Holy Spirit to influence our spirit so that the fruit of the Spirit will enrich our lives and also be manifested more readily to those who encounter us. Because the Christian is called to continue the work of Jesus in our particular time and place, St. Paul's words seem to call upon us to develop a spirituality that will assist us in the process of putting to death the "life according to the flesh" and help us learn to use the freedom that is ours in the service of love rather than in the choice of the "flesh."

Because this particular series of the Pope's reflections begins with Jesus' denial of the value of ritual purity and his emphasis that "life according to the flesh" refers to all the sins we commit, it refutes the arguments of those who equate "flesh" with the body and sex and treat Paul's words about the "flesh" as a reference to the sins of the body. At the same time, these words speak to the task that we have been pursuing in all our spiritual reflections when we emphasize the importance of spiritual maturity—the necessity of being continually aware of the choice between "the flesh" and "the Spirit." When we reflect on how, in the past, we have related our faith to our experiences, we become aware that a variety of different approaches have led up to those times when we have manifested the fruit of the Spirit. Studies of religious imagination have shown that the stories of God that we were told as children have a powerful influence in our lives. Some of us might look back on our own devotional practices and realize that, even though there was always a danger that these devotions could take on a "magical" quality, there were times during which our devotions not only enriched our appreciation for a particular experience in our lives, but also helped us both open our own spirits to the influence of the Holy Spirit and positively use our freedom in order to reveal the fruit of the Spirit. Some of us may have used very rudimentary forms of spirituality in the past, and others may have had a more sophisticated approach to the spiritual life. Nevertheless, St. Paul is urging all of us to use the freedom that Jesus has given us to allow the Spirit to permeate our lives. When we open our imaginations to the possibility of the Spirit, we begin to uncover ways in which the depth of meaning that is contained in our creedal statement is manifested by people who live lives that bear the fruit of the Spirit.

Life according to the Spirit is a requirement for Christian living. The innumerable experiences of mystery in our lives will become true religious experiences for us when the Holy Spirit lives through us and bears fruit in all areas of our lives. Although our major concern in this book is with a spirituality of sexuality, we must appreciate the need to die to "the things of the flesh" in other aspects of our life as well. To appreciate how life according to the Spirit might help us acquire that purity of heart which is the opposite of adultery in the heart, however, we must turn to the Pope's analysis of other Pauline material.

SEVENTEEN
Purity and Life
According to the Spirit

*This is the will of God, your sanctification:
that you abstain from unchastity; that each of
you know how to control his own body in holiness and honor, not in the passion of lust like
the heathens who do not know God . . . God
has not called us for uncleanliness, but in holiness. Therefore, whoever disregards this, disregards not man, but God, who gives his Holy
Spirit to you.* —1 Thessalonians 4:3-5, 7-8

*God arranged the organs in the body, each one
of them, as he chose . . . On the contrary, the
parts of the body which seem to be weaker are
indispensable, and those parts of the body
which we think less honorable we invest with
the greatest honor, and our unpresentable
parts are treated with greater modesty, which
our more presentable parts do not require. But
God has so composed the body, giving the
greater honor to the inferior part, that there
may be no discord in the body, but that the
members may have the same care for one
another.* —1 Corinthians 12:18, 22-25

*The body is not meant for immorality, but for
the Lord, and the Lord for the body . . . Do
you not know that your bodies are members of
Christ? Shall I therefore take the members of
Christ and make them members of a prosti-*

tute? Never! Do you not know that he who joins himself to a prostitute becomes one body with her? For, as it is written, "The two shall become one flesh." But he who is united to the Lord becomes one spirit with him. Shun immorality. Every other sin which man commits is outside the body; but the immoral man sins against his own body. Do you not know your body is a temple of the Holy Spirit within you, which you have from God? You are not your own; you were bought with a price.

—1 Corinthians 6:13b,15-20a

Summary of the Pope's Addresses

As we continue our reflections on the complexity of the concept of purity, we find that the purity of which Paul speaks in the First Letter to the Thessalonians shows itself through man's knowledge of how to "control his own body in holiness and honor, not the passion of lust." Purity, in this context, is a capacity, an aptitude, a virtue that can lead one to abstain "from unchastity" because he who possesses it "knows how to control his own body in holiness and honor, not in the passion of lust." Purity is a practical capacity that allows man to act in a given way while, at the same time, he does not act in the opposite way; purity is a capacity that is rooted in the will mastering desire so that it is capable of acting in conformity with virtue. Thus, purity is a different form of the virtue of temperance.

In the First Letter to the Thessalonians, Paul not only emphasizes the overcoming of the passion of lust, but also turns our attention to the more positive dimension of the virtue of purity—that of controlling one's own body, and, indirectly, the bodies of others, in "holiness and honor." "Abstention" and "control" are closely linked and also dependent on each other; we cannot "control" if "abstention" is lacking. "Control," it seems, confers adequate meaning and value on "abstention," calling for the overcoming of that which not only spontaneously arises in man as an inclination, an attraction, and a value above all in the sphere of the senses, but also has particular repercussions in the affective-emotional dimension of human subjectivity.

Paul considers purity not only a capacity of man's subjective faculties, but also a concrete manifestation of "life according to the Spirit" in which human capacity is interiorly enriched by the "fruit of the Spirit." The honor that arises in man is seen by Paul as a power of the spiritual order and is the most essential power for man's control of his body "in holiness." In this way, purity is a capacity of acting that relates to the multiple impulses "of the passion of lust," to which man sometimes surrenders.

In order to better appreciate the First Letter to the Thessalonians, the Pope turns to Paul's reflections on the church as the Body of Christ in 1 Corinthians, chapter 12, in which, by means of ecclesiological analogy, Paul also contributes depth to the theology of the body. He shows the human body to be worthy of the "honor" that is mentioned in 1 Thessalonians and also teaches those who have received his letter the correct concept of the human body. The thread between these two letters is perhaps the essential link of the Pauline doctrine of purity.

Paul's description of the body is a "realistic" description that contains a fine thread of evaluation and confers a deeply evangelical Christian value on the body. Although it is possible to describe the human body with the objectivity of the natural sciences, such a description is not adequate because it does not describe man who expresses himself *through* the body and *is* the body. But Paul's thread of evaluation considers that the idea of man as a person is indispensable in describing the human body, even though this description does not have a "scientific" meaning, but is simply a prescientific description that would not be possible without the whole truth of both creation and the "redemption of the body" that Paul professes and proclaims. This description is contrary to both the Manichean contempt for the body and the various naturalistic cults of the body.

Paul is considering the human body to be permeated, in all its truth, by the whole reality of the person and his dignity; at the same time, however, this is the body of "historical" man—male and female—who, after sin, is still influenced by the attraction of original innocence. Paul's comments about the "unpresentable parts" and those that "seem to be weaker" point to the same shame that the male and female experienced after original sin, the shame that remains imprinted on "historical" man as the fruit of the three forms of lust. This shame, as we have seen, also contains an "echo" of man's original innocence, a "negative" of the image whose "positive" had been original innocence.

Thus, we see that the "unpresentable parts" are not this way because of their own "somatic" nature, but because there exists in man a shame that perceives some parts of the body as "unpresentable" and considers them this way. The shame that is mentioned in 1 Corinthians 12:23 leads to "respect" for one's own body, the respect that we are urged to keep in the First Letter to the Thessalonians that will control our bodies "in holiness and honor."

Paul's description of the body in the First Letter to the Corinthians corresponds to the Creator's original plan when "God saw everything that he had made, and behold it was very good" (Gn 1:31). The discord in the body, which Paul mentions, is an expression of the vision of man's interior state after original sin. The man and woman of Genesis 2:25 did not feel such a discord. The harmony with which the Creator endowed the body, and to which Paul refers as "mutual care of the members for one another," is a corresponding harmony within "the heart" that is the "purity of heart" which allowed man and woman, "in the beginning," to unite as a communion of persons.

Just as Paul links his description of the human body with the state of "historical" man, he also indicates the way that; on the basis of shame, leads to the transformation of this state to both a victory in man's heart over that "discord of the body," and a purity in which we "control our own bodies in holiness and honor." Connecting the First Letter to the Corinthians with the "honor" of the First Letter to the Thessalonians by using some of the equivalent expressions—esteem for the "less honorable," for example, and "weaker" parts of the body, and the recommendations for "greater modesty" regarding the "unpresentable"—Paul more precisely describes how "honor" in the sphere of human relations and behavior of the body is important not only for one's own "body," but also in mutual relations (between man and woman, although not limited to them). It seems then, that the "description of the human body" in the First Letter to the Corinthians has fundamental meaning for the Pauline doctrine of purity.

Although the First Letter to the Thessalonians emphasizes that purity consists of temperance, the First Letter to the Corinthians highlights the element of respect that is due to the human body. Together, these two letters reveal that practicing purity as a Christian value is an effective way to become detached from the fruit of the lust of the flesh in the human heart. In this context, purity is a capacity that is centered on the dignity of the human body, that is, on the dignity of the person in relation to his own body—to the femininity or masculinity that is manifested in this body; purity also is the expression and fruit of life "according to the Spirit" becoming a new capacity of the human being in which the gift of the Holy Spirit bears fruit. For Paul, there are two dimensions of purity: (1) the moral dimension of virtue and (2) the charismatic dimension of the gift of the Holy Spirit.

In 1 Corinthians 6, Paul speaks of sins that are in opposition to the virtue by force of which man keeps "his body in holiness and honor." These sins bring profanation of the body because they deprive it of the honor that is due to it according to the dignity of the person. Such sins are also a profanation of the temple because the dignity of the body is decided not only by the human spirit, but, even more so, by the supernatural reality that is constituted by the indwelling of the Holy Spirit in man as fruit of the redemption by Jesus. From this it follows that man's body is no longer just "his own," but has an additional source of dignity in the Holy Spirit, who is also the source of the moral duty that derives from this dignity.

Through the redemption, Jesus has imprinted on the body of every man and every woman a new dignity because, through him, the human body had been admitted, along with its soul, to a union with the Person of the Son and the Word. With this new dignity, there has arisen a new obligation because we "were bought with a price." The fruit of the redemption is the Holy Spirit who dwells in man and in his body as in a temple, thereby sanctifying every man and allowing the Christian to receive himself again as a gift from God—a double gift that is binding because "the body is not meant for immorality, but for the Lord, and the Lord for the body." Because every man has received a new supernatural elevation through the Incarnation, the Christian must take this into account with regard to the behavior of his "own body" and with regard to other's bodies.

In the First Letter to the Corinthians, chapter 6, Paul specifies the truth about the holiness of the body by identifying "unchastity" as the sin against the holiness of the body—the sin of impurity. Purity is, in Paul's teaching, an aspect of life "according to the Spirit"; this means that the mystery of the redemption of the body is part of the mystery of Jesus that was started in the Incarnation and bears fruit in purity, which is understood as a commitment that is based on ethics. Awareness of the redemption of the body leads the human will toward abstention from "unchastity," thereby causing man to acquire the virtue of purity.

In addition, the Pauline text indicates that the mystery of redemption bears fruit in man in a charismatic way. The Holy Spirit enters the human body as his "own temple," dwells there, and operates there through his spiritual gifts. Among these gifts, which have been known in the history of spirituality as the seven gifts of the Holy Spirit, the one most congenial to the virtue of purity seems to be the gift of "piety." Purity prepares man to "control" his own body "in holiness and honor"; piety, as a gift of the Holy Spirit, serves purity in a particular way by making humans sensitive to that dignity which is characteristic of the human body because of the mystery of creation and redemption. Through the gift of piety, Paul's words, "Do you not know that your body is the temple of the Holy Spirit within you? . . . You are not your own," describe an experience of both the nuptial meaning of the body and the freedom of the gift that is connected with it and in which purity and its organic link with love is revealed.

Although control of one's body is acquired through abstention, it always bears fruit in a deeper experience of the love that is inscribed from "the beginning" in the whole human being—including his body, which is made "in the image of God." Paul therefore exhorts his listeners "to glorify God in your body." Purity as a virtue, together with the gift of piety as the fruit of the indwelling of the Holy Spirit, brings about in the body the fullness of dignity and interpersonal relations that glorifies God. Purity is the glory of the human body for God—God's glory in the human body through which masculinity and femininity are manifested.

The connection of purity with love, and of purity and love with the gift of piety, is a part of the theology of the body that is little known but nevertheless deserves particular study. There is a continuity between the Pauline doctrine of purity and the notion of purity found in the Wisdom books of the Old Testament in which purity is seen as a condition for finding Wisdom and following it (Sir 23:4-6, Sir 51:1-20). In another text, however, purity is not so much a condition for wisdom, but wisdom is a condition for purity as for a special gift of God (Wi 8:21). Even here, the double meaning of purity as both virtue and gift—the virtue as in service of wisdom, and wisdom as a preparation to receive the gift that comes from God—is present. The gift strengthens the virtue and makes is possible to enjoy in wisdom the fruits of the life that is pure.

For Jesus, those who are "pure in heart" will have the "sight of God," which is the fruit of purity from an eschatological perspective. Paul, from his perspective, speaks of the dimensions of temporality when he writes: "To the pure all things are pure, but to the corrupt and unbelieving nothing is pure; their very minds and consciences are corrupted. They profess to know God, but they deny him by their deeds . . ." (Tit 1:15f). In this use of purity, Paul refers to both the general and specific meanings that have been discussed earlier, demanding a rebirth in the Holy Spirit. Paul's concept of purity is deeply rooted in the reality of the redemption of the body that has been carried out by Jesus. The understanding of purity as virtue and gift that had been inherited from the tradition of the Old Testament undoubtedly helped many listeners understand Jesus' interpretation of the commandment, "You shall not commit adultery," and also served, in an indirect way, to prepare for the Pauline doctrine of purity as life "according to the Spirit." The Pope concludes these reflections by noting how rich and profound the doctrine on purity is in the biblical sources.

The following are the main points for a theology and a spirituality of sexuality and the body that the Pope developed in his four addresses on purity and life according to the spirit.

1. In the First Letter to the Thessalonians, chapter 4, purity as a capacity, an aptitude or virtue, makes us capable of acting in a given way and, at the same time, not acting in the opposite way, thereby having two functions—"abstention" and "control"—that are closely connected and dependent on

each other. We cannot control our bodies in holiness and honor without abstaining from unchastity; at the same time, controlling our bodies in holiness and honor confers value on this abstention.

2. In the First Letter to the Thessalonians, Paul writes about controlling our bodies in holiness and honor, but his theology of the church as the Body of Christ in the First Letter to the Corinthians shows the human body as worthy of honor and teaches us the correct concept of the human body; this link between the two letters is important, perhaps essential, for understanding Paul's doctrine on purity.

3. As Paul's description of the body in the First Letter to the Corinthians, chapter 12, indicates, we who express ourselves through our bodies *are* those bodies, a description that is possible in light of the truth of both creation and the "redemption of the body" that Paul professes and proclaims, which makes his doctrine different from Manichean contempt for the body and naturalistic cults of the body; Paul has in mind the possibilities of the human body, but he recognizes that the shame we, who are "historical" people, experience over our bodies is an echo of man's original innocence, a "negative" of the image whose "positive" had been original innocence.

4. The "unpresentable parts" of our bodies are so not because of their nature, but rather because we have a shame that perceives them as "unpresentable," causes them to be considered that way, and also causes "respect" for our bodies to spring from our shame; the way in which we are to transform the "discord in the body" is the way of purity, of "control of one's own body in holiness and honor"—especially in human relations and behavior with regard to our "own" body and in mutual relations, especially relations between man and woman, but not limited to them.

5. The two dimensions of purity—the moral dimension of virtue and the charismatic dimension of the gift of the Holy Spirit—are closely connected in the Pauline letters, especially in the First Letter to the Corinthians with its reference to the body as a "temple (a dwelling and shrine) of the Holy Spirit"; sins against the virtue of purity are a profana-

tion of the body that deprive our bodies of the honor that is due to them because of the dignity of the person, and also a profanation of the temple because the dignity of the human person is decided even more by the dwelling and continual presence of the Holy Spirit in our soul and in our body as a fruit of redemption.

6. Through the redemption Jesus has imprinted on our body a new dignity that carries with it a new obligation because we have been "bought with a price"; the fruit of redemption is the Holy Spirit who dwells in us and in our bodies, as in a temple, sanctifying each of us, giving us again the gift from God that is binding in its call to our human will to abstain from "unchastity" so that we might acquire the virtue of purity.

7. The gift of the Spirit that serves purity in a particular way is piety, which (1) makes us sensitive to the dignity that is characteristic of the human body as a result of creation and redemption, (2) leads us to appreciate the nuptial meaning of the body and the organic link between purity and love, and (3) brings about in the body such a fullness of dignity in interpersonal relations that God is glorified; purity is God's glory in the human body through which masculinity and femininity are manifested.

8. The idea of purity as both virtue and gift is found in the Old Testament Wisdom books, Jesus' references to the pure in heart, and the Pauline doctrine of purity; the Pauline concept of purity is rooted in the reality of the redemption of the body carried out by Jesus and links Paul's doctrine to the question of how to respond to Jesus' calls in the Sermon on the Mount.

Spiritual Reflections

The Pope's lengthy analysis of St. Paul's treatment of purity as both a virtue and a gift reveals for us how purity is applied to the more specific aspect of sexuality, and also shows how a Christian spirituality of sexuality helps us lead a life that is a manifestation of the fruit of the Spirit. In our previous reflections, we were reminded that we needed to examine our "hearts" if we wanted to respond to the gift of the redemption of the body that has been offered by Jesus and specifically offered as a redemption of our sexuality in the Sermon on the Mount. We know that Jesus calls us to a purity of heart that we acquire when we live a life according to the Spirit rather than a life according to the flesh. And now these reflections on the Letter to the Thessalonians and the Letter to the Corinthians challenge the listeners—challenge us—to die to "adultery in the heart" and live a "life according to the spirit" that will enable us to appreciate the nuptial meaning of the body.

We are, as St. Paul makes clear, justified by faith in the redemption of our body. We have been set free by Jesus to choose to rediscover God's original plan for human sexuality and, in this freedom—always subject to love—we can again take up the *ethos* of creation and experience our sexuality as a sign of eternal love, in other words, as a way in which to be a lover as God is a Lover. But we, too, like Adam and Eve, are free to choose a "life according to the flesh" and "to look lustfully," "to commit adultery in the heart."

Paul, in his advice to the Thessalonians and the Corinthians, directs us towards the cultivation of a specific purity that is both a capacity that we must acquire and a gift of the Holy Spirit that helps us appreciate the link between purity and love. The virtue of purity, which we must cultivate, calls for abstention and control, for the self-mastery we have considered in previous reflections. The gift of the Spirit, piety, makes us sensitive to the dignity of the body and helps us realize the fruit of the Spirit in our interpersonal relationships.

Unfortunately, purity as abstention and control has conjured up for many of us visions of brides in virginal white who have not "gone all the way"; impurity has for so long had to do with "dirty thoughts" and "going all the way." And we could not imagine a situation in which the conjugal union between a husband and wife would be impure. Yet, we must keep in mind that impurity in relation to our sexuality means the same as "looking lustfully," or "committing adultery in the heart." We are to keep our bodies in holiness and honor because we *are* our bodies, and our bodies are "temples of the Holy Spirit." Although this admonition is undoubtedly a stricture against physical promiscuity, in the context of the *ethos* of the redemption we are able to see it as more than advice to avoid bodily sexual sins.

St. Paul is reminding us that, despite the heritage of the three forms of lust, we who have been redeemed by Jesus can freely choose to respond to this gift (grace) of redemption and recognize in our sexuality the possibility of being "in the image of God." We do not have to feel, like Dolores in *The Bleeding Heart,* that our bodies will betray us. We do not have to remain subject to an unruly sexual drive that is self-destructive and ignores the dignity of others. We who have been redeemed by Jesus are exhorted by St. Paul to realize the positive potential of our sexuality by remembering that we (our bodies) are temples of the Holy Spirit and, consequently, we can once again take up the grace of creation and hold our bodies in holiness and honor. St. Paul also reminds us that our new dignity, which we have acquired through the redemption of the body, confers upon us the obligation to be open to the fruit of redemption, to the indwelling of the Holy Spirit, because this new dignity has been bought for "a price." It is a gift that has been graciously given by God but nevertheless requires a response from us.

As we have already observed, the problem most of us have with our sexuality is our inability to be spontaneous, to have an integrated sexual identity. We might, as we have observed, be "abstaining from the things of the world" in certain areas of our sexually related behavior, but most of us do not seem to be able to live according to the plan of God in all the areas that are affected by our sexuality. Personal reflection on our behavior leads us to an understanding of our own particular shortcomings as well as our strengths, and helps us identify what we must do if we are to die to "life according to the flesh" and appreciate the depth of the nuptial meaning of the body. We are challenged by St. Paul, as we have been challenged by Jesus, to transform our personal experience of sexuality so that we might participate in the sexual feast that has been planned by God. In addition, we are challenged to reveal the possibility of this sexual feast to others who, with us, live at this time and in this place. We have seen that we and our society are "groaning inwardly" as we confront the seemingly insurmountable problems that have been caused by the fact that humans come in male and female variety. At the same time, however, our reflections also make us aware of the wonderful possibilities of human sexuality. Armed with the realization that the redemption of the body has been achieved for us "at a price," we feel called to begin this transformation process.

We turn again, therefore, to a consideration of the various areas of our lives that are affected by our sexuality and consider how the "life according to the flesh" in each area might be transformed into a "life according to the Spirit." We begin to identify what change "in our hearts" we must initiate if God's plan is to be revealed in each area. And we see how our religious imagination can be touched by the symbols, images, and stories of our religious tradition in such a way as to inspire us to make the necessary changes.

We had identified seven areas of our lives that are affected by our sexuality. Let us now briefly consider how each of these might undergo a transformation so that we might reveal God in our masculinity and femininity.

1 Bodily self-image. As the Pope indicated in his analyses of the Sermon on the Mount and the Pauline teaching on purity, the Christian, in approaching bodily self-image, can be neither a Manichean nor a subscriber to a naturalistic cult that sees only the biological nature of the body. As Christians, we are called upon to appreciate our bodies, to recognize that our shame regarding our bodies, which leads us to cover our nakedness, is actually a shame that echoes original innocence because it reminds us that we do not fully appreciate the nuptial meaning of the body. We must remind ourselves that this shame has, in the past, led us to think negatively about our bodies when, in fact, it should only remind us that we need to recognize the dignity of the body in the eternal plan of God. A positive body image is necessary if we are to appreciate the sacramental value of our bodies because, as the Pope observes, we *are* our bodies. Our masculinity and our femininity are the way in which we are the temples of the Holy Spirit. We need to develop a respect for our bodies that frees us to use them in a way that will not only enhance our own dignity, but also respect the dignity of others. We need to appreciate that the attractiveness of the human body is a reminder of the attractiveness of God, while, at the same time, we must continue to die to our tendency to use our bodies to exploit other persons. We need to recognize the power of the body as a sacrament as well as our potential to use it in a destructive way. We must give up our Manichean and suspicious tendencies regarding the body and join with God in affirming that "it is good." We must also recognize that, as "temples of the Holy Spirit," our bodies should serve to reveal God and his divine plan to others; our bodies should remind others of the nuptial meaning of the body, of the need to respect the personhood of the other.

Purity of heart is nurtured when we reflect on our own bodily self-image, when we root out our tendencies to view our body negatively and/or to have a naturalistic view that neglects the sacramental dimension of the body. A spirituality that continually reminds us of the story of the beginning, of our redemption by Jesus, and of the indwelling of the Holy Spirit, should contribute to an increased ability to appreciate the fullest dimension of our body—its physical attractiveness and its sacramental value.

2 Giving and receiving affection. As we have observed, the problems that most of us encounter in giving and receiving affection spring from previous cultural fears of both the body and those demonstrations of affection that might lead to bodily "sins." Those who have problems in this area of their sexuality have a profound influence on others with whom they interact, especially their spouse and children. We need to evaluate our behavior in this area and determine whether it is influenced by a negative image of the body, a negative image that ultimately limits our ability to see that all male-female relationships have the potential for revealing the nuptial meaning of the body.

In some ways, the puritanical attitude of American society has decreased to a degree, and now we, like many Europeans, more readily exchange a kiss when encountering a friend or an acquaintance of the opposite sex. But there are other ways of giving and withholding affection that are easily practiced even by those of us who readily exchange a kiss of greeting. Here, too, "abstaining from life according to the flesh" does not mean refraining from demonstrations of affection; indeed, in many instances, it means just the opposite—learning how to demonstrate affection and concern through physical contact, and developing the ability to both genuinely care about those with whom we relate and realize that this caring includes respecting the dignity of the other's sexuality. If we remember that a unity of differences that shows affection and concern is a possible revelation of God, we should be encouraged to learn how to give and receive affection in such a way as to diminish our fear that our bodies will betray us.

3 Male-female roles. The area of male-female roles is the area of our sexuality that causes great problems for us in this modern world. Relationships of appropriation that are based on stereotypes have, for so long, been the model for understanding male and female roles in society that, even now, when there is no longer a need for such strict separation of man's and woman's work, we still find it difficult to give up "our heritage of lust" in this area of our lives. If we are a temple of the Holy Spirit, then we are, each of us, unique persons who deserve to be accorded respect and dignity on the basis of that personhood, not on the basis of how we measure up to some stereotype model of machoism or pseudofemininity. All of us, however, no matter how liberated we might feel we are, still carry a sexist view of masculinity and femininity buried deep within us. We die to "life according to the flesh" when we earnestly strive to overcome our sexist tendencies. In this period of societal transition, it is especially important that we who strive to live a life "according to the spirit" bear testimony to God's plan for masculinity and femininity and overcome stereotypical thinking while, at the same time, we retain respect for those qualities of human nature that have been kept alive in the different experiences of man and woman.

People hoping to develop "purity of heart" must remember, first, the story of original time and, then, the story of the relationship of appropriation as part of a heritage of lust. Those who live "according to the Spirit" must give up this heritage of lust through continual attention to how it manifests itself in daily living. We allow the redemption of the body to be operative in our lives when piety reminds us to appreciate the nuptial meaning of the body in both masculinity and femininity.

4 Family lifestyles. The crossover of attitudes from one area of behavior to another has been obvious in our reflections and is particularly apparent when we consider our understanding of what makes a "good husband and good father" and who is the "good wife and good mother." In this area, just as in the societal understanding of correct male-female behavior, we have developed a stereotypical way of thinking that makes it difficult for a man and a woman to develop a true relationship of intimacy. The call of Jesus to abandon our tendency to "adultery in the heart" specifically highlights how easy it is for us to nurture false images of sexuality in the close circle of the family. We who have been called to die to "life according to the flesh" need to develop a much greater appreciation of intimacy in marital relationships. We need to recognize how we use inherited images of husband-father and wife-mother as a means of avoiding a deeper level of intimacy with our own spouse. We need to recognize the continual requirement of dying to our old self so that we might experience the redemption of the body in our marital relationships.

This dying to the old self demands that we make use of the freedom that has been won for us by Jesus, appreciating that this freedom once again allows us to love the *person* of our spouse in such a way that we reflect the "image of God." This call to reflect and glorify God necessitates that we give up our stereotypical ideas and work with our spouse as a person; both of us must appreciate how the other lives as a sexual being. We cannot be satisfied with the claim that it is woman's nature to do the housekeeping and man's nature to provide the finances; rather, we must see that it is in the unity of masculinity and femininity that family life is allowed to blossom. How the man and the woman contribute to the maintenance of family life varies from generation to generation and from culture to culture, but the strong sexual attraction between the man and the woman serves to remind us that this relationship should be worked out in a way that will allow the personhood of each to maintain its dignity.

We seem to cultivate purity of heart in this area of our sexuality when we are open to new possibilities of husband-wife relationships, when we recognize that, in an advanced technological society such as ours, the growth of marital intimacy requires a willingness on the part of both partners to explore the depth of possibility that is offered in the nuptial meaning of the body. Only then will we open ourselves to the presence of the Holy Spirit who will assist us as we seek to cleave to each other so as to become one flesh in a society in which many people question the possibility of such a cleaving, at least for any long term.

5 Sex education. Evidence abounds to indicate that, despite our increased understanding of physical sexuality, Americans are very remiss in assuming the task of educating their children even in the most rudimentary "facts of life." Perhaps this, more than any other fact, demonstrates the discomfort that most of us experience when we are confronted with issues of our sexuality. In addition, there is the tendency to limit sex education to mere biological knowledge, neglecting the realization that sexuality is a pervasive factor in our existence. Those of us who might be able to convey biological knowledge to our children often fail to realize how we actually influence their developing sexual identity right from the moment of birth.

In this area, we who are parents and educators need to die to "life according to the flesh" by developing a greater ease with our own sexuality and a greater understanding of how pervasive sexuality is, so that we will be aware of how we contribute to the formation of our children's sexual identity. Here, too, as in all other areas of our sexuality, we need to remind ourselves that our bodies have been redeemed at "a price" and that, consequently, we have an obligation to pass on to our children a positive sexual identity. We need to realize that we are temples of the Holy Spirit and that, if we open ourselves to this presence of the Spirit, we will appreciate the gift of piety and be sensitive to the dignity and nuptial meaning of the body. Our sensitivity, then, should help us as we try to offer positive models of sexuality to our children and as we try to share with them our vision of the meaning of sexuality.

We work toward achieving "purity of heart" in this area of our lives when we seek to identify how and why we are failing as educators in sexuality. We need to abstain from that behavior which is harmful for the development of sexual identity in our children. We need to learn the ways in which we can be positive role models of spontaneity. We need to believe in the redemption of the body. We need to remember the dignity of persons whose spirits are linked with the Holy Spirit.

6 Reproduction. Because much of the history of sexuality has been strongly influenced by our societal need for reproduction, we have tended to overemphasize the reproductive aspects of sexuality and, consequently, we have subjected our sexuality to criteria that judge how it influences reproduction. As a result, we have often failed to realize that a commitment to reproduction carries with it a concomitant commitment to the care and rearing of the child. Although there has been much talk about the contraceptive mentality of our modern technological society, there is little evidence to support the notion that children born in previous generations were always afforded the dignity of personhood. It is quite possible that there were just as many people in previous generations who disliked children and would have limited the number of offspring if they could have found a way to accomplish this limitation. The fear of the contraceptive mentality, however, should include the fear of a male-female relationship that does not result in the ability to love the offspring that are born to that relationship.

Recent studies of young adult Catholics indicate that, by and large, they do not have a "contraceptive mentality."[1] But now that people are free to regulate when they will reproduce—whether this regulation is by natural or by artificial means, it is nonetheless a limitation—Christians making decisions on reproduction need to be conscious that their bodies are called to reproduce another "with the help of the Lord." The "new image of God" that a husband and wife may choose to reproduce calls upon a man and a woman to responsibly use their power of procreation so as to create an environment in which the possible fruit of this union might grow to appreciate the meaning of being "in the image of God."

By giving up the Manichean tendency to see the body and sex as only for procreation, we will develop a "purity of heart" as we learn to more fully appreciate how the nuptial significance of the body encourages us to understand the sexual use of our body as a way to form a communion of persons that can, with the help of the Lord, create a new human "in the image of God." Couples who are open to the gift of the Spirit, to the piety that respects the dignity of the body, will come to see that a bodily act that leads to reproduction is part of an ongoing commitment to form a union that will reflect the glory of God.

7 Erotic behavior. Erotic behavior is the glue that binds all the other aspects of our sexuality together because the power of the perennial physical attraction has assured the survival of the species and serves as a constant reminder of the human search for unity. Both the human fear of the power of that sexual drive and the implication of the commitment that is demanded by the unity have led to misunderstandings about erotic behavior throughout our history. When St. Paul speaks of self-mastery, of abstention and control, we have most often considered his words only in this particular sphere of our sexuality; throughout the history of Christianity, we have often interpreted these words, along with Jesus' words in the Sermon on the Mount, as a prohibition.

But we now see that, in the erotic sphere, we die to the works of the flesh and live a life "according to the spirit" when we abstain from all behavior that robs the erotic of its power to aid us in our search for the true, the good, and the beautiful. Because a "communion of persons" that is strengthened by sexual intimacy is one avenue for achieving this goal, we must hear Paul's words as an admonition against Manicheism. In addition, we must come to appreciate that "controlling" the body requires that we learn to use the freedom in the erotic sphere as a freedom that has been won for us by Jesus—that is, in other words, a freedom that is a way of subjecting our strong sexual drive to the demands of love. Purity of heart will be ours when we are open to the way in which piety reminds us that our bodies, which are temples of the Holy Spirit, also have a powerful sexual drive that has the capability of reflecting "life according to the Spirit," that is to say, our sexual drive can reveal God for us in this time and in this place.

The self-mastery that will help us, in the erotic sphere, lead life according to the Spirit is important because, in this area, freedom from "the world of the flesh," that is, the ability to appreciate the positive value of the erotic, reinforces our behavior in other areas and, at the same time, is supported by our cultivation of "purity of heart" in those other areas. As the thread that runs through all of human relationships, the erotic can be the source of inspiration just as it is possible for it to be a destructive force in our lives.

Those of us who hope to live a "life according to the spirit," who want to avoid "adultery in the heart," find, in these reflections on Pauline purity, the challenge to develop a spiritual maturity regarding our sexuality. We have received the "redemption of the body" with its re-invitation to the sexual feast at "the price" of the death of the Lord. We are challenged by Paul's words to cultivate the virtue of purity by opening ourselves to the gift of piety and its respect for the dignity of the human body; thus, we allow the Holy Spirit to ready us for our participation in that feast through which we once again become "in the image of God." We begin to under stand our own responsibility for developing a spirituality of sexuality, and we are now in a position to look to our religious community for ways in which we might be supported in and also contribute to the development of this spirituality.

EIGHTEEN
Purity of Heart

Blessed are the pure in heart, for they shall see God. —Matthew 5:8

You have heard that it was said, "You shall not commit adultery." But I say to you that everyone who looks at a woman lustfully has already committed adultery with her in his heart. —Matthew 5:27-28

Summary of the Pope's Addresses

Before concluding his analysis of Matthew 5:27-28, Pope John Paul II briefly summarizes his previous reflections, which have enabled us to outline a true theology of the body. The Pope's analysis of the original state of innocence has led us to an understanding of the theological truth about man—his being male and female in the image of God, that is, incarnate in the visible and corporeal fact of the masculinity or femininity of the human person. The Pope has also considered this truth about man in the context of hereditary sinfulness when he analyzed Jesus' words in the Sermon on the Mount—words that refer to the man of every time and every place when they proclaim to each one a truth that is valid and substantial for him.

This truth is a truth of an ethical and normative nature. Jesus' interpretation of the commandment against adultery indicates the evil that must be avoided and overcome while, at the same time, it points out the good that will be accomplished by overcoming desire, the good of "purity of heart." In the biblical context, this purity of heart means freedom from every kind of sin or guilt; our primary concern, however, is with that one aspect of purity that constitutes the opposite of adultery in the heart. When we understand purity of heart according to Paul's thought as "life according to the Spirit," we then have a fuller appreciation of Jesus' words in the Sermon on the Mount that warn us against evil and indicate the moral good of human conduct.

We find that Jesus' words have not only an ethical truth, but also an essential truth, an anthropological truth about man; this is why we use them in formulating a theology of the body that is related to, and in the perspective of, Jesus' other reference to "the beginning." Through Jesus' words, the man of original innocence is recalled to the consciousness of the man of lust. Jesus does not try to make the human heart return to the state of original innocence; rather, he is indicating a way to a purity of heart that is accessible even in a state of sinfulness. This is a purity of the "man of lust" that is not only inspired by the word of the Gospel but also open to "life according to the Spirit," that is, it is entirely enveloped by the "redemption of the body" that has been carried out by Jesus. We find that, in his heart, interior man must open himself to life according to the Spirit in order to participate in purity of heart and rediscover and realize the value of the body that has been freed through redemption from the bond of lust.

Our analysis of Jesus' words in the Sermon on the Mount, connected with the text of St. Paul, enables us to shift the meaning of "temperance" toward the positive function of purity of heart and thereby open the way to a more perfect discovery of the dignity of the human body. Purity as temperance matures in the heart of the man who cultivates it and, likewise, tends to mature and strengthen the nuptial meaning of the body. Through mature purity, man enjoys the fruits of the victory over lust by "controlling his own body in holiness and honor," revealing the efficacy of piety, which is the gift of the Holy Spirit whose "temple" the human body is. In this way, a spiritual climate that is different from the passion of lust brings the joy that man finds in more fully mastering himself so that he can also more fully become a real gift to another person.

Concluding his brief summary of the previous reflections, the Pope observes that both Jesus' appeal to the heart and his reference to "the beginning" allow us to construct an outline of a "theology of the body" that is, at the same time, pedagogy. Jesus' pronouncements are pedagogical because they aim at educating man, that is, they set before him requirements, they motivate him toward those requirements, and they point out the way that leads to the fulfillment of those requirements. Jesus' answer to the Pharisees regarding the indissolubility of marriage, as well as the words of the Sermon on the Mount concerning the mastery of lust, contain a pedagogy of the body and therefore prove that the Creator has assigned man his body—his masculinity and femininity—as a task that is also a clear sign of the interpersonal communion in which man fulfills himself through the authentic gift of himself. Having given man the requirements for the task that has been entrusted to him, the Creator also points out to the man and the woman the ways that lead to their fulfillment.

This theology of the body, we discover through our analysis of the key texts of the Bible, is the basis of the best method of pedagogy of the body, that is, the education—more precisely, the self-education—of man. This is particularly important for modern man who has made great progress in the fields of biophysiology and biomedicine, sciences that are, however, only partial in nature because they do not develop the awareness of the body as both a sign of the person and a manifestation of the Spirit. This biological knowledge can arrive at an understanding that treats the body, in a more or less systematic way, as an object of manipulation whereby man ceases to subjectively identify himself with his own body. Man, in this context, ignores the meaning and dignity that derive from the fact that this body is proper to the person. We touch upon problems that often demand fundamental solutions that are impossible without an integral view of man.

Thus, it becomes clear that our theology of the body becomes the fundamental method of pedagogy that is understood under the aspect of a specific "spirituality of the body." The body and its sexuality are given as a task to the human spirit and, by means of maturity of the spirit, become a sign of the person. Man, through his spiritual maturity, discovers the nuptial meaning that is proper to the body, a meaning that is not revealed by lust. Purely "biological knowledge" is capable of helping man to discover the true nuptial meaning of the body when it is accompanied by an adequate spiritual maturity of the human person.

Many experiences of our own time confirm the fact that biological knowledge that is devoid of spiritual maturity often has an effect that is the opposite of helping man discover the true nuptial meaning of the body. It is from this perspective that it is necessary to consider the pronouncements of the modern church. Their adequate understanding and interpretation, as well as their pedagogy, demand a deep theology of the body that we can derive from the key words of Jesus, which we have analyzed at great length and which seek to emphasize the dignity of marriage and family. Jesus was speaking to universal man, that is, to man in all times and in all places. Therefore, the pronouncements of the church, which aim at applying Jesus' words to the here and now, must be reread according to the theology and that pedagogy which is both rooted in and supported by Jesus' words.

The Pope then turns to three short passages, one from *Gaudium et Spes,* 47, and two from *Humanae Vitae*[1]; he sees in them the same concern that dictated Jesus' words on the unity and indissolubility of marriage, purity of heart, and mastery of lust of the flesh, as well as our analysis of the Pauline material. These passages, he feels, clearly show that the theology of the body, which we have developed, is indispensable for an adequate understanding of the pronouncements of the *magisterium* of the modern church. It is indispensable because this theology becomes the fundamental message of the whole Christian pedagogy of the body, the purpose of which lies precisely in ensuring that the "affective manifestations proper to conjugal life" be in conformity with the moral order, that is, with the dignity of the person. Theology, understood as the method of the pedagogy of the body, thus prepares us for further reflections on the sacramentality of both human life and married life.

The following are the key points for a theology and a spirituality of the body that the Pope developed in his two addresses on purity of heart.

1. Jesus' words in the Sermon on the Mount, as well as his direction to the Pharisees to return to "the beginning," coupled with the Pauline view of "life according to the Spirit," proclaim to each of us the ethical, normative, essential, anthropological truth about man that recalls the possibilities of original innocence to us who lust; Jesus' words

indicate for us a way to a purity of heart, "inspiriting" us by the word of the Gospel and opening us to "life according to the Spirit."

2. Although "purity of heart," from the biblical point of view, means freedom from every kind of sin or guilt, we can understand this "purity of heart," which is opposed to "lust of the flesh," in the Pauline context of "life according to the Spirit"; in Paul's letters, purity is not simply abstention or temperance as a negative function, but is a more perfect discovery of the dignity of the human body by which, through mature purity, we enjoy the fruits of the victory over lust, appreciate the efficacy of the gift of piety, and enjoy a spiritual climate that is so different from the "passion of lust" that we find ourselves able to more fully be a real gift to another person.

3. The theology of the body that has been outlined up to this point is, at the same time, a pedagogy of the body that leads to our self-education and makes us aware that our body is a sign of our person, a manifestation of our spirit; through a spirituality of the body, we attain a spiritual maturity whereby we recognize that our masculinity and femininity are given to us as a task to the human spirit in which we are to discover the nuptial meaning of the body. "Biological" knowledge of the body, if it is accompanied by an adequate spiritual maturity, is capable of helping us discover the nuptial meaning of the body.

4. The need for a spirituality of the body—for a spiritual maturity—requires that we understand, interpret, and apply the pronouncements of the modern church from the perspective of the deep theology of the body that has been derived from the key words of Jesus; the purpose of a pedagogy of the body is to ensure that the affective manifestations that are proper to conjugal life will be in conformity with the moral order, with the dignity of persons, so that we may appreciate the sacramentality of both human life and married life.

Spiritual Reflections

As we come to the end of the Pope's analysis of certain key scriptural passages, we see that the theology of the body that he has outlined up to this point finds Jesus' words leading us to a "purity of heart" in which we will both enjoy the fruits of the victory over lust and appreciate ourselves and our sexuality as a real gift for another. Throughout this series of reflections, we have been engaged in a conversation with the creation story of Genesis, with the Law, the Prophets, and the Wisdom literature of the Old Testament, with Jesus' directive to the Pharisees and his words in the Sermon on the Mount, and with the Epistles of St. Paul. These biblical passages have shown us how various doctrines of our Catholic Christian tradition—creation, fall, incarnation, redemption, grace, and the Holy Spirit—have had profound implications for our understanding of the meaning of sexuality. In the process of reflecting on these texts and doctrines, we have encountered a new perspective on the body and on human sexuality—a perspective that is meant to encourage us to discover the positive values of both sexuality and the body as we cultivate a "purity of heart."

The vision of sexuality which begins in Genesis, develops through the Old and New Testament, and continues down through the years "at every point of geographical longitude and latitude," constantly reminds us that we are male and female "in the image of God." Our bodies, our sexuality, were given to us, according to God's original plan, so that we might discover the secret of Love. As we join in unity, we are to appreciate the need to be "disinterested gift to each other." This "nuptial meaning of the body" shows us how to be lovers as God is a lover. Even in "historical time," without the "innocence" of Adam and Eve, our bodies, having been imprinted with the image of God, remind us of the divine plan. The lust we experience is much more than simply the passion that attracts us to the other sex; it is the attitude "in our hearts" that turns male-female relationships into relationships of appropriation for our individual satisfaction and causes us to commit "adultery in the heart." But God has not deserted us; we have not been left with a longing for unity but no hope of attaining it. Through the "redemption of the body," we are reminded that our bodies are "temples of the Holy Spirit." We are to develop a "purity of heart" so that the Spirit can permeate our spirits and enable us to control our bodies in "holiness and honor." Through the grace of the Spirit, we will once again take up the call to be "in the image of God."

The rich storehouse of answers to the problems of human sexuality that we find in our Catholic Christian tradition surprises those of us who have come to expect religious interest in sexuality to be confined to prohibitions and negative interpretations of the body, sex, and women. And unfortunately, even today, we hear little in the way of a positive vision of human sexuality from our pastoral leaders; indeed, many of us do not even look to the church for such a vision at the present time. The compartmentalizing of sexuality—which has been reinforced by numerous statements on birth control but little attention to changing male-female, husband-wife roles, the positive role of *eros* in our lives, the importance of education in sexuality, and so forth—has not helped to create an impression that our religious tradition has an overriding vision that speaks to both the pervasiveness of human sexuality and the positive and negative possibilities of sexuality in the modern world. The value of the vision that has been developed out of these addresses is that the Pope has included a broad perspective on human sexuality, rather than limiting sexuality to concerns about reproduction and erotic behavior.

Jesus' directives to the Pharisees, coupled with his words in the Sermon on the Mount, certainly call for this broader vision as they remind us that the Creator saw sexuality as good. Jesus' reaffirmation of this goodness calls upon us to have a "purity of heart" that will allow us to join with both the Creator and St. Paul as we try to discover the meaning of sexuality and learn to say, along with them, that "it is good." The vision challenges us to a new way of life, to life according to the Spirit, to life in which we are willing to die to all of the attitudes and behaviors that have interfered with our ability to be spontaneous, sexually mature adults. In order to do this, we need to be reflective about our own experiences, we need to sort out those experiences that help us live according to the vision from those that actually contradict the vision; we also need to learn to discern how, in the area of our sexuality, we sometimes choose the things of the world and sometimes choose the things of the Father.

This vision, which grows out of a theology of the body, then serves as a way of assisting us in developing a spirituality, a way of linking the vision to our own experiences, a way of evaluating our behavior in terms of the task that we have been given—to discover the "nuptial meaning of the body." As we mentioned in our initial reflections, we are the beneficiaries of much secular wisdom regarding human sexuality. Such an abundance of knowledge about the physical and psychological dimensions of human sexuality should contribute to the dignity and respect that is due each individual person. Yet, based on our reflections, it does not seem that secular wisdom alone leads us to an appreciation of the nuptial meaning of the body, though we must admit that secular wisdom, coupled with an appreciation of the spiritual dimension of human existence, can be extremely helpful in our search for an appreciation of the real meaning of human sexuality.

We have engaged in these reflections on the Pope's theology of the body and sexuality as a way to develop a spirituality of sexuality that will help us live this life "according to the Spirit," that will allow us to participate in the sexual feast. A spirituality of the body is the kind of self-education that is necessary to maintain our awareness of the fact that our body is a sign of our person, a manifestation of our spirit, that calls us to rediscover the nuptial meaning of the body. In this way, the vision of human sexuality that has been developed out of the theology of the body is a part of the pedagogy of the body; the vision not only educates us but also inspires us and shows us the way to become people whose lives bear the fruit of the Spirit. What is more, the vision gives us a perspective from which to evaluate our behavior in all the areas of our lives that are affected by our sexuality. When we are able to incorporate this vision into our way of thinking about the meaning of life, we then begin to evaluate our behavior in terms of this perspective, and it is in this way that we begin to cultivate purity of heart and to become the spontaneous person that the *ethos* of redemption calls for.

Through our reflections, we have discovered the need for a spiritual maturity, the need for a spirituality that is an ongoing way of linking our experience of sexuality with the meaning of life that has been uncovered in our faith tradition. Now that we have also uncovered a vision of sexuality in that tradition, we need the community of the faithful to join together with us in the continual articulation and celebration of this vision. In addition, we need the communal sharing of this vision as a support for our own individual processes of evaluating behavior. We need the community of the faithful to engage in an ongoing discussion of the implications of this vision and share an appreciation of the vision. We need a community of people, who are open to the gift of piety, to address the problems, concerns, and positive values of sexuality so that not only individuals but also the entire community will reflect "life according to the Spirit."

Just as the Pope points to the need to understand, interpret, and apply practically the pronouncements of the modern church in light of the deep theology of the body that has been derived from the key words of Jesus, so, too, we need to continually remind ourselves—and be reminded by our faith community—that this theology of the body is the criterion by which we measure our sexually related behavior. If we are able to share this vision with other members of our religious community, we will have an ongoing reminder that life "according to the Spirit" requires that we live our sexuality in light of this vision.

In addition, it seems that the vision we have uncovered in our reflections demands that we contribute to the understanding, interpretation and practical application of the pronouncements of the modern Church (the Magisterium) in light of the theology of the body outlined by the Pope. The reflection on our own experiences of sexuality, which has been a part of this development of a spirituality, can, when linked with the experiences of others, aid in this task. Indeed, without the contribution of the understanding of certain aspects of human sexuality uncovered in this type of reflection, the Magisterium would, at times, be unaware of some of the revelatory aspects of sexuality.

For example, in the apostolic exhortation on the family, *Familiaris Consortio,* the Pope refers to the charism of discernment which married people possess by virtue of their participation in the sacrament of marriage.[1] Married people are called upon to contribute to the Church's understanding of marriage and the family through the exercise of this charism, unique to their experience. As our reflections have shown, and as the reflections on marriage described in *Marital Intimacy: A Catholic Perspective* make clear,

231

the bonding power of sexual intimacy plays a vital role in helping marital partners appreciate the relevatory potential of marriage. This experience of sexual intimacy which one psychologist refers to as "the rubber band effect"—if marital partners become too engrossed in their individual concerns, the power of sexual attraction pulls them back both to bodily unity and to attention to each others' needs with a deepening sense of responsibility—is not always appreciated by marital partners. Many marriages suffer from too little passion, rather than from too much. However, as our examination of the experience of sexuality has made obvious, without reflection on the role of sexual intimacy in their marriage, many marital partners will fail to recognize the potential of the gift of body unity. Thus, it would be surprising if the Magisterium, without input from the reflections of married people, would be fully cognizant of this aspect of sexuality.

So, too, the experience of women, who have been the chief victims of relationships of appropriation throughout human history up to and including the present time, is only now being subjected to deep scrutiny by women themselves. Both the positive aspects of this experience—the value of those dimensions of human experience that have been the "territory" of women—and its negative implications—what it means to be the victim of being "lorded over" by another who discriminates against you because of your inferiority and who often thinks of you only as a sex object—will only be understood by the Magisterium when women's experience of sexuality is seen as relevatory. Our reflections on a spirituality of sexuality have made it clear that without an appreciation of such things as pregnancy, motherhood, sexual intimacy, housework, the feminity of God, rape, wife abuse, sexual harassment, and job discrimination as these are experienced by women, the Magisterium will not fully appreciate the implications of the theology of the body which sees humankind "in the image of God," male *and* female.

The important contribution a spiritulaity of sexuality can make to the task of the Church requires that the Magisterium engage in an ongoing dialog on this "basic fact of human existence" with those who have charisms different than those of the teaching authority. Only then can the entire Church hope to be faithful to its obligation to continue to proclaim the "redemption of the body." The Pope's theology of the body and sexuality is a first step in this process. Attention to the need for a spirituality of sexuality at all levels of the Church will continue the task.

After these reflections, we find that we can agree with Eugene O'Neill's remark that "enough is not as good as a feast." We must now be about the difficult process of changing our own lives so that we can participate in the feast ourselves and also encourage our religious communities to celebrate the feast.

Appendix

The summaries of all the Pope's addresses are based on translations found in the English Edition of L'Osservatore Romano. Included in the following list are the date of the Pope's address, the actual title, the headline that identifies each address, and the date of the issue of *L'Osservatore Romano* in which the translation of the address appeared. The grouping corresponds to the chapters in this book that summarize specific addresses.

General Audience Date	Title	*L'Osservatore Romano* Date

Chapter 1: In the Beginning

5 September	"Pope John Paul II speaks of Unity and Indissolubility of Marriage"	10 Sept. 1979
12 September	"Biblical Account of Creation Analyzed by Pope John Paul II"	17 Sept. 1979
19 September	"The Second Account of Creation: The Subjective Dimension of Man"	24 Sept. 1979
26 September	"Boundary between Original Innocence and Redemption"	1 Oct. 1979

Chapter 2: Original Solitude

10 October	"Meaning of Man's Original Solitude"	15 Oct. 1979
24 October	"Man's Awareness of Being a Person"	29 Oct. 1979
31 October	"In the Very Definition of Man the Alternative between Death and Immortality"	5 Nov. 1979

Chapter 3: Original Unity

7 November	"Original Unity of Man and Woman"	12 Nov. 1979
14 November	"By the Communion of Persons Man Becomes the Image of God"	19 Nov. 1979

Chapter 8: Shame and Lust

16 April	"Christ Appeals to Man's Heart"	21 Apr. 1980
23 April	"Ethical and Anthropological Content of the Commandment: 'Do Not Commit Adultery'"	28 Apr. 1980
30 April	"Lust Is The Fruit of the Break of the Covenant with God"	5 May 1980
14 May	"Real Significance of Original Nakedness"	19 May 1980
28 May	"A Fundamental Disquiet in All Human Existence"	2 June 1980

Chapter 9: Appropriation

18 June	"Domination over the Other in the Interpersonal Realm"	23 June 1980
25 June	"Lust Limits Mystical Meaning in the Body"	30 June 1980
23 July	"The 'Heart' a Battlefield between Love and Lust"	28 July 1980
30 July	"Opposition in the Human Heart between the Spirit and the Body"	4 Aug. 1980

Chapter 10: Adultery in the Body

6 August	"Sermon on the Mount to the Men of Our Day"	11 Aug. 1980
20 August	"Adultery according to the Law and as Spoken by the Prophets"	25 Aug. 1980
27 August	"Adultery: A Breakdown of the Personal Covenant"	1 Sept. 1980

Chapter 11: Desire

| 3 September | "Meaning of Adultery Transferred from the Body to the Heart" | 8 Sept. 1980 |

Chapter 16: The Flesh and the Spirit

10 December	"Purity of Heart"	15 Dec. 1980
17 December	"Justification in Christ"	29 Dec. 1980
7 January	"Opposition between the Flesh and the Spirit"	12 Jan. 1981
14 January	"Life in the Spirit Based on True Freedom"	19 Jan. 1981

Chapter 17: Purity and Life according to the Spirit

28 January	"St. Paul's Teaching on the Sanctity and Respect of the Human Body"	2 Feb. 1981
4 February	"St. Paul's Description of the Body and Teaching on Purity"	9 Feb. 1981
11 February	"The Virtue of Purity Is the Expression and Fruit of Life according to the Spirit"	16 Feb. 1981
18 March	"The Pauline Doctrine of Purity as 'Life according to the Spirit' "	23 Mar. 1981

Chapter 18: Purity of Heart

1 April	"Positive Function of Purity of Heart"	6 April 1981
8 April	"Pronouncements of Magisterium Apply Christ's Words to Today"	13 April 1981

Notes

Introduction

1. Some months after the May 1981 assassination attempt, Pope John Paul II again returned to a discussion of a theology of sexuality and the body. From November 11, 1981, through January 1983, the Pope delivered over forty more addresses in which he reflected on how the theology that is implicit in the Bible leads to a deeper understanding of virginity, celibacy, marriage, and the representation of the church as the Bride of Christ.

2. The Pope's addresses deal with the "basic fact" of masculinity and femininity as manifestations of human sexuality and with the model of unity that is presented in the husband-wife relationship of the second chapter of Genesis. He does not address, nor does this book address, the fact that humans have sexual orientations that are other than the basic two of male and female (i.e., homosexuality). Still, the theology of the body and of sexuality that is developed here could and should be applied to situations other than those specifically discussed in these pages. Similarly, the Pope's use of "man," rather than man and woman, has been retained. The Pope uses this term, however, in the generic sense, that is, to mean *mankind*; it should not be understood to exclude women.

3. J.M. Anzia and M.G. Durkin, *Marital Intimacy: A Catholic Perspective* (Chicago: Loyola University Press, 1982).

4. A.M. Greeley, et al., *Parish, Priest & People: New Leadership for the Local Church* (Chicago: Thomas More Press, 1981).

Chapter 1

1. E.J. Roberts, D. Kline, and J. Gagnon, *Family Life and Sexual Learning* (Cambridge, MA: Population Education, Inc., 1978), p. 2.

2. Quoted in Roberts, *Family Life and Sexual Learning*, p. 2.

3. R. E. Leaky and R. Lawin, *People of the Lake: Mankind and Its Beginnings* (New York: Doubleday, 1978), pp. 39-40.

4. D. Johanson and M. Edey, *Lucy* (New York: Simon and Schuster, 1981).

5. Leakey, *People of the Lake*, p. 243.

Chapter 2

1. For a discussion of the various structures of existence that are associated with the evolving psyche see, J. Cobb Jr., *The Structures of Christian Existence* (Philidelphia: Westminister Press, 1967).

2. J.J. Lynch, *The Broken Heart: The Medical Consequences of Loneliness* (New York: Basic Books, Inc., 1977).

Chapter 4

1. Leaky, *People of the Lake*, p. 243.

2. K. Clark, *The Nude: A Study in Ideal Form* (Garden City, NY: Doubleday-Anchor Books, 1956), pp. 23-54.

Chapter 5

1. "Disinterested" is used, in its standard definition, to mean *unselfish* or free of bias and self-interest, rather than in the nonstandard sense of uninterested or indifferent.

Chapter 6

1. M. Eliade, *Images and Symbols: Studies in Religious Symbolism* (New York: Sheed and Ward, 1969), pp.16-18.

Chapter 7

1. Leaky, *People of the Lake*, pp. 239-240.
2. N. Thayer, *Stepping* (Rockville Centre, NY: Playboy Paperbacks, 1981), pp. 174-175.
3. Ibid., p. 15.
4. A. Rossi, "A Biosocial Perspective on Parenting," *Daedalus* 106, no. 2 (Spring 1977): 1-31.
5. W.C. McCready, *Ultimate Values of the American Population* (Beverly Hills, CA: Sage Publications, 1976), chap. 4.

Chapter 9

1. A.M. Greeley, *The Mary Myth: On the Femininity of God* (New York: Seabury Press, 1977).

Chapter 16

1. A.M. Greeley, *The Young Catholic Family: Religious Images and Marriage Fulfillment* (Chicago: Thomas More Press, 1980).

Chapter 18

1. "The happy dignity of these partnerships [that is, marriage and the family] is not reflected everywhere, but is overshadowed by polygamy, the plague of divorce, so-called free love, and similar blemishes; futhermore, married love is too often dishonored by selfishness, hedonism, and unlawful contraceptive practices." *(Gaudium et Spes, 47)*.

"Another thing that gives cause for alarm is that a man who grows accustomed to the use of contraceptive methods may forget the reverence due to a woman, and, disregarding her physical and emotional equilibrium, reduce her to being a mere instrument for the satisfaction of his own desires, no longer considering her as his partner whom he should surround with care and affection." *(Humanae Vitae, 17)*.

"The mastery of instinct by one's reason and free will undoubtedly demands an asceticism so that the affective manifestations of conjugal life may be in keeping with right order, in particular with regard to the observance of periodic continence. Yet this discipline, which is love, rather confers on it a higher human value. It demands a continual effort, yet thanks to its beneficent influence, husband and wife fully develop their personalities and enrich each other with spiritual values . . . It favors attention for one's partner, helps both parties to drive out selfishness, the enemy of true love, and deepens their sense of responsibility." *(Humanae Vitae, 21)*.

2. Pope John Paul II, *Familiaris Consortio* (Apostolic Exhortation on the Family), 5.

Index